ROBIN HANBURY-TENISON, OBE, DL, is a founder and current president of Survival International, the world's leading organisation supporting tribal peoples, and was one of the first people to bring the plight of the rainforests to the world's attention. He has been a Gold Medallist of the Royal Geographical Society, winner of the Pio Manzu Award, an International Fellow of the Explorers Club, a Winston Churchill Memorial Fellow, a Trustee of the Ecological Foundation and a Fellow of the Linnean Society. Among his many publications are: *A Question of Survival for the Indians of Brazil*, *A Pattern of Peoples*, *Aborigines of the Amazon Rain Forest: The Yanomami*, *Fragile Eden*, *The Oxford Book of Exploration*, and his two autobiographies, *Worlds Apart* and *Worlds Within*, as well as a successful quintet of books about long-distance rides he and his wife Louella have made across France, China, New Zealand, Spain and Albania, the latest being *Land of Eagles* (also published by I.B.Tauris).

'The doyen of British explorers.'
SPECTATOR

'Robin Hanbury-Tenison is the champion of indigenous populations everywhere. This is an inspiring book, an evocative, enchanting account of his life among the nomadic Penan tribe of Borneo and how he changed our attitudes towards such tribal peoples for ever.'

Redmond O'Hanlon, author of
Into the Heart of Borneo **and** *Congo Journey*

'Throughout the traditional homeland of the Penan, one of the most extraordinary nomadic cultures in the world, the sago and rattan, the palms, lianas, and fruit trees lie crushed on the forest floor. The hornbill has fled with the pheasants, and as the trees continue to fall, a unique way of life, morally inspired, inherently right, and effortlessly pursued for centuries, has been assaulted in a single generation. In this elegant memoir Robin Hanbury-Tenison reveals the world of the Penan for he was there as a naturalist and explorer long before industrial logging ravaged the forests of Sarawak. It is at once an elegy and a testimony to the folly of greed, and a reminder of just what is at stake in the struggle to protect the remaining tropical rainforests of the world.'

Wade Davis, Explorer-in-Residence,
National Geographic

'A fascinating book. You will see what a beautiful, magical and sci-entifically outstanding place Mulu is. And you will see how much was achieved by the scientists of the Royal Geographical Society's expedition. It led directly to the designation of this unique habitat and ecosystem as a protected reserve and World Heritage Site.'

John Hemming, author of
Tree of Rivers: The Story of the Amazon

FINDING
EDEN

A Journey into the
Heart of Borneo

ROBIN
HANBURY-TENISON

I.B. TAURIS

LONDON · NEW YORK

Published in 2017 by
I.B.Tauris & Co. Ltd
London · New York
www.ibtauris.com

Copyright © 2017 Robin Hanbury-Tenison

The right of Robin Hanbury-Tenison to be identified as the author of this work
has been asserted by the author in accordance with the Copyright, Designs and
Patents Act 1988.

All rights reserved. Except for brief quotations in a review, this book, or any part
thereof, may not be reproduced, stored in or introduced into a retrieval system, or
transmitted, in any form or by any means, electronic, mechanical, photocopying,
recording or otherwise, without the prior written permission of the publisher.

Every attempt has been made to gain permission for the use of the images in this
book. Any omissions will be rectified in future editions.

ISBN: 978 1 78453 839 2
eISBN: 978 1 78672 241 6
ePDF: 978 1 78673 241 5

A full CIP record for this book is available from the British Library
A full CIP record is available from the Library of Congress

Library of Congress Catalog Card Number: available

Text design and typesetting by Tetragon, London
Printed and bound in Sweden by ScandBook AB

For Nyapun and all Penan people.

This book has helped us to understand our heritage. Listening to Robin and our grandfather talk, we heard things we never knew about how our people lived before we settled at Batu Bungan.

Sukia Avit and Kalang Noh, Nyapun's grandsons

Borneo is the place for me.

Sir David Attenborough, 2015

CONTENTS

LIST OF ILLUSTRATIONS

Unless otherwise specified, all photographs were taken by Robin Hanbury-Tenison or Nigel Winser.

MAPS

PLATES

1 Clive Jermy, a botanist and world expert on ferns at the Natural History Museum.
2 Travelling by longboat.
3 Our jetboat.
4 A remote forest river in the Mulu Park.
5 Buttress roots support giant trees on shallow soil.
6 Being greeted at the landing stage at Long Terawan.
7 Nigel Winser and his team about to set off.
8 Lusing, a nomadic Penan, sharpening a blowpipe dart.
9 Nyapun drinking through his blowpipe.
10 Nyapun resting.
11 A Penan child from Long Liau.

by John Hemming

For me, the Mulu (Sarawak) Expedition started with a suggestion by Tom Harrisson: 'As its next big research expedition, why doesn't the Royal Geographical Society follow a year's cycle of the Penan tribal people through their forests in northern Borneo?' This was in 1975, just after I had become the Society's director. Tom Harrisson was the legendary explorer who had led the Oxford University Expedition to Borneo in 1932, and who bravely operated with his Kelabit and Penan friends behind Japanese lines during the war. I was looking for a new field project for the RGS, so I eagerly asked Harrisson to investigate further during a journey to South East Asia. He did this in a series of letters – until he was tragically killed in a bus accident in Thailand. Meanwhile, my close friend Robin Hanbury-Tenison was also in that region, and Anthony Galvin, the Catholic bishop of Miri, introduced him to the wonders of eastern Sarawak. So I enlisted another family friend to join the steering committee for this project: Gathorne Medway (later Earl of Cranbrook), who had a doctorate in zoology, had worked with Tom Harrisson in the Sarawak Museum, had already written the definitive *Mammals of Borneo* and knew those forests intimately.

The expedition was launched, with Robin as its leader and Gathorne director of the Faunistic Survey. We soon decided to focus on the forests around Mount Mulu, a truly remarkable region of karst lime-stone topography, full of dramatic stone pinnacles and gigantic cave systems, with unspoiled dipterocarp tropical rainforests, rich fauna and those admirable indigenous peoples whom Tom Harrisson wanted us to study.

The next priority, as with every venture, was funding. There were fewer sources of research grants at that time, and we could not understand why donors were not rushing to support such an exciting expedition. But we succeeded, during months of fund-raising. We were helped by Algy Cluff, a rich enthusiast for RGS exploration and Borneo in particular, and by Eddie Shackleton (Lord Shackleton KG, leader of the House of Lords, son of the great Antarctic explorer and former president of the RGS – and also with Tom Harrisson on the 1932 Mulu expedition). Many trusts and companies contributed, some with cash, others with equipment or supplies in kind.

Robin and Gathorne set about recruiting what proved to be a formidable team of scientists, led in the field by Clive Jermy of the Natural History Museum. Robin proved to be an outstanding leader – efficient, dedicated, enthusiastic and able to charm and motivate everyone involved in this large undertaking. He had a range of experience that would prove invaluable. He was a working farmer; he knew tropical rainforests; he could handle boats in river rapids, having done a solo river journey from the Caribbean to the River Plate; he understood and sympathised with indigenous peoples; and he was an active environmentalist. Robin and I had, with a handful of others, founded the indigenous-rights charity Survival International, which continues to thrive with Robin as its president.

The Mulu (Sarawak) Expedition was a happy and glorious affair, as can be seen from this book. I have a few memories that illustrate Robin's skills. When Base Camp buildings were being erected, we were determined to use no local wood, but to bring all materials up the river. Some of this was done with a jetboat that could climb rapids, with Robin or Nigel Winser, Robin's indefatigable deputy, at the tiller. But heavy timbers came slung under big Royal Malaysian Air Force (RMAF) helicopters. Everyone charmed the pilots of these aircraft, who were beguiled by head of admin Shane Wesley-Smith and nurse Rosie Sadler, and Robin got on famously with their commanding officer. Air Commodore Sam Welch said that he wanted a little mouse deer for his regimental zoo; Robin saw one as a pet at a Penan longhouse and bartered it from them. Radioed about this, the officer said: 'Great. Bring it down on your next visit.' But Robin replied: 'Mouse deer here at Mulu,' which elicited the reply: 'Message understood. Another helicopter-load of cargo on its way.' Base Camp was always teeming with strange creatures brought back from the field by the scientists, as well as pets and animals rescued from the approaching loggers.

Later in the project, a team from the Sarawak Museum in Kuching paused at our camp before proceeding into the hills to excavate a cave burial. But the tomb from which they removed some artefacts was that of the grandfather of the local Berawan headman! The chief was understandably furious. He vented his anger on our camp and could have expelled us. Robin used all his understanding of indigenous peoples, tact and diplomatic skills to abate the chief's indignation. The expedition's punishment was reduced to payment of a large fine and a pig.

Gathorne Medway once appeared holding a bat and said to Robin: 'I think that this is a new species.' Rightly thrilled at the thought of finding a new mammal, Robin asked Gathorne where we could get this verified – the Smithsonian Institution, the Natural History Museum, the Zoological Society?... Gathorne answered: 'No, Robin. You misunderstand me. If I think it is a new species of bat, it *is* a new species of bat.' He could say that, as author of *Mammals of Borneo* and a world authority on bats.

1   John Hemming at Mulu (left). I am piloting
the boat; on the right is Dr Gerry Mitton.

Many other stories emerged from this exuberant expedition, as the reader will discover in this fascinating book. You will also see what a beautiful, magical and scientifically outstanding place Mulu is. And you will see how much was achieved by the scientists of the RGS expedition. It led directly to the designation of this unique habitat and ecosystem as a protected reserve and World Heritage Site. Tropical forests around Mulu have been destroyed by rapacious loggers. But at least part of the Penan's beloved forests has been saved. Tom Harrisson would be delighted.

INTRODUCTION

I once found a Garden of Eden. The world is full of little Edens, if you just take the trouble to look for them, but many have been destroyed through man's greed and ignorance. Sometimes it feels as though the whole planet has been so polluted and ravaged that there are no Edens left, but they are there to be found by those who step off the beaten track, and some are protected in national parks and by their inaccessibility. So it was with mine. The scientific expedition I was in charge of was to the newly gazetted and almost completely unexplored Gunung Mulu National Park in Sarawak, Borneo, the largest in that state. It is one of the most diverse and interesting places on earth, with almost every conceivable type of rainforest growing on its sandstone and limestone mountains. One of the biggest pieces of limestone in South East Asia, Gunung (Mount) Api, three times the size of the Rock of Gibraltar, towered over our Base Camp. Deer Cave, probably the largest river passage cave in the world, was at the southern end and had already been visited, but we were to find that

2   First view of the Garden of Eden.

the rest of the mountain contained one of the most extensive cave systems yet to be discovered.

On 8 August 1977, six weeks after I first arrived, my 17-year-old daughter Lucy and I found a way through the vast darkness of Deer Cave and over giant mounds of guano crawling with insects to a point where we could see light again ahead. Negotiating steep cliffs in the half-light and fording a deep stream which ran into the cave at that point, we emerged into a wonderland of sparkling brightness filtering through the foliage to glittering clear water below. It was like passing through the looking glass. Although the local Berawan people, who had visited Deer Cave when hunting, said they had seen light beyond the darkness, none admitted to having climbed through and ours may well have been the first human feet to tread there. We named it the Garden of Eden and some of the more intrepid visitors to Gunung Mulu National Park today go there, helped by fixed ropes; but it is still something of an adventure.

As Lucy and I emerged blinking into the daylight, washed off the guano in the clear river and lay in the sun to dry, we saw Prevost's squirrels playing in the tree above our heads. They seemed unaware of us and we realised that we were in a naive place, somewhere that had never before been disturbed by man, so that animals were not afraid.

Indeed, we later discovered that there was no other way into the deep valley formed by the river which disappeared into the mountain, save the way we had come. The sides are too steep to climb and so no one had ever been there to hunt. As if to prove the point, a troop of 25 grey leaf monkeys passed slowly overhead. A large male led the way, followed by females carrying tiny babies clinging to their chests. Juveniles leaped noisily from tree to tree and were clearly being encouraged by the adults. They all ignored us, although the male bringing up the rear paused to gaze curiously at us for a while... Even the fish in the pool where we bathed gathered in shoals around us; the scene was from a Rousseau painting, with lianas looping between the trees and gigantic, lush ferns and other epiphytes growing everywhere there was a foothold. On a patch of soft ground we saw a lot of catlike footprints, some more than 10 centimetres across. These may have been made by one of the extremely rare clouded leopards. They were known to exist in Mulu, although our expedition never had a definite sighting allowing us to record them. Two months later, when visiting a Murut longhouse on the Medalam River on the far side of the park, I was to find the stretched skin of a clouded leopard, which had been killed five months before. Having spent several hours marvelling at this untouched utopia, Lucy and I felt that the time had come to leave, and we tiptoed away, although we and most of the rest of the team were to return many times.

Three months later, we slept in the Garden of Eden for the first time. One of the most extraordinary phenomena at Mulu, and today one of the main draws for tourists, is the mass exodus of bats from the

3   Inside the Garden of Eden.

main entrance of Deer Cave at nightfall. There are 12 species of bat in Deer Cave, the highest number occupying a single cave ever recorded, and, between 5 and 6.30 p.m., as the sun sets, 3 million of them leave the cave mouth in a virtually continuous stream. They then form into extraordinary spirals and whorls, while bat hawks lurk and swoop to pick off the unwary. That night we were the first to record the smaller, but no less dramatic, exodus from the Garden of Eden entrance.

Two other members of the expedition, Henry and Nigel Osmaston, father and son geomorphologists, had followed the valley to the top and found there a magnificent cave which they had named Green Cave, as the entrance was so overgrown with vegetation that the inside was suffused with a green light. They had dropped down the steep slope into the darkness, but had not gone far into the cave itself. With Nigel Winser, ostensibly my deputy but really the man who ran everything and made our expedition the phenomenal success it was, and Shane Wesley-Smith, our wonderful No. 3 (she and Nigel eventually married), I reached the lip of the cave and looked down through the greenery into the interior. Nigel and Shane decided to rest there but I scrambled down, looking back from time to time towards the light until their diminishing figures vanished from sight. The Osmastons had marked the spot they had reached before turning back, as they had no torch with them. I had a small one in my pack and so decided to be the first to venture into the intimidating blackness ahead. Time was short if we were to get back to Base Camp by nightfall, but I paused for a moment as I suddenly felt very alone and afraid. I realised that I was in a profoundly privileged position. How many people get the chance to go somewhere no one has ever been before? It was unlikely there was any real danger in there, but having grown up in a very haunted old house in Ireland, I was familiar with the sensation of being watched and the echoing chamber ahead seemed to be holding its breath, as indeed was I.

I turned on the torch and stepped into the darkness. The ground felt crunchy under my feet. I shone the torch down and saw that I was stepping into a veritable fairyland. Everywhere I looked the floor of the cave was covered in exquisite crystal formations, tiny stalagmites formed by water dripping from the roof high above. It was like a garden of white plants made of calcite, and I felt terrible that I had stepped on a bit of it. Fortunately, there were large areas of bare earth and guano on which I was able to make my way without doing any more damage. Soon the light behind me faded and I groped my way along a stream bed by the rather feeble light of my torch. Later, when exploring some of the many other new caves beneath Api with our expert team of speleologists, I was to use their much brighter carbide lamps, which used acetylene and water. Today these have largely been replaced by more powerful and long-lasting LED batteries, but they were then the best system, giving off a broad, unfocused light. This improved peripheral vision in complete darkness.

I had just a faint little beam and my battery was running low. The thought of being lost in total darkness was frightening, but I hurried on and round a bend until, when I switched my torch off, there was not the faintest glimmer. Standing still in absolute pitch blackness, listening to the sounds of the underworld – a drip here, a squeak there – and wondering what other life there might be around me was a moment of exquisite fear. There is life in these caves, lots of it, especially near the entrance, and wherever swiftlets and bats fly to roost and nest. Their droppings, which form guano, provide a rich habitat for myriad species of insect. Those which made their presence felt most were the giant earwigs which normally live on the cave roof, feeding on the dead skin cells of roosting bats. But they regularly fall off in huge numbers and then, 'frantic to regain their lost hosts, they clamber up any available support – including passing humans'. This was how Philip Chapman, a speleobiologist who joined us later, described them. He spent much of his time crawling over great mounds of guano collecting interesting specimens of cockroaches, beetles, flies and moths. Best avoided were the main predators of this teeming underworld: large (up to 20 centimetres long), fast-running centipedes with extremely long legs and poisonous claws set below the head. Other centipedes produced a bright-green phosphorescent trail when annoyed, while fearsome huntsman spiders pursued juicy crickets which sported antennae 45 centimetres long. Lord Hunt of Everest fame, and at the time president of the Royal Geographical Society (RGS), wrote that his most abiding memory of our expedition was watching John Lewis, a myriapodol-ogist, popping centipedes into collecting bottles as fast as he could catch them, oblivious to the earwigs, cockroaches and spiders which swarmed over his body. And I well remember a great moment when, after returning from a day in the field, we were all eating around our communal table at Base Camp and someone pointed out that Phil Chapman had an earwig on his neck. Chapman, who had not had time to change and wash, calmly removed his shirt to reveal that his entire upper body was coated in crawling earwigs. It said something about the sangfroid our expedition members had acquired by then that no one left the table – unlike on an occasion some months later, when Jo Anderson, a biologist from Exeter University, spotted a giant forest scorpion ambling across the floor under the table. That did result in a mass exodus while Jo and I chased her around the kitchen area and eventually caught her in a plastic box. Jo named her Belinda after a memorable girlfriend, who had done him wrong. The next day she produced 22 live babies, which fed off a milky secretion on her back. Soon afterwards, Jo returned to the UK, taking Belinda and her babies with him, which were sold to Dudley Zoo – for all I know their descendants may still be there.

All this lay in the future as I stood, rigid with fear but revelling in the experience, deep in Green Cave. Behind the tiny sounds was a deep, oppressive silence which seemed to be waiting for something. I became aware of the 1,000 metres of limestone rock above my head. It was easy to feel how claustrophobia could overwhelm one, even in such a big space, if one allowed panic to take over. I switched on the torch. Now I could see the glowing red eyes of giant spiders watching me from the cave wall. A white moth fluttered into the shadows. I started to make my way back to the entrance. There I found Nigel and Shane worried, as I had been away for more than an hour. It had seemed like only a few minutes.

Caves were to play a large and continuing part in the story of Mulu, as there were to be many further expeditions to study and explore them, most led by the great Andy Eavis, one of the world's foremost cavers. Today they are the main draw for tourists and work on them continues.

This is because they are arguably the greatest known cave system on the planet. Sarawak Chamber, deep inside Mount Api, is the largest cave chamber in the world that we know of, being 700 metres long by 400 wide and 100 high. This makes it the most colossal enclosed space on earth, big enough to hold ten Wembley Stadiums, with a much larger roof than anything built by man. Deer Cave is possibly the most sizeable cave passage anywhere in the world. The Clearwater may have the largest volume of any cave system, having more than 130 kilometres of known passage. The total for the caves of Mulu is more than 600 kilometres, and more is being discovered every year. There is a vast amount of fascinating life in them, much still undiscovered, like blind white crabs, which evolved more than 3 million years ago, time enough to lose not just their pigment but their eyes as well. There are even lots of cave racer snakes down there, which feed on passing birds and bats, catching them as they flit past in the total darkness. Above all, it is the caves' incredible antiquity which I find thrilling.

My most fulfilling moment of exploration was when, one day, as we entered yet another undiscovered cave passage deep underground, we came on a sandy beach beside a subterranean river and I walked across, leaving footprints.

'How long ago was this cave formed?' I asked Andy.

'At least 3 million years,' he replied.

'And so mine are the first footprints here of man or beast!' I was able to say. 'Well, if that's not true exploration, I don't know what is.'

Today, the Gunung Mulu National Park is a UNESCO World Heritage Site, with more than 20,000 visitors a year. It is a showcase for the richest environment on earth, and by the time the expedition left in 1978 it was the best-researched tropical rainforest anywhere. As Edens vanish everywhere, it is vital that places like Mulu be protected and understood.

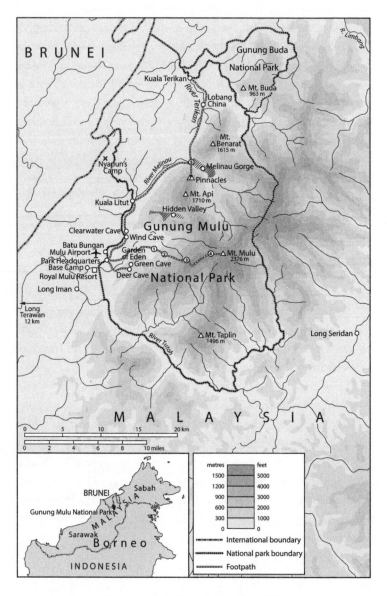

Gunung Mulu National Park, c. 1977.
Note: Gunung Buda was given national park status in 2001.

PART I

NYAPUN

The Punans have a quality of stillness... They melt into the shadows and that is their life.

Tom Harrisson, 'Remembered jungle', in Tom Harrisson (ed.),
*Borneo Jungle: An Account of the Oxford University Expedition
of 1932* (London: Lindsay Drummond, 1938)

4 Nyapun.

CHAPTER I

Meeting

Ten days after Lucy and I discovered the Garden of Eden, something else happened which was to change my life. For two months I and my small admin team had been setting up what was to become the largest RGS expedition to date. Deep in the Borneo rainforest we had built, with the help of an expert group of local Berawan people, a replica of a longhouse to accommodate more than 100 scientists, who were to come and go over the next year; and we had erected sub-camps where they could stay for weeks at a time doing their fieldwork in different habitats. We had cut trails far into unexplored places and we had heard rumours that there might still be Penan, the indigenous nomadic hunter-gatherers of the interior of Borneo, in the forest, but we had seen none, just some faint signs of abandoned camps. For the first time since my arrival in Sarawak there was peace; I was almost alone in Base Camp on a sultry afternoon, sitting on the steps of the house.

Suddenly, out of the corner of my eye, I saw a figure standing motionless in the shade on the other side of our clearing. I felt that if I blinked, he might melt away into the forest. For a frozen moment – I still recall it with a shiver – our eyes met, and he stepped out of the forest, walked over to me and gently took my hand. He was strongly built, not taller than me but with a muscular grace that made his body glide through space as though he were part of it, almost invisible. He told me, years later, that he had been very frightened as he came out of the shadows, but that he, too, had felt that we sort of recognised each other. Clad only in a bark loincloth and carrying nothing but a blowpipe, this man was to become my best friend.

He told me, in halting Malay, that his name was Nyapun, and I understood, as we sat and talked, that his family were camped some way away to the north-east. Early the next morning I trotted behind him for five hours and arrived in a paradise. His two wives and young children looked up like startled fawns as we approached their three *sulaps*, or shelters. None of them except Nyapun had seen a white man before. He said something to them in Penan and, reassured, they went back to what they had been doing. His wives, Itang, the elder, who always looked a bit cross, and the breathtakingly pretty Awing, were preparing wild sago by pounding and sieving it in bark containers; three little girls, Taree, Anyi and Amun, were searching for prawns and small fish in the stream below their camp, the headwaters of the Sungai Lutut. Later the eldest of his ten children, two sons, Lugoh and Noh, returned with a bearded pig (*Sus barbatus*) slung on a pole between them. I stayed with them all day and that night we feasted on roast pork seasoned with salt I had brought and a variety of aromatic forest herbs. Succulent red prawns and tasty little fish eaten whole. Heart of palm with an astringent wild spinach and a syrup-like sago, sweetened with my contribution of brown sugar. I still remember it as one of the best meals I have ever eaten. Nyapun's memory of the evening is that I had given him an orange when we met and that he had kept it and shared it out with his family. He gave each member a segment. They had never seen an orange before, he told me.

The little area between the *sulaps* was lit by flares made of dried palm leaves filled with damar gum. They made it feel as though we were in a great baronial hall and gave off a strong aroma of incense, which may have gone to my head. I certainly felt myself transported into a dream world when they began to dance. First Nyapun, gracefully performing the Penan version of the *najat*, then still a familiar feature of Borneo longhouse life. It tells of hunting and fighting and is performed with a *parang* (machete), which is swished through the air in graceful curves while the dancer sinks to the ground, often maintaining his balance with manifest difficulty. Nyapun was elegant and confident. Then it was the turn of his wives, who astonished me by breaking into a twist which left nothing to the imagination and was accompanied by Nyapun on his three-stringed *sape*, and King, his middle son, on a *keringon* nose flute. The four smallest children, Madya, Suda, Tagam

5   Nyapun's *sulap* on the Sungai Lutut.

and Aren, slept contentedly in the firelight and, later, so did we. I had
never felt more at home.

The next day everything was packed up and I assumed they would
be going off to hunt and gather while Nyapun led me back to my Base
Camp; but instead I realised that they were all coming with us. Their
whole world was condensed into a few rattan *selabits*, their very efficient rucksacks. The smallest children rode on the backs of the slightly
larger ones; Awing carried Aren in a very efficient baby carrier made of
rattan; and we trooped merrily along dry riverbeds and by faint forest
trails until we were home.

There they built new *sulaps* in a dense patch of forest close behind
our Base Camp, to which they came and went freely, the younger children often turning up to play with Katie, the three-year-old daughter of
two of our leading scientists, John and Sue Proctor, who were with us
for the whole 15 months. Little Anyi took me firmly under her wing,
following me around when I was in camp and making it quite clear
that she was in charge of me. Our resident doctor and nurse examined

13

6   Nyapun's family walking to Base Camp.

them all and found that, by and large, they were in exceptional health. None of them had ever visited a doctor before and they were interested in the procedures. Nyapun had a skin rash which was quickly cured. One day Sue, having been dosed for worms, brought in a bottle of formalin with an impressive fat, white, 18-centimetre roundworm curled up in it. Katie had a smaller one. Nyapun and his family were present as we all gathered round to admire them and the Penan were fascinated to be given worm doses and told that they should go home and see if they had any, too.

Sometimes, late at night, when our Base Camp longhouse was quiet after a busy day supporting the scientists as they collected and dried their specimens or set off to stay in one of the sub-camps, there would be a scratching on the door of my *bilek*, my room next to the dining area. I would find that Nyapun's whole family had come to call on me in order to have a party. The children would climb into my big Brazilian hammock and sit in an expectant row, like swallows on a telegraph wire. We would rustle up some cocoa and biscuits from the kitchen, which they shared out equally and never squabbled over, and the entertainment would begin. He and his wives would play to us on some of his musical instruments, or one of his sons would play and

7   Aren, Itang, Tagam and Nyapun.

they would dance. Nyapun was a great musician and he had, of course, made all his instruments himself. They were the *pagang*, perhaps the oldest form of stringed instrument in the world, consisting of a large, hollow section of bamboo, on which four thin strips are raised and tightened and which is only played by women; the three-stringed *sape*, which looks and sounds a bit like a crude sitar; *keringon* nose flutes, made from reeds, which make gentle, melodious whisperings and have special magical connotations through using 'nose breath'; and delicate Jew's harps called *ilut*, fashioned from palm stems, the sound of which always brought a smile. His wives' dancing was extraordinary and totally unexpected. These two demure mothers would start to shake and wiggle in the sexiest way, gyrating to the music like teenagers in a nightclub, and generally reducing the watchers to uncontrollable hysterics. It was so completely out of character and so different to the slow, graceful dances we had all seen the Berawan girls do in the longhouse at Long Terawan. Nyapun's dance, too, was quite different from the *najat* dances of Berawan men, which told of great battles,

15

8   Nyapun's family visiting my *bilek* at Base Camp late at night.

headhunting sorties and triumphal returns accompanied by graceful but fierce waving of razor-sharp *parangs*. His dance was gentler and more contemplative. He seemed to be drifting through the forest in search of the animals with which he had such a close affinity. His *parang* wove a path as though he were exploring much more than reality. And then, of course, it would be my turn to make a complete fool of myself, after which they would all melt off into the night again.

Nyapun, who was a few years older than me, became my constant guide and companion. From his arrival on I never had to worry about getting lost or running out of food when out on patrol, and together we covered most of the park and its surroundings.

When we eventually left, a year later, Nyapun and his family gathered on the riverbank to see us off. One by one, his children came and forced bead bracelets they had made onto our wrists, or hung pretty necklaces around our necks. At last Nyapun and I embraced and the tears coursed unashamedly down both our faces. I knew how much he trusted me to help during the difficult years that inevitably lay ahead for him and his people as they were forced by the Sarawak government to adapt to a settled way of life. I knew how little I would probably be able or allowed to do.

CHAPTER 2

Discovery

I first set foot on the island of Borneo in 1958, when, aged 21 and freshly down from Oxford, I had taken off to roam around the world on a shoestring. Having driven a battered World War II jeep from London to Ceylon (now Sri Lanka), I wandered on through Burma, Thailand and Cambodia, mostly alone, an object of curiosity to locals who had not yet seen a tourist. Little did they know what was to come. As a result, I had the temples of Pagan entirely to myself and I spent a week alone among the ruins of Angkor, living above a shop in Siem Reap since there were no hotels there yet.

Travellers were still a rarity. Embassies and district officers were pleased to see a new face and invited me to stay. When I reached Sarawak, after crossing the South China Sea to Brunei in a cargo boat from Singapore, I was passed along the coast from one lonely colonial officer to another. I expressed a desire to visit the already-famous Niah Caves, where the legendary Tom Harrisson, of whom more later, was excavating prehistoric remains. He was being assisted by a young British zoologist, Gathorne (Lord) Medway, who had been working there in solitary splendour for the previous six months. To my acute embarrassment, an enthusiastic young district officer sent a radio message saying 'Fellow Old Etonian on his way'. My reception was predictably frosty. This extract from a letter to my mother, dated 22 February 1958 and sent from Hong Kong, tells what happened next:

> Since writing, I've been in Borneo, or rather the colonies of Sarawak & North Borneo [now Sabah] and the Sultanate of Brunei. The most exciting thing I did was to visit the Niah Caves, of which you may have heard. There, far up an inaccessible river and across some

miles of frightening wild jungle, which I crossed in a hurry by myself on a slippery plank walk less than a foot wide, late in the evening, starting at every deafening cicada and surrounded by strange unlikely noises, I arrived to find Gathorne Medway (my age, shaggy, bespectacled and quite charming, very learned on bats, birds and 'human remains'), sitting high up in the cave's mouth, unexcited by the arrival of the first white man for ages, as he could not be distracted from counting bats – he was at 1,500,001. So I sat down too, streaming with sweat – Borneo is very hot (moist) – and then stayed in the cave in Gathorne's 'house'. This was a platform on stilts, with walls but no roof, which meant that the occasional dropping of guano fell on one during the night. However, the bats and swifts involved made up for this by keeping the cave clear of mosquitoes. The caves are famous for a variety of reasons, which more or less follow upon one another. I had been in a hurry to get there before dark – apart from fear of night in the jungle – because of the incredible sight I had heard about, and with which I was rewarded, which occurs at sunset. As the million upon million bats of innumerable species, some special to the cave, leave in a cloud, the equally numerous swifts come in to roost and the sky is black with flying things and a fantastic medley of twitterings and cheeps. The swifts make birds' nests, which are periodically collected by intrepid Chinese, who climb into the blackness on endless single bamboo poles, lashed together indefinitely – a very skilled and dangerous business. Birds' nests, for soup, do not exist in China.

As a result of all this the floor of the cave – vast, cavernous, and in places descending, apparently, literally into the bowels of the earth – has, over the centuries, gathered deep guano, which also, from time to time, is collected by Dayak tribesmen, who carry up to 200 lbs [90 kg] down the steep, tortuous path to the river. Below the guano are preserved the remains of some of the earliest prehistoric men in the world – 40,000 BC – which puts Java Man in the shade. And this is what the expedition is all about, and it's really rather exciting. I saw one newly discovered skull being painstakingly unearthed by means of tiny brushstrokes with a paint brush. [According to

Tom's biography, *The Most Offending Soul Alive* (1998) by Judith M. Heimann, the first Borneo Man skull was found on 7 February 1958 – this must have been the one I saw being unearthed.]

The next day I was put to work by Gathorne on his sideline interest – lice. My job was to collect, alive, a couple of dozen female bats' lice of a certain species, and then cut open their abdomens to discover how many babies they had (they don't lay eggs, and I had, of course, to find pregnant ones). This I thought I did rather well, as they were very 'horrible wriggling creatures' and were about an inch long. I was then flown out by a Shell Co. helicopter, which was very kind of them – I had gone in by river, which was slow. [Tom Harrisson flew in on that helicopter on 12 February, and so I met him then, very briefly, for the first time. He had G. H. R. von Koenigswald with him, the famous German Dutch palaeontologist, who had worked in Java before the war, finding skulls of Java Man (*Homo erectus erectus*). These were, in fact, from a species very much older than those being excavated in the Niah Cave when I was there, perhaps as old as 400,000 BC, but very interesting as they may have been the first hominids to use fire.]

In Sarawak I also visited a Dayak longhouse, where I was most courteously received and fed on a splendid variety of rather peculiar fruits, strong liquor – rice wine, but much stronger than arak – and nuts. They are a delightful people, tattooed from head to foot, and very happy and friendly. Usually, each man carries everywhere with him, tucked under his arm, a splendid, brilliantly coloured cock which, now that headhunting is forbidden, they sacrifice at every opportunity.

This was my first visit to a Borneo longhouse, but I was to spend quite a lot of time in different ones over the subsequent years. This one was Iban. They are the most numerous of the Dayak people, numbering nearly a million throughout the island of Borneo. Known originally as Sea Dayak, since they lived mostly along the coast, often practising piracy, they were the people rebelling against the then sultan of Brunei, Omar Ali Saifuddien II, in 1841. When James Brooke, who was to become the first Rajah Brooke, defeated them, he was given the title of Rajah of Sarawak by the sultan, who also ceded complete sovereignty of the country to him.

Longhouses, called *rumah panjang* in Iban, are wonderful structures, perhaps the best-designed communal houses in the world – and the longest, some measuring up to a kilometre and housing several hundred people. I remember being told proudly on several occasions that no one could hit a golf ball the whole length of the longhouse I was staying in. As the world record for a golf drive is 471 metres, this was probably true. They are built on stilts to avoid flooding, often on a riverbank, with access up a slippery notched pole from the water's edge. The most characteristic feature is the way they are divided right down the middle into a wide public area, like a raised and covered street where children can play safely and old people sit to watch the world go by; and a continuous row of private living quarters, *bileks*, on the other side. Behind these are often bridges across to further individual buildings which serve as bathhouses, latrines and kitchens, thus reducing the risk of fire, as well as attracting insects away from the main house.

They are graceful buildings, blending into the landscape between river and surrounding forest. There is a tremendous sense of community.

9   A Sarawak longhouse.

Traditionally, the headman, or *tuah rumah*, lives in the middle of the longhouse, with the most senior-ranking families next to him and so descending to the lowest in the hierarchy at either end. The area in front of each *bilek* is private and domestic work, such as pounding rice and weaving baskets, is undertaken there in pleasant commune with other households doing the same thing, so that there is a pretty constant chatter running up and down the gallery. This is also the space where guests are invited to sleep. One of the inconveniences of being a guest in an Iban longhouse, I found, was that the fighting cocks which they so prized also lived in this area, and they practised their deafening crowing at all hours of the night. Other livestock, mostly pigs and chickens, lived underneath the house and rootled about collecting any food which fell through the slatted floor.

I was once at a two-day cockfighting festival at an Iban longhouse at Long Medalam on the Limbang River. The atmosphere was that of an English village fete, with colourful stalls selling drinks, sweets and

10   An Iban fighting cock being prepared for battle.

fruit, and great activity in the roped-off ring. Here urgent men with wads of notes solicited bets while the next contestants fussed over and showed off the finer points of their cocks. Then the tying to the left leg of each of a lethal and razor-sharp curved blade, followed by holding them out towards each other so their ruffs extended, and the betting reached fever pitch, all being marked up on a blackboard.

The fight itself only lasted a matter of seconds, usually, as one rapidly disembowelled or gravely injured the other. The loser is always killed and eaten. It is not an attractive sport, I have always thought, bringing out the worst in people, like boxing. There were a lot of increasingly drunk young men and so I left after about eight fights – they took place very rapidly, accompanied by a lot of shouting. I went back to the longhouse and spent a much more enjoyable time surrounded by children, to whom I issued balloons, making them sing for each one, which they loved. That night, sleeping on the hard floor of the balcony was awful, a complete contrast to the relative comfort of the Berawan longhouse at Long Terawan – where, admittedly, I had usually been made drunk – let alone to the luxury of a hammock in a Penan *sulap*. The Iban *pengulu* or headman was a bore and the food was pretty filthy, but the surviving cocks were unbelievable. There was one tied outside every door – that made nearly 30 – plus the ones roaming free outside. And they crowed all the time, hardly stopping all night, urgently, differently, hysterically, deafeningly, so that one's senses reeled. I think I would have gone mad if I had had to spend more than 18 hours there. But that was a rare unpleasant experience.

One of the great things about longhouses is that they take up very little space. A whole village is accommodated in one raised, covered street. Nearby are the *padi* fields for cultivating rice as well as some vegetables. In front is the clear river with a row of longboats tied up and ready for fishing and hunting trips up- and downstream. Behind is undisturbed woodland teeming with game and other forest produce to provide a rich and varied diet. Under ideal conditions it is hard to imagine a better way of life, and it is no wonder that elaborate rituals and entertainment became such a feature of longhouse culture. Sadly, due to massive and unsustainable logging by outsiders in recent years, today most of the forest surrounding most longhouses has gone and there is little game to be had. Erosion has caused the rivers to become muddy and devoid of fish. The soil has washed away and life is no longer sustainable without income from outside. Ironically, most of this has come from working in the dangerous and ill-paying logging camps, which are bringing about the very destruction at the heart of the problem. I don't pretend to understand the legal and political shenanigans which have brought this state of affairs about, but I can't help thinking that if the rights of the indigenous peoples of Borneo to their lands had been recognised, as has happened in parts of South America, they would have protected it better and prevented the loss of most of their forests.

11   A Mentawai shaman on the island of Siberut performing a ceremony to drive away bad spirits.

The clan houses of the Mentawai people of the island of Siberut off the coast of Sumatra, with whom I was to stay a few years later (1973) while researching a book about the tribes of Indonesia's Outer Islands, were much smaller and designed differently. Called *umas*, they were strongly and elegantly built from wood and palm thatch, with a wide veranda in front, open on three sides. There, the men would sit repairing arrows and making fishing lines, while the women wove hammocks and nets. Inside was a large, wide room with a wooden dance floor where ceremonies and celebrations took place. Further back, stretching away into the darkness, were the cooking fires and sleeping places for the 30 to 80 families living communally. The rough-hewn plank walls were covered in bas-relief carvings of crocodiles, gibbons, storks and deer, while from the rafters hung the skulls of pigs and monkeys; deer antlers and bones; big black gongs representing wealth; drums and musical instruments; feathers and bows and arrows, as well as bundles of herbs and dried food pickling over the big central fire, which was built on sand and flat stones.

The Mentawai people reminded me a lot of the Choco Embera Indians of Panama and Colombia, with whom I had been travelling the year before when part of the Darien Gap expedition. They had the same peaceful approach to arrivals and departures as most Amerindians: no great performance of handshakes and shouting, just quiet conversation as we sat together discussing things. The men preferred to wear bark loincloths, which they said were more comfortable than cloth ones, while the women just wore sarongs. Most of the men were intricately tattooed all over their bodies, and they all had bright, inquisitive eyes, pale-brown skin and ready, fresh smiles. We sat cross-legged on the split-bamboo floor eating sago, plantain and pork and dropping scraps through the cracks to the pigs penned below. One evening the *kerei* or shaman of the *uma* I was staying in performed two long ceremonies. The first was to drive away bad spirits from a sick child. Colourfully draped with strings of beads, wreaths of flowers and bunches of feathers, he had brass bangles on his arms, and with his right hand he insistently jangled a small silver bell. In front of him were a bowl of red and white hibiscus blooms and a little box containing beads, tiny bottles, pieces of cloth and other small objects. A white cockerel with a bright-red comb was brought and put into his hands. It lay quite still while he stroked and talked to it as it stared up at him with bright, beady eyes. More chickens were brought and a pig was tied up outside. Later, they were slaughtered one by one, but even while the chickens' necks were being wrung and the pig's throat cut, the *kerei* stroked them and talked to them, explaining that this was being done only because the people were hungry and needed to eat. He apologised to their spirits for the necessity of disturbing them and, strangely enough, the animals lay quiet and did not struggle. While the carcasses were being prepared for cooking, the *kerei* examined the entrails, carefully parting them and searching for omens. Everyone sat quietly waiting for the verdict and then laughed with relief and began to chatter happily when he said that all was well and the child would live. Later, the *kerei* made a long speech to the animals in the dark jungle outside. Once again he was apologising to them for the necessity of taking their lives, this time during the hunt which was to take place the next day. The hunter, who was to go in pursuit of a deer, stood silently with head bowed, listening intently. The next evening he told me that he had gone far into the forest to a place he knew and had been thinking about the night before. There he had found a deer waiting for him to shoot with his bow and arrow. He said that its spirit had understood and that it had shown no fear.

The longhouses of the Ot Danum, another Dayak people, on the Kapuas River in Kalimantan, were also smaller, but built more along the lines of Iban ones. With only 20 or 30 rooms, they were highly decorated with carvings, and sometimes had carved figures outside, like heraldic beasts. These, I was told, were commemorating ancestors and protected the community from malevolent spirits.

In the early 1970s, fundamentalist Protestant missionaries were rapidly converting the Ot Danum, and at one of the first longhouses I visited I found a depressed atmosphere with the people ashamed and embarrassed by their culture. But when I explained that we were not missionaries and would really like to see them dance, they shyly brought out their gongs and flutes and started to play. The long gallery became

12 Carved figures outside an Ot Danum longhouse.

crowded with people, their faces illuminated by a few oil lamps, which threw shadows into the dark corners of the rafters, where paddles, fish traps and pots were stored. Five men, stripped to the waist, played the gongs but, to the shame and anger of the older men, none of the young men was prepared to dance. At last a few tried, rather half-heartedly, but it was clear that they had forgotten how, and they giggled as they clumped about and nudged each other. Then, unexpectedly, a short, dark boy of about 16 was pushed forward. He had a singlet with a butterfly painted on it and the moment he started to dance his intensity and concentration stilled the chatter. Wheeling and dipping like a bird in flight, he leaped and twisted over the uneven floor, fluttering his arms and bending to touch the ground. At the end he stood silent with head bowed. We were told that he had only recently arrived from a distant longhouse deep in the interior to attend the school being set up by the missionaries. I have seen many men and women dance pleasingly in longhouses throughout Borneo over the years, but the memory of that confident, graceful boy from far away has stayed with me as a perfect vision of how it should be done. It is sad to think that, as with the other boys there, his dancing would probably soon be 'taught' out of him by the missionaries at the school.

By contrast, the Toraja of Sulawesi, whom I visited next, build rows of extravagantly ornate houses with towering roofs made of thousands of matched pieces of bamboo laid one upon the other like tiles and sweeping up in a great curve similar to the prow of a ship at either end. They are massively constructed of hardwood. No metal nails are used, but the whole is securely slotted and pegged together. Outside, every visible expanse of wood is painted or carved in strong colours; red, white, black and yellow are favoured, and the pattern designs are often surmounted by a pair of buffalo horns. The interiors are small by contrast, and their significance is as ancestral homes rather than as meeting places. Communal life among the Toraja mostly takes place out of doors, funerals being by far the most significant and elaborate ceremonies. The sacrifices and feasts can last for months and are not designed so much to satisfy the mourners or furnish symbolic food for the deceased as to impress the gods whom he will be joining with his importance so that he will be able to intercede effectively on their behalf. I was lucky enough to attend the culmination of the funeral rituals for a great Toraja man who had died some three months previously. Several hundred people had come from far and wide to view the body, which was tightly wrapped in layers of coloured cloth, neatly sewn at the ends to make a regular shape like a bolster, and to partake of the feast, which was being prepared in his honour. Three buffaloes, several pigs and a few chickens were being prepared, and each of the arriving guests carried a green bamboo tube filled with palm wine (*tuak*), which the Toraja make from a tree called *induk*. Although the drinking and dancing was to take place in the open air, the atmosphere was not unlike that of a good longhouse party.

Further west during my travels through the Outer Islands of Indonesia in 1973, I was able to visit the remotest of the surviving tribes of the interior of the island of Ceram in the Moluccas, the Hua Ulu. An Italian anthropologist, Valerio Valeri, and his Swedish wife, Renée, the first Europeans to be allowed in, had been there for 18 months, and thanks to them my first wife Marika, who was to die of cancer in 1982, and I were welcomed. Notorious as energetic headhunters, the Hua Ulu were left alone by the coastal people and the authorities, and they had vowed to take the heads of any missionaries who tried to convert them, but we felt safe in the company of the first outsiders to be accepted by them. Their houses were built on stilts, open along one side like miniature longhouses, and were decorated with remarkable carvings of a high quality no longer found elsewhere on the island. The Hua Ulu were a fiercely independent people and proud to show us how their young men were learning to carve the complex traditional spiral and geometric designs, as well as to reproduce lifelike animals. For the uprights supporting each house a species of tree fern was used. This wood is most suitable for being worked and we saw surprising contrasts with bas-reliefs of realistic crocodiles, pigs' heads, lizards and birds interspersed with surrealist impressions of great beauty and charm. The *baileu*, or clan house, had the finest carvings around its base, above which rose a magnificent and spacious hall with a wide wooden dance floor under a sweeping tightly interwoven roof, which reached down to the level of the platform.

They brought us palm-wrapped parcels of rice and fish preserved and seasoned with harsh salt dried from seawater, freshwater prawns, bananas, sago, green leaves and a quantity of wild pig which smelled very strong. Marika, who was the cookery editor of the *Sunday Telegraph* and interested in trying anything culinary, unwrapped the pig meat and turned up her nose, but Valerio said that it was a rare honour for us to have been given this and that we must eat every scrap. The flesh was rotting and there were thick white maggots crawling through the fibres. She did her best to conceal the smell with lime juice and red peppers and cooked it well in a blackened pot, but all her skill in adding disguising flavourings could not mask the stink of rotten meat or hide the plump whiteness of the maggots which still lurked in the flesh and, even though they must have been suffocated by the heat of cooking, still looked as though they might crawl across our plates.

The surreal paradox was that we were eating off elegant celadon Ming plates, which at that time took the place of currency with the Hua Ulu. The Chinese had been trading with the Moluccas for centuries and examples of these 500-year-old pieces of porcelain were, back in the 1970s, to be found throughout the islands. Some would have been kept as family treasures, others dug up from Chinese graves. These people, who were regarded by the dominant Indonesian society as primitive and backward, had been practising their own rich culture and associating with peoples from different societies, like the Chinese, for hundreds of years. Yet, as so often everywhere in the world, their government was obsessed with making them conform to their idea of what constituted 'civilisation'. When I travelled a couple of years later through unexplored eastern Sulawesi with a friend who had studied ceramics under one of the great Japanese masters, he was able to make quite an important collection of this ware from people in the remote interior, who were prepared to trade it for some of our equipment, such as torches and mosquito nets.

13   A Hua Ulu family in the interior of the
island of Ceram in the Moluccas.

The sago gruel given to us by the Hua Ulu, which we ate with three-pronged wooden forks each made from a single twig, finely smoothed and split at one end with the prongs splayed out, helped to wash it down, but it was probably the most unpleasant thing I have ever had to eat. We were closely watched by men in red turbans, which denoted that they were married, and bark loincloths; the women in colourful sarongs took a deep interest in us as strangers, while the children never shouted or followed us around. These were strong and self-contained people, but Valerio told me that the authorities were already beginning to take an interest in them, obsessed with persuading them to move down to the coast; change was not far off.

After Ceram we travelled through the interior of the Indonesian part of the island of New Guinea, called by the government Irian Jaya, but now properly known as West Papua. It should never have been part of Indonesia but, once again due to an obsessive desire to make everyone conform, we were to see brutal examples of people being forced to change their ways. 'Operation Koteka', a plan to clothe and 'civilise' the Dani people of the Baliem highlands, famous for their spectacular penis sheaths or *kotekas*, was in full swing. As I wrote in my subsequent book, *A Pattern of Peoples* (1975), it was 'so paternalistic, ill-conceived and puritanically prejudiced in its priorities as to make one gasp that it could have been drawn up in the twentieth century'. But I kept a copy of the pamphlet published by the Indonesian government and, rather than comment, shall simply provide a quotation from it so that the reader can see what I mean:

> Socioeconomic conditions among the island inhabitants are distressing. They live on the products of nature they gather briefly every day, and on the produce of their primitive cultivation, shifting from one place to another [...]
>
> The people remain strongly attached to tribal traditions and customs. This attachment constitutes an impediment in our effort to lead them on the path of development, of social unity and progress in living standards.

The chiefs who are, at the same time, warlords, leaders and guardians of tradition and culture, occupy a central position in the tribes.

Their housing is extremely poor. Huts are built of tree poles with thatched roof, primitive structures with no attention to hygienic or aesthetic factors. The people sleep on the floor, on a bedding of grass, around the fireplace for protection against the cold.

Our objects include teaching people the importance of having decent living accommodation according to normal village standards, as well as to build houses using locally available materials [...] to dress neatly, to cultivate plantations, to care for their animals, to use Indonesian in a limited way, to sing Indonesian songs, to know the names of the Indonesian islands, to cook their food, etc. [...] so as to facilitate the work of officials in guiding and influencing the people towards attainment of the main objective and, at the same time, to render government administration easier.

Dom Moraes, writing in *Asia Magazine* (March 1972) about the Baliem Valley, sums up Operation Koteka:

Its aim, in fact, is to change the Dani, whether they like it or not, though the Indonesians don't think of it like that. They will deliver trousers to the Dani in much the same mood as that in which Saint Paul delivered Epistles to the Lacedemonians [...] It is bound to be enforced eventually. Money will come into the valley with clothes. The old free life will be finished, and [the Dani] will become another backward race looked after by a supposedly paternal administration. More children will attend more schools: but what will they learn there which will be of any use to them if they continue to live in the valley? Possibly quite a lot, as the valley changes: but the happiness one feels in the Dani now will have departed, it will have flown beyond the mountains, and nobody will know where they can find that blue bird a second time.

Operation Koteka concentrated on trying to get the Dani to wear shorts and shirts, which were issued in large quantities. But the men

14   An old Dani man in the Baliem highlands in
West Papua with a *koteka* (penis sheath).

used the shorts as hats and the women the dresses as carrying bags and
the campaign was eventually abandoned. The oppression of the Dani,
however, continues to this day.

A couple of years later, in March 1976, we were back in Borneo
seeking the best site on the island for the planned RGS expedition
designed to make the first full-scale study of a rainforest. I had heard
of an extraordinary, virtually self-contained ecosystem in one of the
remotest, least explored and still-pristine places on the island, the
Maliau Basin. Totally separated from the outside world for centuries,
it is an area almost completely encircled by insurmountable cliffs and

was only known from occasional sightings from aeroplanes. Although some locals might have penetrated the area, no archaeological record has been found establishing any permanent residency ever in this zone. The first account of the Maliau Basin by Westerners was in the late 1940s, when a small plane almost crashed into the cliff wall, and it was not until 1988 that a modern expedition would be undertaken, revealing glorious waterfalls and an abundance of wildlife.

I wanted to investigate the logistics of getting there, and the closest point of entry looked like being a then rarely visited and barely navigable river inhabited by Murut people, who lived in longhouses along its banks: the Sapulut. I had also heard of a legendary limestone outcrop, the Batu Punggul, which I was determined to reach. Our boat was old and leaky – the holes packed with bits of grass pushed in with a screwdriver – and the river full of rapids, which we had to drag it over, as the water was low. But the river was delightful, with trees covered in what looked like orange blossom hanging over the water, where it was reflected, and it was stimulating to go where few outsiders had been before. Our guide was a strong young man called Lentil, who looked after us solicitously – especially Marika, who was struggling with the rather arduous travelling conditions, but who showed her mettle when it came to the drinking, of which we had been warned.

The Murut longhouses were smaller than Iban ones, only having about ten families per house. They were still very traditional then, rarely visited by outsiders and hard to get to because of the rapids. Reached, as were all riverside houses in those days, by a precarious notched pole, the buildings had walls made of bark, peeled off the tree trunk in one strip; there were still human heads to be seen up in the rafters among the various deer antlers and pigs' jawbones. The Murut, whose name means 'People of the Hills', had been legendary headhunters, among the last people to give up the practice, and no young man could hope to gain the hand of his beloved unless he presented at least one head to her family. Headhunting almost died out due to government and missionary activity in the 1930s, but was enthusiastically taken up again during the Japanese occupation in World War II.

We were fed on bowls of rice with big dishes of deer meat in a broth and a huge pot of sago and vegetables: aubergine, beans and wild spinach. There was a pervasive smell of rice wine; in this case it was *tapai* made from tubers of cassava. It was stored in large Chinese jars and we had been warned that we would have to drink lots. This was done through a straw, which is a well-known way to get drunk fast, and the alcohol content is about double that of wine. After we had eaten, we were made to drink. Gongs were banged and there was much laughter and ceremony as we were led to the row of jars, made to sit on stools in front of them and shown how to drink. Leaves were stuffed into the mouth of each jar and a notched stick was carefully forced down through them with a rattan straw beside it. The liquid is forced up above the leaves and the rule is that you have to drink until it is down to their level. This is much harder to do than it looks, as the jar bulges out at that point and so you have to drink an excessive amount, thereby getting rapidly drunk, which is the whole point of the exercise – and seemingly unavoidable, as it gives your host so much pleasure. Marika held her own with the toughest of the warriors and earned their respect; I was made to drink until I felt like death and passed out. It was not reassuring to be told that the jars were often destined to be used as funerary urns.

We did reach Batu Punggul eventually, after dragging our boat through endless rapids. We stopped on a gravelly beach surrounded by thick mist, out of which strange rock formations loomed. Gradually an enormous, white, sheer-sided skyscraper of rock began to take shape, towering over the thick surrounding forest and reaching way up into the sky. I told our Murut companions that I wanted to climb up to a cave we could see through the mist and then, hopefully, to the top. They said it was impossible now. In the past there had been a fallen tree up which they had been able to climb, but that had gone. After a difficult scramble, hanging on to roots and sharp, thorny lianas, we did make it to the cave, to be greeted by a huge spider, one of the biggest I have ever seen. It was about 20 centimetres across. I went nearer to photograph it, but was pulled back and told that if it bit me I would be dead in five minutes. It seemed unlikely, but I decided to let it be.

There were lots of swiftlets nesting and bats roosting on the roof of the cave, open holes through which the sunlight now shone and, high up on a ledge, bright-green luminous moss which glinted like fairy gold. I tried to climb up to the top of the *batu* (rocky outcrop) and was defeated, but I reached a point where I was rewarded by views across undisturbed forest as far as the eye could see. Batu Punggul is today a popular tourist site, but I doubt the views and the forest are as pristine as they were 40 years ago.

It was clear that the Sapulut River could not at that time provide a suitable access route for a major expedition into the Maliau Basin, titillating though the prospect was. The logistical obstacles which needed to be overcome were just too great. Today there is a dirt road to the cliffs, scientists are starting to do research and some adventure tours are even planned. I will be leading one soon after this book is published.

It was on the Tinjar River in Sarawak, later on my recce, that I found a whole unspoiled river lined with perfect, functioning longhouses in a still-pristine environment at a day's paddling distance from each other. We started from Marudi, then a charming, isolated little river town with no road to the outside world. I was to get to know it very well later when it became our nearest shopping centre and collection point for scientists joining the Mulu expedition. Above the town is the pretty Fort Hose, built in 1883, overlooking the big, brown Baram River, down which occasional large barges, some two or three storeys high and made of clapboard, passed at a snail's pace towing a never-ending streamer of logs lashed together and bobbing like corks when passing another boat's wash. The forest inland seemed then so infinite, and these extractions so small, relatively, but they were the beginning of the process which, over the next 20 years, was to rip out Sarawak's heart. Already, they told us, the quality of the water had changed, becoming muddier from erosion. The old Kenyah names for the Baram River are 'Juice of the Pineapple' and 'Silver Snake'.

Bishop Galvin, of the Mill Hill Missionaries, was making a tour of his remoter parishioners, and a Dutch priest, Father Herman, was to come with us. Our guide, Lawing, arrived to greet us in Marudi's main square. He was an old man with a shaved forehead and a long pigtail tied in a neat knot. A wide grin revealed his blackened teeth behind his lips, red from betel juice. He took the bishop's hand and kissed it passionately. The most modest and gentle of men, Anthony Galvin was frequently greeted this way by his flock, who clearly adored him. Around us were tightly packed shops, all it seemed selling exactly the same things. The pattern was broken by an exotic thatched Chinese temple with a colourful gateway, full of dragons and with ornate walls and curvy roofs. Next to it was 'The Great Wall Dentist' and then 'The Speedy Tailor', where one young girl sat alone at a long row of old-fashioned Singer sewing machines. Ominously, along one side of the square was another row of machines: giant diggers belonging to a timber company, poised to inflict devastation upriver. They looked like praying mantises.

Our boat was much larger than the one we had used on the Sapulut River. It felt palatial, with a corrugated-iron canopy under which we could all sit in reasonable comfort on our baggage. Over the next few days the bishop and I were able to have long conversations about the possibilities and difficulties of mounting a major scientific expedition into the interior. As we turned into the Tinjar River, we passed people washing in little bathhouses on rafts off the riverbank. Every now and then we glimpsed dark-green openings where the trees met overhead and tempting overgrown watery ways flowed into the main river, inviting us to explore their secrets. From here emanated the cool, earthy, leafy smell of damp jungle. Now passing boats were only small dugouts with neatly woven rattan testers to shade the occupants from the sun and rain. When in the open, both men and women wore the wide, shallow, colourful, circular hats made of an almost parchment-like leaf, bound at the edges with cotton, decorated with beads and with a neat skullcap underneath to keep the hat firmly fixed in place. Often their boats were so low in the water that the rim was invisible and it looked as though the people were actually sitting in the river. Logging had not yet begun on the Tinjar and the water was clear. Many kingfishers, some quite large, flew along beside us and various hornbills regularly darted across from bank to bank. We were to see and learn to identify all eight species found in Borneo over the next

couple of years, but now it was just sheer pleasure to watch their lei-
sured flight with their huge beaks hanging down in front like the nose
cone of a landing Concorde. The most spectacular are the Rhinoceros
hornbill, the national bird of Sarawak, whose loud wing beats were a
familiar sound above the canopy, and the helmeted hornbill, known
as the 'kill-your-mother-in-law bird'. This is because of its strange and
funny call. It starts with a series of loud *tocks*, which sound a bit like
a stilt house being chopped down. This is followed by a crescendo of
wild and increasingly hysterical laughter. Legend has it that a man, who
disposed of his mother-in-law by cutting down her home and then
hacking her to pieces, was punished by being changed into the bird
and condemned to relive forever his unholy glee as he committed the
terrible deed. Their casques, whose ivory is locally called 'golden jade',
are still much sought after by the Chinese for making into jewellery.

During the afternoon it would nearly always rain heavily, the drops
bouncing off our boat's tin roof like hailstones. This was often followed
by a sensational sunset of pure streaks of lime green, citrus yellow, palest
tender blue and geranium red. It was time to arrive. On one occasion,
we came to a stop below a muddy bank, above which stretched a huge
longhouse. At first there was silence, the house appearing deserted, until
the sound of stamping feet and chanting began to crescendo above us.
Suddenly a shotgun was fired and a crowd appeared far above on the
bank cheering and clapping. A gaggle of small boys scrambled to grab
our baggage. We had to be helped up the narrow-notched poles leading
up from the water's edge over the deep mud. At the top to greet us was
a very pretty girl with ear lobes reaching down to her shoulders, so tight
and thin that they looked like stretched pink rubber bands, but giving
her wonderful posture as she stood tall and was careful not to make
violent movements. They were dragged down by two highly polished
and very heavy brass weights. Behind her, a row of young men in cotton
cawats or loincloths, their long black hair hanging down their backs to
their waists, held bottles of milky rice wine (*borak*), while an equal row
of bare-breasted and shyly smiling girls, almost all with stretched ear
lobes, held full glasses out to us, which we were compelled to drink. As
soon as they were empty, the young men filled them again. Several wore

highly decorated circular hats, some with hornbill feathers hanging from them. Many were tattooed: the men with the traditional Kenyah designs of swirling patterns on their throats, shoulders and legs, the women often with glove-like intricate, lacy motifs on their hands and arms. Meanwhile the chanting and gunshots continued, welcoming the much-loved bishop and his guests.

We were led to seats on the veranda of the longhouse with our backs to the river. A tray of glasses was put in front of us with two bottles of arak, the stronger, clear, distilled form of rice wine, just in case we had not already had enough. An old man, heavily tattooed and with bright-red lips from the betel he was chewing, came and sat down cross-legged next to the tray. Everyone gathered round. He closed

15   A Kenyah girl on the Tinjar with stretched ear lobes.

his eyes and began to sing, swaying slightly. It was a song of welcome, poetry sung in a high-pitched voice in an archaic version of the Kenyah language, and the bishop translated quietly as he sang. Fathers sat with children in their arms or holding their hands, while other groups of children sat motionless and entranced. Sometimes they joined in what seemed to be a chorus. He bade us welcome to the rice and what food they could offer us and invited us to drink with them.

'You have come up the Tinjar, the Lemon River, to visit us. You come at a good time, when the moon is like a pregnant woman. You are young and we wish you a long life and many children.'

Addressing us each in turn, he sang: 'You [Marika] have hair like a cloud of yellow butterflies; you [me] are strong as a tiger; you [the bishop] are like a great tame hornbill. Please protect us and help us to make good *padi* [hill rice]. We moved here from the Usun Apau and now we are poor. We are shaped like the hairy caterpillar. You are strong like the centre of a *prau* [dugout], keeping us safe from the waves. We have nothing. We are so ashamed of what we have to offer you. We wish you a long life, so that you will walk with a stick.'

Then, with his eyes closed and a very serious expression: 'We prophesy this and may God curse us if what we say is not true. We want you to live close together, under one shirt. Robin is a man. He is going on a long journey, but Marika is left behind, so she must fly in an aeroplane and circle above us, seeing where he is and that he is safe.'

As soon as he finished singing we were made to drink more arak, the girls kneeling in front of us and politely offering us large, full glasses. When we tried to refuse, they gently but firmly put their arms around our necks and literally forced the liquid down our throats until we were quite drunk, which, again, seemed to be the object of the exercise and made everyone laugh and smile contentedly. We were now led into the *bilek* of the Tua Rumah or headman, his personal accommodation, which was in the centre of the longhouse, facing, like all the other *bileks*, onto the wide veranda, and we were fed. They apologised that they had not been able to kill a wild pig in time for this feast, but we had fresh and smoked deer, chicken soup, small smoked fish from the river, and huge bowls of sticky rice and a different sort packed in banana-leaf parcels. Drink alternated between sweet coffee, *borak* and arak. After eating, we all went out to the back of the longhouse, where there was a platform with a tap from which flowed delicious fresh, cold water piped from a mountain stream. The forest beyond, into which a network of paths led, was the loo. We just walked as far as seemed to make sense and the regular heavy rains and teeming insect and plant life rapidly took over, so that everything was soon clean again. Only at night was answering the call of nature rather less pleasant, as the fire ants came out. Wherever one stopped they would find one within seconds and their bites really hurt, resulting in an undignified and hurried return to the longhouse.

An idyllic series of longhouse visits took us right up to the headwaters of the Tinjar and into the narrow, clear, pale-green Nibong River, whose fresh, sweet water ran fast down off the Usun Apau. Here we made slow progress, ascending many rapids through tumbling, broken water. Often the rocks almost met in the middle and there were trees brought down by the rains lodged diagonally across the stream. We started to find small Penan huts on the bank, always with some cleared land, burned stumps and trunks of larger trees up the steep slope behind. These were Penan beginning to make the difficult transition from a nomadic way of life to the much harder one of settled agriculture and growing hill rice. At the furthest one we were able to reach, Long Liau, I parted from Marika and the bishop, who were to return downriver to Miri, where his cathedral was, and wait for me to return after I had walked with a group of young Penan across the foothills of the Usun Apau to the upper reaches of the Belaga River, a tributary of the Rejang. This would involve crossing from the fourth to the third of Sarawak's administrative divisions, skirting the highlands of one of the then least explored regions of Sarawak.

I gave the headman of Long Liau a small heap of presents: tobacco, salt, soap and matches, and explained that I should be grateful for two or three young men who could come with me and show me the way. He looked me over carefully and at last pronounced that I looked strong and fit and that he would be happy to help me. The rest of that evening passed tranquilly. Unlike the hectic all-night parties usual in Kenyah longhouses, there was no dancing or heavy drinking.

Long before dawn the household was, mouse-like, on the move and, stimulated by the prospect of the long walk ahead of me, I had packed and repacked my few possessions, double-wrapping film and cameras against the wet and adding quantities of silica-gel crystals. We set off by dugout canoe up the now very shallow Nibong. After a while we dragged the dugout up the bank, hid it in the undergrowth and began to walk. As in much of Sarawak, the terrain consisted of a series of steep ridges, up and down which we climbed. Between them we followed the course of streams, often wading knee- or waist-deep with occasional halts to remove leeches.

We rested at the Lobang River, where rice and water were put on to boil over a small fire. Sigau Pajun, an older Penan who had appeared from nowhere while we were walking and simply joined us, unpacked a small throwing net from one of our rattan backpacks and began to cast it at the point where the calm water surged between two rocks. Working his way upstream, he was soon out of sight. He returned carrying eight

16 Dragging our dugout up the Nibong River as we set out to cross the watershed between the Tinjar and Belaga Rejang rivers.

fish of about a kilogram each, which were cleaned, scaled and boiled in a few minutes. Having been assured by the headman of Long Liau that my companions had enough rice for our needs and that we would catch or hunt meat on the way, I had brought only salt, tea and a bar of Kendal Mint Cake as basic luxuries, as well as tobacco to give as a present. The salt now proved invaluable, seasoning the bland flesh of the fish and drawing appreciative murmurs from the Penan. We slept that night in an abandoned *sulap*, hurrying for the last few kilometres as clouds gathered and the nightly rainstorm prepared to fall on us.

When we reached the Belaga River we found a diminutive dugout hidden by some previous Penan. Since it was so small, and leaked badly, two of our party left us to walk back across the watershed to the Nibong. It was just able to carry Gelang, Kaleng and me, but as there was only one paddle Kaleng carved another with his *parang* out of a small softwood tree. He took exactly five minutes to make it, from felling to final decorative shaping.

The river was narrow, with trees meeting overhead and lianas trailing in the water. Monkeys crossed from side to side and one fell into the water ahead of us in its alarm at catching sight of us. Here we were far beyond the limit of settlement, several weeks by dugout canoe from the sea, and the Belaga is notorious for its rapids, in which many have died. However, we were fortunate that the water was high and we were able to shoot many of the smaller rapids. When the current became too fast and waves threatened to swamp the boat, Kaleng and I carried the baggage along the bank, sometimes along tracks, sometimes having to cut our way, while Gelang paddled through the white water alone. Long Urun was the highest settled Penan longhouse on the Belaga. My arrival caused a major sensation since they had had few visitors and a European was an extreme rarity. Women and children ran up from the riverbank shouting to call the men out of the longhouse and a large crowd gathered around me as I settled myself in the centre of the gallery. Kaleng and Gelang left me there to return home, having established that other Penan would take me on downriver.

Five young Penan boys agreed to take me down the Belaga to a Kenyah longhouse above the fierce rapids at Sambop, which mark the limit of normal navigation. They were a cheerful band who refused to take me or anything else very seriously. Most of the time they laughed and gossiped, clowned when I took their photographs and broke into snatches of song.

They spoke little Malay, but language was seldom much of a problem. Only hunting brought intense stillness and concentration. Game was incredibly plentiful on this little-visited stretch of river, and drifting quietly with the current was the best way to see it. In the evenings we stopped, apparently just anywhere, and I would watch them build a *sulap* from scratch. In less than an hour an area of virgin forest was converted into a comfortable campsite with a totally waterproof house and rice, fish and wild boar ready to eat. Each Penan knew exactly what to do and without discussion performed his allotted role. Balan Utang, the only other adult, would disappear to hunt a pig; his son, Ugat Balan, chopped a neat pile of firewood with his *parang*, finely shredding the outside layers of certain logs to create an effect like cutlet frills and so provide kindling. Supau Leding, who sported an atypical little military moustache, and Gud Lisang, whose ear lobes were being stretched by thick and heavy earplugs, rapidly assembled the framework of the *sulap*. Two tall, forked uprights stuck firmly in

17   My young Penan companions clowning at being photographed.

43

the ground and two lower ones, each with a crossbar, formed the roof support. The floor was made of matching poles laid side by side across two thicker ones, so leaving a space of about 2 centimetres above the ground. The first layer of the lean-to roof consisted of a similar row of slender poles cleverly hooked side by side to the top crossbar by having an uphill slice cut into them near the end. Meanwhile Toi Parin, the youngest boy, was collecting palm fronds.

After an astonishing 20 minutes of intense activity the camp was practically complete. The fire was lit, the *sulap* almost finished and a leech- and mosquito-free cleared area around us. After a brief discussion between the two architect–builders, Toi dropped his last load and stretched. He walked over to a nearby tree, cut a slice of wood off it and brought it to me to smell. It was sweet and refreshing, like lemon-flavoured custard. I remembered how the Choco Embera Indians in Panama, when hauling a heavy dugout over another watershed, used to stop and apparently draw strength from the smell of certain lianas which they rubbed on their hands.

18   Making camp the Penan way in the evening.

19 Kaleng, one of the young Penan who accompanied
me through the Usun Apau foothills.

While the rice cooked over the fire, all, including the returned, successful hunter Balan, set to work to weave the waterproof roof covering. The Penan name for the palms used for thatching is *kebopah*. Each fan-like frond is knitted together with a strip of fibre from the stem. This was a slower job, and it was half an hour before the roof was complete. Then the rain came and we sat in a row in total shelter, without a drop coming through, as Supau stirred the rice and we watched the storm lash the river below.

This was my first proper experience of travelling for weeks as the Penan did when hunting, and I loved every minute of it, secure in the knowledge that I was safe in the hands of the most competent hunter-gatherers to be found anywhere.

CHAPTER 3

History

THE RAJAHS BROOKE

For 105 years, from 1841 to 1946, Sarawak was ruled by the Brooke 'White Rajahs' as a private fiefdom. They had a policy of leaving the indigenous population largely alone and interfering as little as possible with their lives. Adventurers, speculators and missionaries were banned, and even the more economically developed coastal people were prevented from encroaching inland. Scientists and travellers, who were really explorers in those days, people like Harry de Windt and Marianne North, were encouraged. The one thing they drew the line at was the tradition of headhunting. This had played a vital role in the lives of many of the longhouse peoples and forbidding it interfered profoundly with ritual observances, let alone the prestige of young men seeking a bride. But, on the whole, the successive rajahs were popular for their unobtrusive administration, and life was a lot safer. The story of how they came to be there is a deeply romantic one, unique in the annals of European colonialism.

In the sixteenth century the Sultanate of Brunei was one of the most powerful states in South East Asia. It controlled modern Sarawak and Sabah, the Sulu Archipelago and part of the Philippines, as well as trading far afield: south to Java, west to Malacca, east to the Moluccas and north to Siam, today's Thailand. The first Europeans arrived with the Portuguese explorer Magellan, whose navigator, Pigafetta, described riding on elephants caparisoned in silk and a royal palace protected by brass and iron cannon, where the inhabitants wore gold-embroidered clothes and had jewellery of pearls and precious stones. In 1578 the

Spanish, who were by then well established in the Philippines, attacked and captured Brunei, but only managed to hold it for 72 days before withdrawing due to sickness. Brunei endured a slow decline as the colonial powers took over much of its traditional trade, until at the beginning of the nineteenth century things began to fall apart. The Land Dayak and the coastal Malays were rebelling against the heavy taxes being imposed by the sultan and seeking independence. There was much intertribal fighting between them and the seafaring Iban.

In 1836, James Brooke, the 33-year-old son of a British High Court judge in India, inherited £30,000 on the death of his father. This was the equivalent of about £3.5 million in today's money. With it he bought a 142-ton schooner and, with the support of the new RGS, which had only been founded in 1830, he set off in 1838 in search of adventure and exploration. On arrival in Kuching, he found the uprising in full swing and the sultan's representative beleaguered. In an extraordinary piece of military diplomacy, he defeated the rebels with hardly a shot being fired, and they surrendered on condition that he become rajah of a Sarawak that was independent of Brunei, where the sultan would continue to rule. Ironically, the small state of Brunei, which was all the sultan eventually had left to him, proved to be where most of the oil would subsequently be found, so that, 150 years later, his descendant became the richest man in the world. Meanwhile, the first Rajah Brooke, effectively an absolute monarch and unconnected to the British Empire, took control of a country with a well-populated coast and a largely unexplored interior. He was to be the inspiration for both Kipling's *The Man Who Would Be King* and Conrad's *Lord Jim*. His state flag was based on the Brooke family coat of arms, a St George's Cross in red and black, and this remained in various forms until independence in 1963.

Under his rule peace was brought to the region and much important scientific work was initiated, most notably by Alfred Russel Wallace, who visited Sarawak in 1854 and, just as we were to go on our expedition, stayed for 15 months. In his book *The Malay Archipelago* (1869), Wallace writes: 'I was hospitably entertained by Sir James Brooke, and lived in his house whenever I was at the town of Saráwak in the intervals of my journeys.' He spent both the Christmases he was on the island with the rajah, 'who possessed in a pre-eminent degree the art of making every one around him comfortable and happy.' They used to climb together up to the summit of a little nearby mountain where there was a

> rude wooden lodge where the English Rajah was accustomed to go for relaxation and cool fresh air [...] A cool spring under an over-hanging rock just below the cottage furnished us with refreshing baths and delicious drinking water, and the Dayaks brought us daily heaped-up baskets of Mangusteens and Lansats, two of the most delicious of the subacid tropical fruits.

In return, Wallace named one of the most attractive butterflies in the world, the Rajah Brooke's birdwing, after his host. His description of it reveals the breadth of his skill both as an observant scientist and as a writer:

> This beautiful creature has very long and pointed wings, almost resembling a sphinx moth in shape. It is deep velvety black, with a curved band of spots of a brilliant metallic-green colour extending across the wings from tip to tip, each spot being shaped exactly like a small triangular feather, and having very much the effect of a row of the wing coverts of the Mexican trogon [a Latin American bird] laid upon black velvet. The only other marks are a broad neck-collar of vivid crimson, and a few delicate white touches on the outer margins of the hind wings.

He was also deeply impressed by Brooke's style of government:

> Equal justice was awarded to Malay, Chinaman and Dyak. The remorseless pirates from the rivers further east were punished, and finally shut up within their own territories, and the Dyak, for the first time, could sleep in peace [...] it must ever be remembered that he held Saráwak solely by the goodwill of the native

inhabitants [...] he ruled them, not for his own advantage, but
for their good.

Wallace, who has always stood out for me as the greatest of the great
explorers, was an indefatigable collector. He was able to accumulate a
vast quantity of beetles during four months spent at an opencast coal
mine, where a clearing had been created with many felled and rotting
trees surrounded by dense forest. This was ideal collecting habitat
and the results were staggering: 'by paying a cent each for all insects
that were brought me, I obtained from the Dyaks and the Chinamen
many fine locusts and Phasmidæ, as well as numbers of handsome
beetles.' He was averaging 24 new species a day, and ended up with
a collection of several thousand. This was the era when scientists like
Wallace were beginning to reveal the astonishing richness and diversity
of nature. I found it extraordinary and rather alarming that, 125 years
later, when our scientists were collecting in Mulu, some of them were
still finding the same diversity and the same numbers of new species.
I remember our German mycologist, Walter Jülich, telling me that he
was collecting more than 50 new species of fungi every day for three
weeks. Since then, so much of the rainforest has been destroyed and
with it huge numbers of never-to-be-known species, each of which had
taken many millennia to evolve. That has to be wrong by any standard.

Just after the country celebrated 100 years of Brooke rule in
September 1941, the Japanese invaded and initiated a reign of terror. A
'Sarawak Provisional Government in Exile' was established in London,
lasting until September 1945, when the country was liberated by
Australian troops. Sovereignty was restored to Charles Vyner Brooke,
the third rajah, but in spite of much opposition, he was forced to bow
to British government pressure and cede his rights, so that Sarawak
became a British Crown Colony on 1 July 1946. Malcolm MacDonald,
governor general of Malaya, officiated at the ceremony marking the
end of Sarawak's independent statehood. He was later to be one of the
original patrons of Survival International, the charity of which I was
a co-founder, and to pen the foreword to my book on the tribes of
Indonesia, *A Pattern of Peoples* (1975). In it he wrote:

Can the tragedy which has overcome, and sometimes completely destroyed, many such societies during the last few centuries as a result of the encroachment of Western and other alien peoples and concepts be avoided? Can what is good (but not what is bad) in their traditional ways of life be preserved and combined with what is good in their true interests (but not what is bad) in more modern cultures? It is a very difficult, but very important and urgent problem.

I myself have watched a similar dilemma being tackled among the Iban and other tribal peoples in Sarawak, next door to their neighbours in Kalimantan whom the author describes in one section of his book. In spite of the still lingering inclination of the tribal elders when I first knew them in the late 1940s to take heads – a passion which they were no longer allowed to indulge! – those Iban and the nearby Kayan and Kenyah were among the most likeable, and in some ways actually while in others potentially talented, characters whom I have known anywhere round the Earth. Their skills in certain handicrafts and in music and dancing were delightful; their brains were often excellent; and their ethical code of personal conduct had quite a lot to recommend it. They were also then, because of their simple though ample and usually satisfied desires, the happiest people whom I have ever met. I must not expand on that theme, and I will only say that the transition of their younger generation from their customary old, rather jungley ways to more up-to-date, partly urban ones is proceeding not too badly, although considerable difficulties and previously unthinkable frustrations now and then arise.

In my judgement we sophisticated peoples, with our excessive worship of materialist technology, have just about as much to learn from them as they have to learn from us, if our world is to be saved from disaster. I hope that Robin Hanbury-Tenison's writings, as well as similar activities by other individuals and groups dedicated to a great cause, will help bring us to our senses before it is too late.

Sarawak remained under British rule until independence in 1963, when the Federation of Malaya was formed. Unfortunately for Sarawak, under international law offshore petroleum resources belonged to the federal government, and so it was deprived of its main asset. The forests were the only major resource remaining, but they, as a result of short-term greed, have been devastated by massive extraction over the last 40 years, thus ripping out the very fabric of the country.

TOM HARRISSON

The European name most associated with Sarawak after Brooke was that of Tom Harrisson. He had led an Oxford University expedition there in 1932 and, in January 1945, was parachuted into the interior with seven Australian special forces soldiers to mount a rearguard attack on the occupying Japanese. He informed the local Kelabit, and later all the other peoples of the interior, that the ban on headhunting, which the Brooke administration had imposed, was lifted in the case of the Japanese, an announcement greeted with huge enthusiasm by all, as they had suffered greatly during the occupation.

His story is extraordinary. In some ways it goes to the heart of why Borneo in general and Mulu in particular matter. On the 1932 expedition he learned to appreciate and understand the indigenous peoples of Sarawak's interior. He studied their ways and fell in love with their gaiety and wit, while developing an admiration, which never left him, for their intimate knowledge of and affinity for the rich environment then still surrounding them. He made several journeys through the rainforest with them, most memorably a stiff walk, involving a portage (dragging a dugout over the watershed) and boating over many rapids between the headwaters of the Tinjar and the Belaga, a tributary of the Rejang. It was 44 years later, in 1976, while on my recce for a site for the RGS expedition, that I was to become only the second European to make this journey, travelling with that delightful group of young Penan from Long Liau, as described in Chapter 2.

Tom claimed that it was on this trip that he had his first heterosexual experience. The Kenyah women, with heavy brass rings suspended from their long, elegant ear lobes and, partly as a result, the most graceful, poised and serene bearing imaginable, were in those days well known for extending generous hospitality to those who visited their longhouses, if they fancied them. Tom Harrisson was notorious as a womaniser and left several illegitimate children in Sarawak. No such favours were extended to me when I followed in his footsteps. For a start, as I have described, I travelled up the Tinjar with my wife, Marika, and Anthony Galvin, the delightful Catholic bishop of Miri. And on the two-week walk across the watershed I was accompanied by an enthusiastic group of young Penan, which made the atmosphere more like that of a Boy Scout camp.

Tom next arrived on the island when he was dropped by parachute into the Plain of Bah, in the very heart of Borneo and close to the then Dutch (now Indonesian) border, on 25 March 1945. This was a large area, some 6–900 metres above sea level, inhabited and cultivated by the Kelabit people, the remotest of all the tribes of Borneo, who, most unusually, irrigated their fields and so were able to harvest two crops of rice a year. Largely self-sufficient, they traditionally made cloth from bark and produced excellent iodised salt from saline springs. This they traded for steel for making *parangs*, the indispensable long knives carried by every man, as well as cloth, metal pots and medicines. It was one of the very few open areas where a parachute drop was possible, since most of the island was covered in dense forest. They had spotted it on one of several long reconnaissance flights at the very limit of the Royal Australian Air Force's four-engine Liberators' range. The plane that finally dropped them there never made it home.

As a major in 'Z Special Unit', the Australian equivalent of the Special Operations Executive (SOE), he was in command of seven tough and experienced New Zealand and Australian soldiers, who were about to become the first Allied troops to be parachuted behind Japanese lines on the island. Next to drop after him was Sergeant Fred 'Sandy' Sanderson, a Eurasian Australian, who spoke Malay. Sanderson was to spend much of the next six months in an area based on the Limbang River, close to Mulu. As well as two radios, which were damaged in the drop but subsequently repaired, and more than a ton of arms and equipment, they brought with them 50,000 fish hooks and a quarter of a million needles to pay for local food and labour, money not being much use in the deep interior. Some of the needles ended up being used for defence on later military excursions in the forest, being set in bamboo and hidden in the ground around camps.

Their mission was to gather information about Japanese occupying forces and troop movements prior to the coastal invasion planned for June; to disrupt enemy supply routes without being detected; and to train the local population as guerrilla troops. By the simple expedient described earlier of telling his hosts that the embargo on headhunting, which had been imposed on them some years before by the Brooke administration, was lifted as far as Japanese were concerned, he soon had the exuberant support of everyone in the interior, including, as it turned out later, the nomadic Penan. Tom and all the others were always called by the respectful honorific title *tuan*, meaning 'lord', given to very important people. It was a deliberate recognition that Tom and the others represented the pre-Japanese authority of the Brooke regime. The resulting skirmishes with the columns of heavily armed Japanese troops escaping the coastal bombardment must represent one of the most successful covert campaigns in World War II. Many weapons, rifles, carbines, Sten guns, Bren guns, handguns and high explosives were dropped and used with spirited effect by the Kelabit and Kayan. But the most effective weapons proved to be their own traditional ones: the *parang*, a short sword or machete for taking heads and, above all, the blowpipe or *sumpit*, especially after Allied troops had landed on the coast and the Japanese were escaping inland and planning to re-form and counter-attack.

Using blowpipes and able to move silently and invisibly through the surrounding forest, they were able to pick off the soldiers as they followed narrow paths in single file or hacked their way through the undergrowth. The great advantages of blowpipes are their silence and their use of poison. If you miss with your first dart, it is probable that your victim will not notice the faint swish as it whizzes past and you can have another go. With all the other stinging things around, he may not even notice when he is hit and will walk on until the poison takes effect and death follows within the hour. The poison is made from the sap of various trees and comes in diverse forms: glucoside, which stops the heart, and strychnine, which causes muscles to spasm and so brings on asphyxiation. These poisons are used on arrows and blowpipe darts all over the world, but the Penan varieties are said to be the most powerful. I have seen them being prepared by Yanomami Indians in Brazil as well as by the Penan, and they used to be widely utilised as arrow poison in Africa, too.

It must have been terrifying and dispiriting for the escaping Japanese columns as they trekked through terrain they found utterly inhospitable. Sometimes whole groups were picked off as they forded a river, the survivors being felled one by one later as they tried to escape into the undergrowth and soon became lost. Many committed suicide in despair by hanging themselves with their belts, and for some years after the end of the war grisly remains were still to be found suspended from trees in remote places. One of the main escape routes taken by Japanese heading upriver from the oil town of Miri and attempting to cross over the watershed between the Tutoh and Limbang rivers led through what is today the Gunung Mulu National Park and right past where I was, many years later, to establish our expedition Base Camp. The local Berawan paramount chief, Temenggong Baya, who gave me permission to build our own longhouse on the very edge of the newly created park, told me the place was called 'Long Pala', meaning 'the place of the heads', as so many had been taken there. This was also the route taken in earlier years by Kenyah headhunters seeking trophies from their Iban enemies on the other side, and today it is a popular tourist route called 'the Headhunters' Trail'.

Tom's group of guerrillas was credited with almost 2,000 Japanese killed, with the loss of only 11 lives. Four of these were murdered when acting as peace envoys under a white flag, trying to persuade Japanese to surrender. When they did finally surrender, and in Borneo several units continued to fight for a couple of months after Hiroshima, the extent of the atrocities they had committed finally came to light. Many of the local population were tortured to death in an attempt to get them to reveal where downed American airmen were being kept, or summarily executed when suspected of supporting the guerrillas; but the worst cruelty was inflicted on the thousands of mostly

Australian and British prisoners of war, many of whom had been among the 100,000 who surrendered at the fall of Singapore. There were several dreadful camps on the island, where starvation, beatings and executions were standard, but by far the worst was the Sandakan camp, where more than 2,500 prisoners were housed in appalling conditions. As the war ended and invasion approached, they were taken on one of the worst 'death marches' on record. The 1,900 then still alive, all malnourished and many seriously ill, were made to walk 260 kilometres inland. Fewer than 200 made it to Ranau, where they were forced to build a temporary camp. All were executed when peace was declared and before help could reach them. Only six Australians, who escaped, survived to tell what happened, and what the Japanese had tried so hard to hide.

There is a dreadful symmetry in these two stories, which were unfolding alongside each other in 1945, with neither side fully aware of what was actually going on. The Japanese in North Borneo were trying to eliminate all trace of the 2,000 or so Australian and British prisoners of war, so that the world would never know how brutally they had been treated. Tom Harrisson and his unit across the border in Sarawak were successfully killing about 2,000 of the Japanese troops escaping into the interior, so that they would not be able to link up with those running the death marches to the north. If Tom had known just how dreadful the total massacre being perpetrated within marching distance was, might he have abandoned the relatively easy business of picking off frightened and lost escaping Japanese soldiers and hurried to try to save those being harried to their death? I suspect he might. Those Japanese who did make it to the interior and held out until the war was over were safely repatriated.

This legendary story inspired the 1969 novel *L'adieu au roi* by Pierre Schoendoerffer, which was later turned into a film by John Milius – *Farewell to the King* (1989), starring Nick Nolte and James Fox. All seven soldiers who parachuted in with Tom survived, but several were traumatised by the experience and the dreadful atrocities they witnessed. Sandy Sanderson suffered nightmares for the rest of his life.

Tom Harrisson's own book about this time, *World Within*, published in 1959 and still in print with Oxford University Press, tells the story and also reveals his growing fascination with and love for the people of the interior. I have a proof copy with Tom's final corrections in it, which was given to me by Sir Anthony Abell, governor of Sarawak in the 1950s, when it was a Crown Colony, who also gave me good advice when we met in 1977, just before our expedition began. There is a letter from him tucked into the book, which says: 'Here is Tom Harrisson's rather disorganised book – you may find some of it interesting and useful [...] I hope all goes well.'

After the war, Tom became curator of the Sarawak Museum and made it into one of the finest of its kind in the developing world and the institution that really put Sarawak on the map, thanks to his huge energy and eclectic interests. In 1962 he was awarded a Gold Medal by the RGS in 1962 for his work in Borneo – just as I would be, 17 years later, in 1979, after the Mulu expedition. He was an amazing man with a great zest for life, who also made many enemies and had a reputation for explosive outbursts. It was therefore with some trepidation that I joined him for tea at the Travellers Club in November 1975, soon after the idea of an RGS expedition to Borneo had first been mooted. I had met him before, of course, 20 years earlier, although both of us had forgotten. I told him that I was most interested in studying the Penan, the elusive hunter-gatherers of the interior, and that I hoped to base our expedition in their territory and study their ways. 'There are no nomadic Penan left in Sarawak,' he told me firmly, as soon as I raised the subject. 'Seek as you may, you will not find any!' I was taken aback, as I was sure there were still some who had not been settled, but I dared not argue with him and I listened meekly as he gave me some anodyne advice on mounting an expedition. The only really useful thing I remember him saying was that the leader had to make himself deeply unpopular in order to draw the fire from internecine battles among the other members. This was something he had himself practised to good effect. In his book *Borneo Jungle*, he wrote: 'If you don't want a lot of enemies, don't go on a lot of expeditions.' Subsequently I did my best to emulate him, as it actually is good advice. Although I didn't carry it to his extremes and have always remained on the best of terms with everyone I have travelled with, I worked on the principle that the price of glory was the absolute understanding that one's role was to take the blame for all failures. A decade before Mulu, I had been a lowly member of an expedition by hovercraft from the Amazon to the Orinoco, where there was no single leader. In theory, we were to be led by a nice modest scientist, but he lacked all leadership qualities and concentrated on his research; there was the organiser, who had had the idea and raised the money, but he was a Machiavellian journalist who enjoyed manipulating people; and there was the splendid captain of the hovercraft, who confined himself to running a tight ship. As a result, most of the evenings were spent in endless, often acrimonious discussions with little being resolved. I remember observing this and swearing that if I was ever to lead a large expedition I would not do it that way. On the Mulu expedition I was supremely fortunate in having a powerful and distinguished committee back at the RGS, who gave me their unequivocal backing and a free hand, as well as a totally loyal and incredibly hard-working small team of helpers, led by my indomitable deputy, Nigel Winser.

At the time of our Travellers Club meeting, Tom was going through a pretty bad patch, having been banned from Sarawak and unfairly accused of stealing artefacts from the museum. I suspect he was bitter, even jealous, when faced with this naive, relatively youthful expedition leader planning to swan into what he, with every justification, regarded as his exclusive territory. I knew that he had a deep respect for the Penan, whom he describes in *Borneo Jungle* as 'probably equal with or superior to any other people on earth', and I wish I had been able to get to know him better and gain his trust and so his good advice, but he was killed two months later, in January 1976, when the local Thai bus he was travelling in crashed into the back of a timber lorry.

I learned more about Tom later from the biography by Judith Heimann written some years after his death: *The Most Offending Soul Alive*. He was a very contentious figure and expert at making enemies. I particularly enjoyed the stories of his battles with anthropologists, as I have had a few of my own. A particular foe of his was Edmund

Leach, later Sir Edmund, who was to become president of the Royal
Anthropological Institute during Survival International's early years,
so that I had a lot to do with him. In Tom's case, Leach incensed him
by dismissing certain important rituals associated with headhunting as
merely 'occasions for individual and group boasting' – and that after
only a month in Sarawak, mainly in Kuching! Tom's researches into the
various people he lived and worked with always took into account the
situation in which they found themselves and the impact of the outside
world, whereas social anthropologists like Leach confined themselves
to examining traditions. In my case, when in 1971 I was preparing for
Survival International's first ever field trip, to visit 33 Indian tribes
in Brazil, I mentioned that I was hoping to reach the Yanomami, the
largest unacculturated group in the Americas, described, in the title of
a 1968 book by the American anthropologist Napoleon Chagnon, as
The Fierce People. Leach's response was to say: 'Oh, I shouldn't bother
to visit them. They are so backward that the sooner they die out, the
better,' a remark that shocked me to the core and stiffened my resolve
that Survival should fight such views, as it always has. Tom also exposed
other examples of ways in which anthropologists had been found to
say things which subsequent research found to be inaccurate.

Shortly after my spat with Leach I was in New York, where I managed to secure an interview with the formidable Margaret Mead,
who had become world-famous as a result of her book *Coming of Age
in Samoa* (1928), which was full of racy facts about the sex lives of
the young people she studied and became a bestseller as a result. Her
research was later found to be largely the result of a trap set by her two
24-year-old female informants, who had made up the information they
gave her on sexual mores, but she was still at that time the best-known
anthropologist in the world. I found her in one of the Gothic attics
of the American Museum of Natural History. I had to grope my way
through an unlit and dusty library, where I was in constant danger of
tripping over and breaking some of the many and probably priceless
artefacts littering the floor. In an untidy office with a view over the
rooftops of the city I faced a small, beady-eyed dumpling of a lady, who
sailed into attack as soon as I came through the door. She could not

be blamed for jumping to the conclusion that I was a crank do-gooder representing a group of woolly-minded idealists who thought that Indians should be preserved because they were pretty. She fired questions at me and then contradicted me before I had time to elaborate. No questioning of her criticisms was allowed and much was assumed without my saying so.

The main point that got up her nose, without it having been mooted by me, was that 'primitive peoples' were better off as they were. She said she was 'maddened by antibiotic-ridden idealists who wouldn't stand three weeks in the jungle', which was a little unfair in my case, I felt. The whole 'noble savage' concept almost made her foam at the mouth. 'All primitive peoples,' she said, 'lead miserable, unhappy, cruel lives, most of which are spent trying to kill each other.' The reason they lived in such unpleasant places, like the middle of the Brazilian jungle, was that nobody else would. She did not accept for one moment that they had any special reason for being protected. Those still running away in the jungle were the ones who had encountered the most unpleasant savagery from Europeans and, even though they might not be in direct contact now, if they could possibly get hold of any aluminium pots, they would use them. It was the memories of the horrors they had suffered which kept them from seeking contact.

She said that to protect them on the grounds that they could teach us anything was nonsense. 'No primitive person has ever contributed anything, or ever will,' she exclaimed. She had no time for suggestions of medicinal knowledge or the value of jungle lore. She was not impressed by curare and stated that quinine was 'a positive disaster, as it meant that Englishmen took their wives with them to foreign parts, whereas previously they had interbred happily with the natives'!

Her tirade was so remarkable that we began to warm to each other, and she suddenly changed tack and said that if there had ever been a time when a movement such as ours stood a chance of being listened to it was then – that the climate was right, as it had not been for decades, for us to be reasonably effective. In the end I took her by taxi to her next appointment and began to see that she was not the dragon she had first appeared to be, but brilliant, capable and, under her gruff manner, highly likeable. We parted very amicably with her offering 'any help she could give'. Perhaps the most famous quotation attributed to her is: 'Never doubt that a small group of thoughtful, committed citizens can change the world. Indeed, it is the only thing that ever has.' I have often wondered if she was thinking of Survival's subsequent success when she said this, and I regret that I never tried to contact her again before she died in 1978.

CONFRONTATION

In the 1970s most people associated the island of Borneo with the undeclared mini war Britain had fought there between 1963 and 1966, during what came to be known as 'Confrontation'. The issue was Indonesia's hostility to the incorporation of Singapore and the British Crown Colonies of Sarawak and North Borneo (now Sabah) into the new state of Malaysia. Indeed, one of the reasons the colonial legislature of Sarawak gave its grudging consent to joining Malaysia in 1963 was the threat that Indonesia might swallow up Sarawak. After successfully taking over the Dutch part of the island of New Guinea through a largely discredited referendum, President Sukarno felt emboldened to attempt to expand his country's territory northwards to include the whole of the island of Borneo, almost three quarters of which, Kalimantan, was already part of Indonesia. At the height of Confrontation more than 14,000 British troops were deployed throughout Sarawak and Sabah, and there were innumerable skirmishes as they repelled Indonesian soldiers attempting to infiltrate the long mountainous and heavily forested frontier. There were also many training exercises, often in remote upriver areas such as the unexplored lowland forests surrounding Mulu. One Victoria Cross and 48 Military Crosses were awarded, mostly to Gurkhas, and many young British soldiers who served there returned with fond memories of their charming local guides, who had fought alongside them and shown them how to live in the rainforest. One such was a subaltern in the Grenadier Guards, Algy Cluff, who went on to find the Buchan

Field, one of the biggest oilfields in the North Sea. He was so impressed by his Iban guides and the Penan he met while in the field that he offered the RGS a grant of £10,000 to mount a research expedition to the island. This was the trigger that sent me off on my recce to find a suitable venue. Originally, the loose idea was just to study the Penan, but this rapidly morphed and grew into the largest scientific research programme the Society had yet undertaken, later to be described in the *Daily Telegraph* as 'one of the most ambitious scientific expeditions ever mounted by the RGS'.

Coincidentally, Nyapun, the hero of my story, had his own brush with British troops, as we shall see in the next chapter.

CHAPTER 4

Penan

Another brain I wished to pick as I prepared for our expedition
was that of Rodney Needham. He was professor of Social Anthropology
at Oxford from 1976 to 1990 and one of Britain's leading anthropologists. During World War II, as a 21-year-old captain in the Gurkha
Rifles, he was wounded during the Battle of Kohima in north-east
India. After studying Chinese at the School of Oriental and African
Studies (SOAS) he read Anthropology at Oxford and did his first
fieldwork living with the Penan for 14 months in 1951–2, when he
was 28. I went to see him in early 1977 at All Souls, where he was a
fellow and my cousin, John (Hanbury) Sparrow, was warden. As with
my meeting with Tom Harrisson, he was extraordinarily unhelpful
about the Penan and it is only while researching this book that I have
gained an inkling as to why that might have been. He seems to have
given only one interview about his time with the Penan (conducted
in 2000 and published in the *Borneo Research Bulletin* in 2007), but it
is very revealing. In answer to the question 'Will the Penan survive?'
he replied:

> No. They are not surviving now, because the forests have been logged.
> They have been driven out of the forest and into government camps
> where there is usually no work for them, and they live in squalor and
> misery. They themselves say they are dying out.

Later in the interview, he was asked about who defended the Penan, and
he replied: 'Nobody, really [...] There is no effective way of defending
them. There just isn't [...] Not by force. Not by law.' He was asked next
if that was why he thought they were doomed, and he replied:

The government can expropriate enormous tracts of forest just by publishing a notice in the *Sarawak Gazette*, in Kuching, which of course the Penan don't see, and which if they could see, most of them couldn't read [...] and if they could read, it would be out of date by the time they saw it. So their rights are gone. No [...] It's a distressing story.

Rodney Needham never wrote up his notes on the Penan fully or published his thesis, having made the familiar researcher's mistake of dashing off on another intriguing project before the previous piece of work was completed. In Needham's case it was an opportunity to visit the island of Sumba in eastern Indonesia. There, after only 12 days of intense research into marriage patterns, he eventually published an important book on 'asymmetric alliance', an obscure but important subject in academic anthropology. He seems to have always regretted his failure to publish material on the Penan, and this may account for his reticence on the subject.

The Penan have been the worst victims of the deforestation holocaust which has descended on Sarawak over the last 40 years. The various Dayak longhouse societies, which were disrupted as the forests were cleared and their rivers polluted, were better able to cope with the reshaping of their lives, almost always without proper consultation. Many gained employment working in the logging camps and, later, palm-oil plantations; others were reasonably happy to move to coastal towns and capable of adapting to new environments and ways of life. Sadly, many of their leaders were also corrupted by the huge wealth being generated by the timber industry and sold their birthrights. I still believe that longhouse life, when surrounded by the natural richness of a vibrant rainforest, is about as good as it gets in human affairs and that it was a crime to force this change on them, but they have adapted and survived.

Not so the Penan. The rapid transformation forced on them has, by and large, impoverished them. Yes, many can now go to school and, now that the initial discrimination against Penan children is diminishing, some are doing well and using their natural talents to succeed in the outside world. But much has been lost in the process, and the glory and pride of their previous life is, for some, gone forever, although even those who have been settled for decades still rely on their forests for 70 per cent of their needs. Without their forests, this was inevitable, but had their forests not been cut down they could have had the best of both worlds. As proud guardians of an environment they cherished, they could have been recognised as the knowledgeable experts they were, teaching scientists about the incredible diversity and wealth of the rainforest while benefitting from what the outside world had to offer: medical help and appropriate education. And, of course, we would all be benefitting from the survival of the great forests, as would the whole environment.

It is not too late to make some amends. There are still large tracts of land in Sarawak, particularly in the highlands towards the Indonesian border, which have not been logged and which ought to belong to the Penan. Left to their own devices, they are the best conservationists, as they have strict rules against over-hunting and have managed and protected their lands for generations. Both the settled and still nomadic or semi-nomadic Penan want their land rights to be recognised by the government, so that they can prevent logging, palm-oil plantations and dam building on their land. Unfortunately, both past and present Sarawak state governments have completely refused to do this. Creating national parks and protected areas is admirable, but they are not the solution to saving the rainforests or its inhabitants, human and animal. If Penan land rights had been recognised and respected since independence, such protection would not have been necessary because the people living there would have done the job for us, as they have throughout history. Forests and biodiversity are not best saved by outsiders coming in and taking them over. The key reason there is so much biodiversity in the first place, which makes the forests so valuable and worth turning into a park, is that there have been people looking after it in a symbiotic relationship for ages. And, what is more, as we were increasingly to learn on our expedition, their knowledge and understanding of it far exceeded our own superficial scientific analysis.

There is no reason why the Penan should not be able even today to have their rights restored, to remain nomadic or semi-nomadic, as guardians of their own territory, but also to have access to medical facilities and schooling, on their own land and on their own terms, for their children. The education should be appropriate to their needs, close to home, in their own language and on subjects that are relevant and useful to them. All too often today, Penan children have to travel long distances to board among communities who regard them as inferior. And the only transport may be logging trucks, whose drivers sexually abuse the girls. It is only the bigotry of those who believe that settled agriculture is a more 'developed' way of life that prevents this solution, and that attitude is, of course, enthusiastically supported by those with a commercial interest in cutting down the forests.

It is really difficult for Westerners to understand the Penan way of life at all, as we have not been nomadic for millennia. Nonetheless, our lives were similar for most of our evolutionary existence and so, as a result, there is something about being a hunter-gatherer which touches a chord in all of us. They have been evolving at the same pace as we have, but down a different path, choosing not to build cities and become dependent on a material culture, as have most of us since permanent agriculture began, perhaps as much as 12,000 years ago in China and 5,000 in Europe. Agriculture led to cities and all the cultural trappings of what we call civilisation, but there is much more to culture than buildings and the technology that makes books, pictures and musical instruments possible. The essential poetry, magic, mystery, joy and wonder of life can be experienced and developed in many other ways, as anyone who has been lucky enough to spend time with a nomadic group of hunter-gatherers will testify. For a start, until the outside world intrudes, there is a security and confidence in existence which we settled people find hard to comprehend. Everything needed to fulfil all of life's physical and spiritual needs is to hand. Death and accidents do occur, of course, but until then everyone knows from childhood how to survive and enjoy life without any outside help. Whatever is needed can be made by anyone. There is food all around and materials for shelter. This is something we have lost. Increasingly,

Western man has become utterly dependent on things made by others and incapable of creating the simplest objects himself or making the basic ingredients of his food. Today we have reached a stage where we are so dependent on energy that if we were, for whatever reason, suddenly to be without electricity, chaos would reign after about 48 hours. Not so with hunter-gatherers.

In the case of the Penan, their life cycle appears deceptively simple: they pursue the herds of wild boar and gather the wild sago, each of which will replenish their energies before, a year later, the cycle is complete. It is in reality much, much more complicated than that. For a start, no group will encroach on the territory of another, and the routes of their annual migrations will be affected by many factors, including where the boar go and when the sago and wild fruits ripen. Hunting is very important and determines much of their movement. Sambar, barking deer and mouse deer are shot with blowpipes, as are five types of monkey, a dozen varieties of squirrel, certain birds and sometimes snakes, especially python, which may grow to a great size. But wild boar are the most valuable because they are a source of fat, which can be stored when cooked, as well as meat, which can be dried over the fire. Their fine, long, polished blowpipes have a spear at the end with which to finish off wounded prey. The poisoned darts are tipped with a whole variety of different substances, but predominately the latex of the *ipoh* tree. The poison can be extremely powerful and effective, killing game within minutes, even from a small scratch. Nyapun used to tell me, when we were hunting together, to be very careful not to touch the darts, although he did also say that he had an antidote. He had several hunting dogs, stocky little animals with sharp noses and a white flash across their chests. They would track the boar and then chase it when wounded until the poison took effect, holding it at bay until the Penan with the blowpipe caught up and dispatched it finally with his spear. Sometimes, a baby monkey may be caught – usually by accident, as they are very careful to select the most appropriate prey from a group – and kept as a pet. These, as well as baby birds, bats or perhaps a sun bear cub, will become part of the family and no one would ever consider killing or eating them. This is something I have observed among very many tribal societies in South America as well as in the Far East. I remember a Protestant missionary once telling me how frustrated he was that he could not persuade 'his' tribe to domesticate animals, such as chickens or pigs, for food, as they would never dream of consuming them. Another quality the Penan share with many other tribal peoples is that everything is always scrupulously divided among the group, however little may have been hunted or gathered. Every morsel of the animal is also eaten, the offal, eyes, brain and bone marrow being recognised as the most nutritious parts, which are usually given to the children. These parts also provide the minerals and salt they need and make up for the fact that they eat few if any green vegetables, although they do harvest lots of different fruits in their season. I found that rather surprising, as our Berawan workers used to gather quantities of excellent wild spinach, which became a staple in our diet. There is no Penan word for 'thank you'. It is simply assumed that everything will be shared.

There are, however, more than 30 words for the sago palm. With some the raw heart of palm can be eaten direct from the tree and, of course, this is a well-known delicacy in the West. Six varieties are harvested and processed to make sago. This is quite hard work, probably the most arduous thing the Penan do – and, of course, it is mostly done by the women. Once the mature palm has been felled by a man and split, the internal pith is dug out and pounded with water on a mat to remove the sago, which trickles down into a lower mat. These are made of such tightly woven rattan, often bearing an intricate pattern, that they are watertight and the milky fluid is retained. This is then dried over a fire and the starchy flour stored in the woven rattan bags familiar to any tourist who visits Sarawak, where it will keep for weeks. When needed, it is simply cooked with water, in which it congeals to form a sticky brown purée, a bit like runny pasta, which is eaten with wooden, two-pronged forks. I found that it was much improved by the addition of salt or sugar, both of which the Penan always welcomed as gifts.

Fishing is traditionally mostly done by the women and children, as I saw on my first contact with Nyapun's family. The little streams and forest pools teem with life, including delicious prawns and small fish, as well as frogs, snails and monitor lizards. Today, as most Penan have been settled near to larger rivers, fish is becoming more important in their diet. An enormous number of other things are gathered by the Penan from the forest, which really does provide almost everything they need. Virtually every plant has a name and a meaning, even if it may not have an obvious use. John Dransfield from the Royal Botanic Gardens at Kew, the world authority on palms and rattans, spent three weeks with us, raising the inventory of known palm species from ten to more than 100. I had allocated him a helper, a young Penan called Leloh, who had arrived soon after Nyapun. He proved to have an extraordinary knowledge of palms and rattans, having names for more than 200 different sorts, as well as an understanding of their varied uses for food, medicine and poisons, as well as for making rucksacks, hammocks and furniture. He did not have Latin names for these plants and some of them were the same species at a different growth stage but, as John said, Leloh, a teenager, was a far greater practical scientist than he would ever be. Tribal peoples have a long-term view of the environment. They occupy the only places left on earth where ecosystems which include people are still coherent. They play a key role in protecting vital habitats in a way no one else, even those with the best intentions, seems able to do. The Penan regularly use at least 30 different plants as medicines for dressing wounds, treating rashes, curing stomach aches and headaches, counteracting poisoning and reducing fever. Others can be crushed to make soap or dyes for the elegant sleeping mats, baskets, and leg and arm bracelets all Penan wear. Long strips of bark are beaten to an exquisite softness and made into comfortable *cawats* or loincloths, which Nyapun assured me were far more comfortable than cotton ones. Everything has a use – especially bamboo, from which water containers and quivers for poisoned darts are fashioned. Originally, their blowpipes were made of bamboo. Only since they have been able to trade for iron and even smelt it themselves have they been able to produce the much more efficient and accurate wooden versions, as these require laborious drilling with a long metal bar through a solid piece of one of a dozen different sorts of hardwood.

Because they move so often, usually at intervals of between ten days and three weeks, nomadic Penan houses are very simple and can be erected very quickly. Usually, they are built high up on ridges where there are fewer mosquitoes and sandflies and where they are safer from falling trees. This may mean that water has to be fetched in bamboo tubes from a stream far below, but the Penan drink very little, getting most of their liquid from their food, especially sago. I have seen Nyapun stop when crossing a stream on a fallen log and suck water up from below through his blowpipe but, unlike today's tourists, a Penan will not normally carry water when travelling. A house, or *sulap*, is made out of just a few stakes rammed into the ground, between which a platform of crossbeams, tightly tied together with strips of rattan, is laid. Above this there is a roof of palm leaves, and a fire, over which meat will be smoked, is made on a flat stone. When I returned to Mulu for the first time after 20 years and tracked down Nyapun again, we filmed him making an 'instant' house, as he used to do for me when we were travelling together. Within well under an hour he had, single-handed, made a neat, waterproof shelter in which we could have happily spent a dry night. Hygiene in the forest is a simple matter for nomads, as waste material biodegrades rapidly and the Penan seldom stayed in one place long enough for it to build up and start to smell.

Before Nyapun first came out of the forest and took me to meet his family, we saw abandoned *sulaps* in the forest as we created the trails, which were to be the main routes between our expedition sub-camps. These were pointed out to us by our Berawan helpers, who said that it meant there were Penan around, but that it was unlikely we would see any. The Penan move through the forest in a different way from even the most skilled among the settled people of Borneo. They hear and feel everything that is going on around them and they are influenced by each sound and movement. As we have seen, they seldom stay in one place for more than a week or two at a time and once they have moved on there is virtually no trace of their passing. There were signs, but it took a sharp eye and a knowledgeable local for us to spot them. The Penan leave messages for each other as they travel through the forest. A stalk bent over, stripped at the end and with little pieces of twig tied to it can be a whole letter, if you understand the significance of each bit: the direction the main stick is pointing indicates where the group is heading; two bunches of leaves hanging down says 'we are two families travelling together'; a leaf may be folded in various ways to mean 'hurry' or 'we are hungry'; three knots in a strip of bark tied to the stick means the journey will be three days, and so on. Travelling with Nyapun, he would often point out old messages, now virtually invisible in the foliage, and tell me what they once signified. We grew to love the rainforest, and it was largely through our Penan companions that we came to understand it. For a while it was our whole life, a world of greenery, giant ferns and hanging lianas, bounded by rivers and mountains, in which one could sometimes glimpse a scarlet rhododendron or hear the beating wings or the harsh cry of a rhinoceros hornbill. Mulu was largely unexplored and we lived in a state of high excitement as each day produced new species and we penetrated unknown valleys. I remember the shock I felt when, having cut a fresh trail one day into a remote and inaccessible piece of forest we thought not previously visited by man, we came on a shallow river. There, playing unconcernedly in the water, dabbling under stones for shrimps, were Anyi, Nyapun's pretty little six-year-old daughter, and her baby sister. They looked as self-assured and tranquil as any children playing in a suburban sandpit. All our combined academic wisdom, modern equipment and safety rules suddenly seemed absurd and artificial beside such serenity and harmony.

I have described the various musical instruments Nyapun made and played and the ways he and his family would come and dance with me late at night sometimes at Base Camp. Music is important to the Penan. There are few more haunting sounds to be heard than the faint melody of a nose flute coming from a *sulap* on a starlit forest night. Standing and listening, invisible between the buttresses of a great *meranti* tree, I felt that I was close to the Penan understanding that nature itself has a soul. This lies at the heart of their deeply held religious belief, their animism. When we travel, we are intruders in the territory of resident spirits, who need to be placated. We need to listen to our dreams and carefully observe the omens, which a wise man will recognise from the flights of birds and the calls of animals.

20 Nyapun playing a *sompoton* made from eight bamboo pipes inserted in a gourd, through which he sucks and blows.

The Penan have traded for generations with the outside world, at the same time making it clear that they wish to live in peace deep in the forest. The Brooke government, and later the British colonial administration, used to arrange trading missions called *tamu* far up the rivers, to which the Penan would bring their wares. One of these annual trading locations was on the Tutoh River at the mouth of the Melinau, where we had our Base Camp. A government official would preside over the trading to make sure that there was fair play, and this role is still remembered with affection by the people. Manufactured goods such as knives, cooking pots, shotguns and bales of cotton for making sarongs and shirts were brought upriver.

One product brought out of the forest by the Penan used to be damar gum, such as Nyapun's family used for lighting their *sulap*. It is today a valued ingredient in eco paints, as it is completely non-toxic. Bundles of good-quality rattan, as well as mats and baskets made from that material, were probably the main produce they would bring, and these are still today the most familiar Penan goods to be found for sale both in remote Penan settlements and in shops in the towns, even in the airports. Monkey gallstones, which used to be a popular Chinese medicine, hornbill casques, deer antlers and bushmeat are less likely to be found today, as is *gaharu* wood, perhaps the most valued of all the forest products. This dark, scented wood is only found as an abnormal growth on *Aquilaria* trees when it is infected with a type of mould, probably following an injury or insect attack. Used as incense and as a medicine, it is one of the most expensive natural products in the world and can fetch as much as $100,000 a kilogram today. Just think how rich the Penan could be if they could still find it in their depleted forests, but it is now rare – because the *Aquilaria* trees, although protected, have mostly been felled by loggers.

Originally, it was only the massive hardwood dipterocarp trees of the lowlands, with which Sarawak used to be so blessed, that were felled. These are the great forest giants of the lowlands, some 500 species of which used to cover large areas below about 1,200 metres above sea level. It is a magical forest to walk through, often with little or no undergrowth and only gentle rays of light filtering through from the canopy to illuminate a wonderland. It is like being in a magnificent cathedral where the spreading buttress roots echo the cornerstones of the columns and the soaring trunks the pillars, while the underside of the upper storeys of vegetation can look like a vaulted roof. It can be very quiet in the semi-darkness between the trees, which adds to the sense of reverence. Then, without warning, often mid-afternoon, there will be the sound of wind far above. Rapidly this can turn into the most violent of storms, bringing branches and even trees crashing to the ground and followed by an overpowering deluge of rain. In no time the floor of the forest is awash with water, rivulets turning to instant rivers, which wash away soil and leaf litter. But the roots bind it all, as they have done forever, and although the main rivers will run yellow briefly, the integrity of the woodland is not damaged. Standing under these great trees, overwhelmed by the power of the rainfall, I was made forcibly aware of the way the trees held everything together, essential to the fabric of it all. No wonder it all falls apart so cataclysmically when this covering is removed and the erosion is allowed to run its course.

Travel is easy, silent, stress-free and awesome. Following Nyapun when walking fast among tall trees, I had to keep my wits about me because he would suddenly freeze without warning when he saw something stir above us. In slow motion, he would reach into the quiver at his waist, remove a dart, pass it across his lips to moisten it and gently insert it into his blowpipe. For an age both of us would be rooted to the spot as he awaited his moment. Often it didn't come and the troop of monkeys would move on; but occasionally the right animal of the right sex would be visible for long enough for him to get it. And he was totally discriminating about which prey to pick, never killing mothers or babies or the lead male. Aware of how many there were in a troop, he would leave it in peace if the number dropped below about 20. There were two species of macaque and three of leaf monkey or langur. The commonest leaf monkey, the maroon, was often seen and sometimes would come and shriek at us above one of the sub-camps. The silver was the rarest and seldom seen. The grey was the least studied and there was some doubt as to whether there might be two species, one restricted to high ground. Our chief zoologist, Gathorne Medway, was studying this problem, and in order to solve it he needed to examine an adult female, which would then be preserved and sent to the Natural History Museum in London. He asked Nyapun if he could obtain one for him next time he went hunting for his family and showed him a picture, explaining his precise requirements. Remarkably, Nyapun, who had returned to his old camp near the Brunei border, where I had met him, far outside the park, returned four days later with exactly what he had been asked for. He had selected from a shy and elusive troop and shot with his blowpipe a perfect mature female, which was neither pregnant nor carrying a baby – a feat which even the Berawan, let alone a European armed with the most sophisticated weapon, would find virtually impossible.

Twenty years or so after independence most of the primary lowland forest had been logged and the law was changed to encourage the exploitation of smaller and smaller trees for processing into plywood. Bulldozers penetrated further into the interior, often clearing tracks along steep ridges with catastrophic results, as landslides and erosion caused watercourses to silt up. Worse for the Penan was the damage this caused to their precious sago palms, which tend to grow along ridges, as do many of their large fruiting trees. The technique for dragging the wooden huts in which the logging crews and their families lived on giant skids was pioneered by James Wong who, in the 1980s, not only owned the largest timber company in Sarawak but was also, ironically, that state's minister for the environment and tourism. I had a run-in with him in 1987 when I was heading an International Union for Conservation of Nature (IUCN), Friends of the Earth and Survival International delegation to Malaysia to investigate why environmentalists were being gaoled under ancient British terrorist laws for demonstrating against excessive logging. For an hour or so I was subjected to some pretty nasty abuse about my motives: 'You scientists know nothing of the rainforest; you just want to keep the Penan in human zoos.' I finally asked, rather despairingly, if he did not agree that deforestation might cause some climate change. Wong replied: 'I play golf. I prefer it when there is less rain!' That remark, sadly, came to epitomise the attitude of all too many South East Asian politicians over the next few decades. He also said of the Penan: 'We don't want them running around like animals. They have to settle down; otherwise, they have no rights.' This attitude was endorsed by the then prime minister of Malaysia, Datuk Mahathir Mohamad, who stated: 'We are asking them to give up their unhealthy living conditions and backwardness for better amenities and a longer and healthier lifestyle.'

Opposition to the phenomenal rate of logging in Sarawak grew during the 1980s and 1990s, but, in spite of massive international interest and campaigning, nothing changed. In fact, things got much worse as palm oil became the most widely used vegetable oil on the planet and the highly lucrative industry boomed. While the secondary forest left behind after all the larger trees have been removed is bad enough, converting the land into sterile plantations has been a catastrophe.

The Penan, in desperation, took to barricading logging roads. Their right to their land has never been recognised by the Sarawak state government. The reaction was violent, and in 1987 more than 100 were arrested and sent to prison. This is a terrible experience for a nomadic hunter-gatherer, but they are continuing to resist both logging and the other threat to their environment: vast hydroelectric dams, which will flood many villages belonging to the Penan and other indigenous peoples, as well as destroying yet more priceless forest. The forest is a rich resource and, if properly managed, lasts forever. We cannot live on electricity.

One European who became a major thorn in the side of those opposing the Penan was an eccentric Swiss shepherd called Bruno Manser. Although I didn't meet him at that time, he came to Sarawak first as a result of my Mulu expedition, when he joined a subsequent caving expedition in 1984. He then spent much of the next 15 years studying the Penan, writing and illustrating copious notebooks and living as one of them, probably more intimately than any outsider had ever attempted before. When the logging road blockades began, he helped to organise them, and this was what really upset the government authorities, who declared him *persona non grata* and arrested him twice, but he escaped both times, once by diving into a river and swimming across, carrying his blowpipe. In between his long spells in the rainforest, he travelled to Europe and the United States, campaigning on behalf of the Penan and for the logging to stop. On one of his visits to London, I found myself at a conference where I was invited to share the stage with him and Ghillean Prance, then director of the Royal Botanic Gardens at Kew. We spoke beforehand and I found him gentle and charismatic before, unrehearsed and impromptu, we all said our pieces about our varied experiences with tribal peoples. I would like to have known him better as there was no doubt that he was hugely influential and dedicated his life to the Penan, who adored him, but we never met again, and, in 2000, after illegally entering Sarawak from Kalimantan, he disappeared while travelling by himself in remote forest near Batu Lawi, a 2,000-metre limestone pinnacle, which he had said he intended climbing. His body has never been found and many believe he was killed by those who had been hunting him for so many years and whom he had annoyed so much. Even today his name is such a red rag to the authorities that it is unwise to mention him in Sarawak. Prime Minister Mahathir even wrote to him a couple of times, saying that it was 'about time that you stop your arrogance and your intolerable European superiority. You are no better than the Penan.'

And: 'As a Swiss living in the laps [*sic*] of luxury with the world's highest standard of living, it is the height of arrogance for you to advocate that the Penans live on maggots and monkeys in their miserable huts, subjected to all kinds of diseases.'

Shortly before we left Mulu, Nyapun chanted an epic poem to us. Locally known as *lakus* and in Malay as *pantuns*, these flattering narratives about us were familiar from the evenings we spent at the Berawan longhouse from which we had recruited most of our workers. The smallest indigenous Kenyah sub-group, the Berawan liked to drink a lot of *borak* (rice wine) and also to get us drunk and make us dance. The songs they sang about us and our great accomplishments appeared on the surface to be entirely complimentary, but we soon learned to recognise the underlying wit and the observations about our fallibility, which always ran through them as a salutary undercurrent: 'You are a great lion from a great country and you have come here to show us, who are only poor and stupid, how to live properly and understand our world better. Of course, you can't walk across a pole bridge without falling off, nor can you look after yourself alone in the forest, as you do not know which plants are edible, but you are so much cleverer than us and we are so lucky to have had you here to teach us.' Always the subtle sting in the flattery, which of course made it all so much less embarrassing and more enjoyable.

Nyapun spoke in archaic Penan, using imagery and proverbs, which he said only he and older men would understand. He then translated it into Berawan for Barah, a very bright, Penan-speaking Berawan, to put into Malay. Zaina Anwar, a Malay visitor from Singapore, then put it into English for us. It appeared not to have any critical undertone. If anyone knew my failings and inadequacy in the forest, he did, since we had spent so much time together, often alone, when I was entirely dependent on his knowledge and skill. But this was all loving, affectionate and delivered with a sort of nobility, as if he were honouring us for having spent time on his land. There was also an undercurrent of sadness at our parting and anxiety about what lay ahead for his people after we were gone. During his lifetime, huge changes had been occurring in Sarawak and beyond in the big outside world: a world war and invasion of Borneo by the Japanese; the opening up of the interior of this, the third-largest island in the world, to researchers; independence from the British; and another war, this time with Indonesia. Through it all, he and his family had lived on as true nomads. They were all provided for by this very strong man who, when I first met him, was caring for two wives and ten children, all in the best of health. My suspicion is that he would leave the forest from time to time to trade resins, rattans, animal skins and feathers, and valuable bezoar stones from monkeys' gall bladders, and to acquire the few goods his family needed or desired or could not make themselves: cloth for sarongs (although he had previously told me that the beaten-bark loincloth he wore was softer than any cloth), salt, sugar, metal pots, and so on. This would have been how he learned his Malay, which was about the same as mine when we met. But until then he had kept his family isolated, only meeting other Penan. Our meeting changed everything for them. The sense of responsibility has weighed on me ever since.

After we left, he and his family were forcibly settled near the park. He campaigned against the deforestation, helping to barricade logging roads, and he went to gaol. In those days some 95 per cent of the lowland rainforest of Sarawak was undisturbed and there were still many Penan following their migratory routes, living off the herds of wild boar they hunted and the wild sago they gathered. Today only 5 per cent of the lowland rainforest is left and there are only a few entirely nomadic Penan. An environmental catastrophe has been perpetrated on Sarawak, from which the Penan living in and around Mulu were, to some extent, protected. But no land was given to them, so that they have had to watch not only as their rich environment was destroyed, but also as their very right to live on it was taken from them. In Brazil, for all the errors of the past, land occupied by tribal people is theirs under the constitution and large tracts of forest have been demarcated for different tribes. These territories represent much of the remaining intact Amazon forest, as can be clearly seen using satellite photography and overlays. Many of the remaining green areas, where the forest has not been removed, have long, straight boundaries. This is because the relatively recent mapping and registering of Indian lands often used straight lines as arbitrary frontiers between Indian territory and areas where loggers have moved in and cleared away the forest, originally making way for settlers but now more often for vast herds of cattle or soya-bean farms. If the indigenous people of Sarawak had been treated in the same way, much of the insane, rapid deforestation of the last 40 years could have been avoided.

Here is Nyapun's *pantun*, shortened and edited. It was sung to Mark Collins, Nigel Winser and me on Mark's last night, 18 July 1978.

'This song is for Mark, Robin and Nigel, and for everyone from England. You are like the hornbill because you came to show us a new life. Before you came we lived in the darkness but since you came we have been happy and our lives have been better. You came from a far country, taught us good things and we have loved being with you and living with you.

'In the past, even though we lived in the difficult forest here, we had not been everywhere in the country round about. But on this expedition we have learned with the scientists to go to new places, even on the limestone, where we never went before.

'Before you came we never had work like this and we were never able to earn money to buy extra food. But since we have been with you English people we have been able to buy things we never had before.

'Now the expedition is about to finish and everyone, even the small children, will cry because you are going away. But now we are happy because we have enough food.

'Since you came here from England you have brought a good life to us with medicines and by caring for the sick people, even sending them to hospital when they are sick. We have thought of you as kings, because no one has understood and cared for us before.

'The people of Sarawak, even the government, used to come here sometimes, but even though many were very kind, you people have been kinder.

'Robin came here and led us into a peaceful place, so we call him the hornbill that shows us the way to fly high and far.

'You are like the full moon which shines light on us, which is why we have wanted to stay with you and not go back into the jungle. As long as you are here we will stay with you.

'You have shown us how to be all together and now, working together here, we are all much closer than before and we are all friends. You came here by aeroplane and you have taken us up in helicopters and shown us many things and we have nothing to give you in return. We have been very happy working with the scientists all over and when we go back to those places we will cry when we remember. We have been so happy, never so happy before, and when everyone is gone we will be like dead people because there will be no more life in us after you are gone.

'Before, whenever we the leaders told everyone what to do they never followed us. Now you have taught us how to co-operate and now they listen to their leaders and work together. We will teach our children how to live together peacefully.

'Your hands and our hands will always be clasped together and this is how we will always remember you.'

Nyapun then changed his tempo, and suddenly I started listening intently as he told us his extraordinary life story:

'When I was Lugoh's age [his eldest son, then about 17, making Nyapun 50 at that time] the Japanese were here and Tuan Sandy [Sanderson – see Chapter 3] arrived here. I had a very good time with Tuan Sandy and we chased the Japanese up the *batu* and took their heads. I took my family to Bario [an area in the Kelabit Highlands of Sarawak] with Tuan Harry [Tom Harrisson], who came here later.

'Then he left and nothing much happened until Tuan Rodney [Needham] arrived. I travelled for many months with him, visiting my relations. Then he left.

'About ten years later, my brother and I were hunting along the Melinau River when we saw a lot of white men in uniforms coming up the river in boats. My cousin Sugun was with them and showing them the way. Now the Penan cannot be seen by outsiders. They have charms which make them invisible. But my cousin saw us on the bank and called out that these were good people and we should not be afraid. And so we watched them setting up camp and then, without disturbing the sentries, we went into the tent of the headman and asked him what he was doing.

'Then we saw no more Europeans until you arrived.'

During all the months Nyapun and I had travelled together through and around Mulu he had never given any indication of his extraordinary history and the fact that he had been involved in three of the seminal things to happen in that part of Borneo. We didn't talk a lot. We had no great need to, as both his and my Malay was not up to intimate conversation, so that we spent most of our time in companionable silence. When not walking, Nyapun would be busy preparing our camp, or he would go off hunting. I would be writing my diary. We had never discussed headhunting, a practice not generally associated with the Penan, although they were known to do it occasionally for ceremonial purposes, and I was amazed to think that this most gentle of men could have enjoyed it as a boy. Had he really, as a young man, hunted Japanese soldiers escaping into the interior at the end of World War II? Had he used his blowpipe with poisoned darts and, perhaps, taken their heads? When I asked him about it many years later, he denied it.

If he had travelled with Rodney Needham, he must have watched and learned how a scientist gathered information long before we came on the scene. And he had spent time with a British Army unit on exercise – the 'white men in uniforms' were most likely the Royal Green Jackets, who arrived in 1965 during Confrontation, the undeclared war between Britain and Indonesia, who opposed the creation of Malaysia. (I would like to have seen the colonel's face when Nyapun and his brother walked into his tent. The CO may have been Colonel – later Field Marshal – Edwin Bramall, who took command of the 2nd Royal Green Jackets when they were deployed to Borneo in 1965, although he couldn't remember the incident when I taxed him with it recently. He confessed that, since he was well into his nineties, his memory was not as good as it was! And just at that time he was being disgracefully persecuted by the police in their enthusiasm to expose high-profile paedophiles, a case that was later dropped.) No wonder he preferred to stay with his people in the forest, doing what they had always done. But now I understood what a remarkable life he had led and I realised that he must have been far more aware of what we were up to than I had given him credit for.

He was telling us of the four most important meetings of his life. For dramatic effect he implied that there were only these four, but there must have been others. He also included a lot of overt flattery, which is traditional in these celebratory odes and which I have learned to take with a large pinch of salt, but touching nonetheless. He was one of the wisest men I have ever met, a true shaman and guardian of his people's wisdom and with a rare stillness and inner confidence. I think he knew at the time how significant these four meetings were and that was what he was telling us. It took me almost 40 years to work it out. This book is my attempt to tell his story as he wanted me to, and to try to link the various threads.

When I went back to see Nyapun 20 years later, in 1999, he told me how he, too, had been put in prison for trying to stop a road: 'When the logging companies left, there was no more forest and the animals had gone. I had wanted to talk to the companies, to negotiate with them. I thought we could share the land, so that they could get their logs and we could keep some of the land to make it safe for the animals. But they told me I was wrong. I said: "Everyone has to have somewhere and we have nowhere." I wanted to make sure there would be a place for my family and descendants, but they said they wanted everything. They were going to log the whole area. That was the reason I was thrown in gaol. There was a big dispute. All the Penan people said the land was theirs, but the government said they had the right to permit logging, because the land really belonged to them. They came to arrest me in a helicopter and told us we would be in gaol for a month. They let us go after a week and two days.'

About 300 Penan still lived a nomadic life in the forests of Borneo then, but Nyapun and his family had, by 1999, been settled to live in a 'Penan village' near the tourist hotel, which had been built near the site of my old Base Camp. Instead of being treated with the respect they deserved as rainforest experts, as we had hoped, they could only get menial jobs and sell their bead bracelets to visitors. Their right to

21   A Penan blockade on a logging road.

hunt was still recognised, but the forests had been felled right up to the edge of the park and the wildlife outside had mostly disappeared. As nomads they had been given no land and this was at the heart of their problem, as it is for most tribal peoples. If the forests can be restored, something that is happening in a few places, and if Nyapun and his family, and all other Penan families, settled and nomadic, can have the right to the land returned to them, then they may regain control over their lives. The knowledge and understanding of the rainforest is still there in Nyapun's children. Let us hope that they may be allowed to pass it on to his grandchildren and, perhaps, to share it with us. We of the developed world may survive the problems being created by a shrinking planet. Without the protection of their forests, the Penan will not. It is their life and home.

CHAPTER 5

Expedition

A s is so often the case, it was a series of linked coincidences that brought about our expedition to Mulu. One day in 1975 my wife Marika and I received a letter from Borneo addressed to us both at our hill farm in Cornwall. It was from Anthony Galvin, the bishop of Miri, saying that he had just read our respective books on our recent travels among the tribal people of Indonesia (my *A Pattern of Peoples* and Marika's *A Slice of Spice*), which had just been published. He complimented us on them and invited us to come to the island he had lived on for more than 30 years and, with him, visit some of the many and diverse people living there. That evening, before we had had a chance to reply, one of our oldest friends came to stay. John Hemming had recently taken over as director and secretary of the RGS (I was on the council). He had been talking to another friend of ours, Algy Cluff, who had started a successful oil company and had just made a new expedition grant to the Society. Because he had served in Sarawak during Confrontation and had grown to love the country and its people, he hoped his grant could be used to promote exploration in Borneo. The idea for what was to become the RGS's largest scientific expedition to date was born.

In 1976 Marika and I went on a wide-ranging recce of the whole island of Borneo to search for the ideal expedition site. We had already travelled deep into the interior of Kalimantan. This time we penetrated some of the remoter and least studied areas of Sabah, which was called North Borneo when I first went there in 1958, Brunei, the oil-rich sultanate, and Sarawak. It was there that we accompanied the bishop on a tour of the longhouses far up the Tinjar River, until I left Marika to return with him while I crossed the watershed to the Rejang in

Tom Harrisson's footsteps (see Chapter 2). I went across the edge of the Usun Apau plateau, the legendary inaccessible homeland of the Kenyah and Kayan people, which seemed promising as somewhere to investigate further. I recently found in the 40 boxes of Mulu archives in the basement of the RGS a letter that Bishop Galvin wrote to Marika and me just after that journey. These extracts reveal what my thinking was at that stage and also some of the enchantment of our time together:

> I feel [...] that Robin will come back next year to open up something really new, something vital not only to the Kenyahs and Kayans but to Sarawak and Malaysia. I sense the strong will and determination to see the Usun Apau put firmly on the map once more. Let's hope the tedious negotiations which must be gone through will bring you both back here next year [...]
>
> I am confident that you will get full support from the ulu [jungle] people if you open up just one little pathway to the Usun Apau. More concretely, if all goes well, I will announce your arrival at the end of the year to our people in the ulu when we have our big meeting at Long San. There you will have a chance to address all the chiefs and aristocracy of the Kenyahs from L. San to Liu Mato.
>
> Enough of the plateau! I found such a lot in common with both of you – your deep sense of cultural values, your patience with tedious journeys, which can be such fun when shared by good companions, your openness to other religions and beliefs. These are the foundations on which Survival International can survive. God knows what avenues all you have been doing so far will open up in the future. The principles on which you work can be readily taken up by anthropologists, by missionaries, social workers, by anyone who has dealings with other people. [Sir Edward] Evans-Pritchard used to say he only learned how to live with his fellows at All Souls through learning to live with the Nuer and Azande!
>
> I think of you both tonight on your long flight back to London and work. Orion is right overhead, the Southern Cross is just visible over the Lambir hills and over the Tinjar I can see lightning. Somewhere in the jungle, our friends will be huddled around wood

fires, spinning yarns about the strong 'tiger' man and his wife with golden butterflies for hair. The rain will patter gently on wooden shingles, the crickets combat bravely with bullfrog and the myriad tropical midnight sounds. But now you to your lambs and I to my sheep and may He who shelters us all keep us in the fold of His arm.

Anthony Galvin was one of the wisest and most saintly men I have ever met. I have always said that it was he who first inspired me with a love for the people of the interior of Sarawak and a desire to do something to help them. Although, as we will see in a moment, a different plan took shape, it was his passion and trust in me that gave me the confidence to make it all happen. He came to stay with us in Cornwall the following summer and we enjoyed showing him our farm and the lambs I had been hurrying home to tend. We talked of all that was about to happen and how much we would be seeing of each other soon. A couple of weeks after that he died suddenly of a massive stroke. He was 57. I found out later that he was famous for having saved Pope Paul VI's life in Manila in 1972 when an assassin broke through the security and managed to stab the pontiff with a knife. Galvin, who was standing nearby, grabbed the man, a mentally ill painter, and pinioned his arms.

I began the flight home thinking that maybe I could put together an expedition to the Usun Apau. Although the logistical difficulties would be formidable, it was the best site I had found on the whole island of Borneo for an expedition base where a multidisciplinary research project into tropical rainforest could live and work and benefit the people, but it was far from ideal. It was only in Singapore, where we stopped on the way home, that everything fell into place.

We dined in Singapore with an old friend, Ivan Polunin. He was the youngest of the three remarkable Polunin brothers. Nicholas, a botanical explorer, was one of the earliest and most ardent environmentalists. He founded, and directed until his death, the Foundation for Environmental Conservation, based in Geneva. Oleg, also a botanist, was the author of many field guides to the plants of Europe, the Himalayas and elsewhere. Ivan, a leading doctor, photographer and documentary film-maker, was an ebullient character, a polymath who helped David Attenborough, among many others, when he came to the Far East. We were joined by Dr Robb Anderson, a distinguished forester and old Borneo hand. I was later to learn that he had an impressive war record with the Black Watch, having been awarded the Military Cross in Sicily for charging a German armoured car single-handed, firing from the hip and causing it to retreat; a bar was added to this decoration later when, following the Normandy landings, he captured the Hooge Bridge during the battle for Le Havre despite having had a bullet pass straight through him, narrowly missing his heart. He was notoriously taciturn and sported an impressive moustache, which fascinated his Iban assistants in the forest. An apocryphal story of theirs tells of how they watched wasps disappear up one of his hairy nostrils only to emerge from the other. It is said that Robb never even twitched.

Over supper Robb literally changed the course of my life. First of all, he asked me if I had found what I was looking for. I replied that I had several ideas for suitable expedition bases in Sabah, Brunei and Sarawak, and that I was compiling a report for the RGS. The Usun Apau looked promising, but I had not found anywhere that was perfect yet. 'In that case, you need seek no further,' he told me sternly. 'I have just finished gazetting the largest new national park in Sarawak and it is the ideal place for you. It holds virtually every possible tropical habitat and it is virtually unexplored. It is called Mulu.' I had, of course, heard of this new national park, but I had not been able to go there. He soon persuaded me that he was right.

He then explained to me why our proposed research was of vital importance. It is a well-known fact that a tropical hardwood tree takes about 100 years to mature. The job of the 'conservator of forests' – the title by which the head of the Forestry Department was known under the Brooke and British administrations in Borneo, Burma and elsewhere, and that was still in use – was to adhere to a simple formula, observing a sustainable harvesting system whereby only 1 per cent of the national forest was logged each year and then carefully restored and allowed to regrow. That way, the forest production of valuable hardwood should last forever and, although the countries were undoubtedly being exploited, the forests were protected. Since independence, however, there was increasing pressure on the elected government, whose window of opportunity might be a short one, to grant larger concessions, often to foreign timber companies and, as was being widely reported in the media, as a result of massive bribes. Only by demonstrating how extremely fragile the tropical forest ecosystem was and therefore how tenuous the future for tropical timber, Robb believed, could there be any hope that sensible long-term policies would be observed.

Sadly, this was not to be. Sarawak's only readily exploitable resource was its forests. The revenue from the massive oil deposits off the coast went to the federal government, leaving the state government with a strong temptation to change the forestry rules. The head of the Forestry Department soon became the 'director of forests' and the rate of logging accelerated. As I have already pointed out, when we were in Mulu about 95 per cent of the lowland tropical forest in Sarawak remained intact. Today only 5 per cent is left.

Many good babies have been thrown out with the dirty colonial bathwater.

The history of deforestation throughout Borneo since decolonisation really is disgraceful. The richest biological environment on the planet, demonstrably in urgent need of protection, was systematically plundered, so that between 1980 and 2000 more roundwood was harvested from this relatively small island than from Africa and the Amazon combined. Even more forest was destroyed by fire or, worst of all, conversion to plantations, which causes the almost total annihilation of life and diversity, and with no chance of regeneration, since the oil palm is a 'terminal' crop – nothing will grow on that land once, as will happen one day, palm oil is no longer needed. An 'ecological desert' is created. At least with careful logging there is a chance of secondary forest being regenerated and, if this is done properly, it can in time be almost as rich as the now increasingly rare, pristine, old-growth forest. The establishing of a palm-oil plantation, by contrast, is not a pretty sight. The topsoil is scraped from a large area and used in nurseries for the oil-palm seedlings before they are planted, leaving bare subsoil. The result is a brutal, apocalyptic spectacle with nothing living or moving as far as the eye can see except for diggers, scrapers and trucks driving the workers home. Swathes of dead and wasted trees are left to rot. Sarawak has the highest density of logging roads and has developed the most effective techniques for penetrating the rugged forest hinterland, with the result that large parts of the interior now look from the air like wrinkled skin, devoid of trees and riddled with tracks. Originally, oil palms came from West Africa, but they were brought to South East Asia at the beginning of the twentieth century. Today 85 per cent of the immense quantity of palm oil consumed globally is produced and exported from Indonesia and Malaysia, more than 60 million tons, mostly not sustainably. The impacts on the environment have been disastrous, with a third of all mammal species now considered critically endangered, most notably the orang-utan, 90 per cent of whose habitat has been destroyed in the last 20 years. It has been estimated that 50,000 have died as a result of deforestation for palm-oil production in the last two decades. This destruction also results in the emission of immense quantities of smoke into the atmosphere, and has made Indonesia, which overtook Malaysia in 2007 to become the world's top producer of this cheap, edible oil, the third-highest emitter of greenhouse gases in the world – and almost all from the burning of forests! The establishment of palm-oil plantations is often promoted as a way of bringing prosperity to undeveloped rural regions in Borneo, but in reality the industry often has devastating effects, allowing powerful corporations to take away the land owned by indigenous peoples and replace their previous sustainable lifestyles with poorly paid indentured labour and other human-rights violations.

It is essential that the remaining areas of primary and secondary forest be given proper protection and put in the ownership of those who will cherish and maintain them, while still exploiting their produce sustainably. The best people to do this are the indigenous inhabitants, especially the Penan, and there is no logical reason why they should not be granted some of their remaining undisturbed land to own and manage. It happens elsewhere in the world, with spectacularly successful results. As discussed in Chapter 4, indigenous territories are the greatest barrier to Amazonian deforestation in South America, as is clearly revealed by satellite photographs. These show clear, straight lines where green, demarcated tribal lands separate the bare red laterite soils of overexploited cattle land and soya-bean plantations, which are just as sterile biologically as those that grow oil palms. Survival International has successfully campaigned for the demarcation of many areas which would otherwise have been cleared. Some of these have been for small groups of uncontacted Indians, the remnants of once-thriving and independent societies, who would disappear or be reduced to a handful of traumatised and lonely survivors without their land. In Brazil, the minister of justice has the power to protect their territory permanently, and in 2016 we mounted a petition which successfully persuaded him to do so for a group called the Kawahiva, who were teetering on the brink of extinction as loggers encroached on their forest. Not so in Sarawak, where the great idea of *bumiputra*, meaning 'sons of the land', a founding principle of Malaysian independence intended to protect the interests of the indigenous people, seems not to apply to the Penan. The whole history of the failure to recognise the land rights of the people of the interior of Sarawak has been sad, unfair and nonsensical. As both the people and the government of Sarawak begin to recognise the urgency of stopping the total destruction of their priceless birthright, it is not too late to grant the Penan the land they need and so resolve two serious problems at the same time.

The full story of the Mulu expedition is told in my book written at the time, almost 40 years ago: *Mulu: The Rain Forest* (1980). We were invited by the Forestry Department of the then Sarawak government to prepare a 'Management Plan' for the newly created Gunung Mulu National Park because they already recognised its importance, and they gave us wholehearted support throughout. About a third of our members came from Malaysia. Some of us, the lucky ones, lived there for almost 15 months. Others came and went, staying for a few weeks or a few months to study and record every aspect of the environment. Our scientists were the best in their fields, chosen for their skills and enthusiasm rather than for their expeditionary experience. Many went on to be world leaders in their academic disciplines, rising to the top of their chosen specialities. (Appendix 2 to this book lists them all.) They were selected by an eminent committee at the RGS, whose greatest virtue in my eyes was that it stood up for me as leader at every turn and endorsed all we did, even when we made mistakes. John Hemming, the director, whose idea the expedition was, oversaw everything with consummate skill and pulled all the strings together. The key player in maintaining the integrity of the expedition's scientific work was our chief scientist, Clive Jermy, a botanist and world expert on ferns at the Natural History Museum. His diligence and wisdom were the key to the success of our work and the whole project's subsequent reputation.

We all fell under the spell of the forest. It is overwhelmingly luxuriant, a noisy cacophony of sound and endless variations of green. Mystery lurks behind the foliage: an infinity of undiscovered teeming life; plants, animals and insects new to science, waiting to be discovered. High above in the canopy the diversity is even richer and less known, while far, far above, near the summit of the sandstone Mount Mulu, are moss forests where one has to crawl through tunnels of vegetation festooned with trailing fronds, deep squelchy mud and contorted roots to emerge into a fairyland of variegated pitcher plants. On the high limestone of Mount Api there is no water save when it rains, and that instantly disappears through innumerable cracks. Here, just across the deep chasm dividing the two soil types, an entirely different vegetation is to be found: while the bare limestone is devoid of even the smallest plants, so that great cliffs shine bright in the sunlight and can be seen for many miles, wherever there is a crevice and humus, shrubs and *Leptospermum*, members of the myrtle family proliferate, while in places woven mats of *Pandanus* cover the ground and provide a habitat for other plants.

Our nearest shop was in Marudi, an isolated settlement on the Baram River, to which no road then led. A fort was built there in 1883 by the second Rajah Brooke, Charles Brooke, when the sultan of Brunei ceded the Baram region to him. Originally, it was named Claudetown, after Claude Champion de Crespigny, the first resident of Sarawak's third division. He it was who first suggested that the oil which seeped through the earth along the coast and was used by the locals to caulk their boats and light their lamps might have a value, but the Brooke government ignored him and the first oil well was not drilled until 1910. Today, oil provides 30 per cent of Malaysia's revenue. Marudi is also believed to be the location of Somerset Maugham's story 'The Outstation' (1924), which brilliantly captures the claustrophobic atmosphere of remote colonial administration centres.

Normally, the journey upriver to Mulu from Marudi past 14 sets of rapids could take three days, but we had a New Zealand jetboat, which had been donated and delivered in person by the inventor of jetboats, Jon Hamilton, and his son, Michael. In it, we could do the journey in three hours, much to the amazement of the residents of the handful of longhouses on the way. Up the wide, muddy Baram we turned left into the Tutoh, rushing down from the Kelabit Highlands, and then left again into the pristine waters of the Melinau flowing under a canopy of trees out of the Gunung Mulu National Park. Many years before our expedition, there was a small fort at this junction, where the Penan came to trade on the rare occasions that they emerged from the forest. When Eddie Shackleton, later the patron of our expedition, climbed Mount Mulu for the first time in 1932, he made his headquarters there in what he described as 'a dilapidated and empty wooden fort which the Sarawak Government had built [...] as a rallying-point and place of meeting with the wild wood dwellers' (from 'The ascent of Mulu', Shackleton's chapter of *Borneo Jungle*, edited by Tom Harrisson). He also was given the permission of the third rajah, Charles Vyner Brooke, to call the summit of Mulu 'Oxford Peak', since that expedition was organised by the Oxford University Exploration Club. That name had lapsed by the time we arrived.

There is a huge body of material arising from the time so many of us lived in that wonderland and were privileged to investigate it for the first time. As well as my book, there is the detailed 'Management Plan' we had been commissioned to write by the Sarawak government; there are about 1,000 scientific papers published in learned journals all over the world; and there are the films: *Mysteries of the Green Mountain* (1978), made by the late, great Barry Paine for the BBC, and *The Lost*

World of Mulu (1999), made later by me for Channel 4. Together, these sources tell how we investigated every aspect of what was often described as the richest environment on earth and made it for a time the best studied rainforest anywhere. Lord Shackleton, a past president, said that ours was the most successful expedition to be sent out by the RGS in modern times. But this book is about more than that. Mulu was a life-changing experience for everyone who was there. Looking at my diaries from the time and the archives of photographs Nigel and I took has made me realise just how important it all was, not just for me but for so many others. Not only were we lucky enough to spend so much time in the most wonderful and fascinating place on earth, but our efforts in trying to understand it and tell everyone about it – scientists, politicians and the caring, campaigning public – helped to spark the global movement to stop the destruction of rainforests. We have failed dismally to overcome the powerful vested interests and deeply ingrained corruption which surrounds the logging industry, but without the rainforest movement there is no doubt that the situation would be even worse today.

PART II

DIARIES

I can say with confidence that this expedition, in terms of harmonious and effective team work, was quite outstanding.

The Rt Hon. Lord Hunt of Llanfair
Waterdine CBE, DSO, president, RGS

I kept a diary religiously during the 15 months we spent in Mulu. I have always believed that this is just about the most important thing to do on an expedition, as memories fade so quickly. Long after everyone else was asleep there would usually be just two lamps still lit: one belonged to Nigel, who would be dutifully working on accounts, labour lists for the next day and the hundred and one problems, large and small, which our admirable scientists managed to dream up; and the other was mine, as I stayed up writing letters and reports – and my diary, at least two pages every day, and often much more. Transcribing them almost 40 years later, I find that much of what I wrote and which seemed so important at the time was a boring chronicle of the logistics of the day. Fetching and carrying scientists, Berawan workers and stores. Three-hour speed runs in our splendid jetboat down to Marudi and back, whizzing effortlessly over the 14 rapids on the Tutoh, through which Nigel and I vied for the status of best navigator. With only a 10-centimetre draught at full speed, it was fairly easy to avoid rocks and logs, but the penalties of failure were dire. The boat, being made of fibreglass, would split or crack on impact. Sharp rocks could lie just below the surface and floating logs were invisible, so that we had to be constantly alert. It was much easier going up- than downstream. Our finest moments were when we passed occasional longhouses on the bank where, having heard the sound of our motor far off, children would gather on the veranda and shout: 'Robin [or Nigel, as the case might be] and his jetboat!' They were still talking about it in 2015 and bewailing the fact that the journey up from Marudi usually still took a couple of days with, especially at low water, regular stops to push through the rapids and repair shear bolts.

Some of the entries are, however, more interesting, capturing something of the excitement and passion we all felt at the time. I begin with a very early entry, from the day after I first arrived at the entrance to the park, having struggled upriver by longboat, as the jetboat had not yet arrived.

GLOSSARY

atap	palm fronds used in thatching
babi	pig
barang	baggage
batu	rocky outcrop
bilek	room
borak	rice wine
cawat	loincloth
gunung	mountain
jamban	latrine
kerangas	tropical heath forest with acidic, sandy soil lacking in nutrients
kuala	mouth of a river
makan	food
parang	machete
pengulu	headman
selabit	rucksack
sulap	shelter
sungai	river
Tua Rumah	headman
ulu	jungle

FRIDAY 24 JUNE 1977. Temenggong Baya Malang [paramount chief of the Baram district] has given me permission to build our Base Camp longhouse at Long Pala, the 'place of the heads' just on the edge of the park. This is on condition everything is removed when we leave next year. [Abdul] Manaf Sairi from the Forestry Department in Miri has already arrived with six men and is starting to clear the site. I have a sketch of what I want to build and I have to decide exactly where it is to go. I have brought a big ball of pink string. I paced out the rough dimensions about thirty metres back from the riverbank and marked it out with the string tied between trees. I tried to do this so that the minimum number of trees would have to be cut down.

[The man I put in charge of building our Base Camp was a Berawan called Usang Apoi from Long Terawan, the nearest longhouse to us, some 20 kilometres downriver. During the next year we were to employ about 150 people from there. Usang was a flawed genius. He could build a house or a longboat by eye, simply measuring everything by handspans, cutting the wood with a chainsaw or adze and finishing in an astonishingly short time. But he had a weakness for drink and women and so was not suitable to be our headman. Instead, I appointed his half-brother, Engan Nilong (also known as Tama Bulan, the name he took on the birth of his first child), a gentle, strong man whom everyone respected and who could be completely relied on to sort out any problem.]

The place is full of leeches, but the leech guards are effective. [These were white-cotton overstockings which we all wore to begin with and which stopped leeches getting up our trousers. As time wore on most of us abandoned them and simply wore shorts, because then leeches were easily seen and scraped off with a knife.] At dusk I climbed the small batu behind the camp. There is a good spot at the top with a view across to Gunung Api and I listened to the night noises. Crows were cawing like at an English rectory, hornbills passed below and there was a weird rushing sound from the millions of swiftlets returning to Deer Cave, which is said to foretell good weather.

22   The view into the park from the *batu* above Base Camp. All the canopy forest in the foreground, being outside the park, has now been clear-felled.

FRI. 8 JULY. [By now the jetboat had just arrived and our longhouse was half-built.] Today I visited the settled Penan village of Long Iman on the Tutoh River with Jon and Michael Hamilton and had a long talk with the headman, Tuwau Labang, about his daughter, Sara, and another girl, Arun, coming to work for us when our longhouse is finished. He is concerned for their safety surrounded by Berawans and foreigners. I gave him my word that I would protect their honour personally! I also arranged to buy some chickens from him. We then took a young man, Ubang Kang, as a guide and tried to go up the Tutoh rapids with Mike [Hamilton] driving. A lot of water coming down after rain in the night and quite alarming turbulent water. Passed S[ungai] Langsat (edge of park) after about 4 mins, then came to a major rapid, marked on the map, Batu Mulong. Frightening, but jetboat passed with ease. Then on and on through broken turbulent water where it's hard to see rocks – touched one or two – until S. Tajum on right. Must have been v. near S. Tapin but decided to turn back. Stopped and photographed at Batu Mulong. Gave Penan some beads. Back at Base Camp house is coming on – 1st crossbeam up today, most of timber has been collected. It is beginning to take shape. Should be lots of storage space underneath. In p.m. Mike and I drove to Nam Hua timber camp above Long Linei to collect 2nd-hand zinc. Very dirty, dusty, nasty work for two hours sorting out pieces under the house. Spiders and v. large scorpion – 2nd biggest I've ever seen. Managed to get 140 pieces onto the jetboat and, though very full, it carried them back to Base Camp with ease in 1 hr 10 mins – same time as going down empty. River well up. Long discussions with Manaf in evening. Decided Forestry and other Sarawak people should contribute [M$]3.50 equivalent in food per man per day and we would all eat together. Must arrange separate kitchen and cooking utensils for anything coming in contact with pork for Manaf's sake, as he is a Muslim. He is a good man to negotiate with.

MON. 18. Nam Hua timber camp. Hard morning spent sorting the sub-camp timber, which was being donated to us, into heaps, tying it into bundles with wire. Stores, zinc, kerosene, tools, etc. all comes to about 15 tons. I hope helicopters can cope. Still got a cold. Fast run up to Base Camp. River much lower and shallows more interesting. Boat went well – 2 hrs to Base Camp. Longhouse now beginning to look like something. 1½ bileks roofed and kajang [roofing material] going up. Usang says there isn't going to be enough kajang – I must try and get some more – also zinc. Generator working at rest house. We also installed a floodlight up on tree over beach. Wrong siting of generator house – will have to use as store for collections of insects, etc. Everyone in good spirits and work going ahead (11 men) a little faster, but it's going to be a race to finish by the end of next week. Nigel & I planning to sleep in the longhouse for the first time tonight. Mike Singer made the first entry into the expedition log today and he has collected some nice insects. Must talk to him and tape-record about his work. Andrew Mitchell went up the batu to record with a parabolic mike. Halfway up the shallows on the Tutoh I saw a large herd of wild pig crossing the river. There were lots of small striped ones being escorted by the adults and it would have been easy to shoot some with gun or blowpipe. But we just enjoyed the spectacle. Mike found among other things a dead ant with what I claimed was a unicorn's horn growing out of the top of its head, but he says it is a fungus which killed the ant and grew out through its head. He told a revolting story (he tells many) of a particular protozoan parasite which needs to use ants, sheep and snails as hosts. Many inhabit each ant but one sacrifices itself for the others so as to get into the sheep as follows. It enters the ant's head, where it forms a cyst and dies, thereby causing the ant to climb, presumably in great pain, up the tallest blade of grass it can find and itself die, gripping the very top. There it is very accessible to sheep, which thus pick up its surviving colleagues inside the ant, who pass through the sheep and then enter a snail somehow, before getting back into an ant.

Tue. 19. Helicopter day. [By now we had cleared, or were still clearing, helipads at all the proposed sub-campsites, and we were waiting for the timber to build the huts. This was Borneo ironwood or belian (*Eusideroxylon zwageri*), which is impervious to termites, and can last up to 100 years after being cut (the huts are still there!). It was donated to us by one of the timber camps and is now very rare.]

On its first flight the helicopter failed to find Camp 4 or Camp 3 so it had landed at Camp 1 and dropped Camp 4's stuff there. I flew in with the next lot of Camp 4's timber, found Camp 3, thought it was Camp 4 and dropped timber there. It was very noisy and frightening flying, but we found a tiny helipad on a ridge, with Lewin [a Berawan] looking scared and wanting a lift home. It was hard, sweaty work. We took half the next load to Camp 1 and the remainder to Camp 3, then on to find, but not stop at, Camp 4 on the very top of Mulu. Manaf at Camp 1 said he had hurt his leg and wanted out. The next and last load was to Camp 5 and then back to Camp 1 to collect

Manaf. I had fantastic views of Api and the gorges behind. The heli was having problems with its tail pin (scary) and not coming next day, so Manaf and I went to Marudi where we parked the jetboat on the mudbank in the kampong [village] and found Gerry [Mitton] and Abang [Abdul Hamid] already arrived by express. They were staying in Hotel A. I was in the rest house. We all dined together. Gerry is our first doctor and very smart in a yellow trouser suit. She has been given a whole lot of sponsored clothing by a company in South Africa, where she has been working with Dr Christiaan Barnard [famous for performing the first successful human heart transplant ten years before].

WED. 20. Sped up to Long Terawan, where I left Gerry in the jetboat with strict instructions not to try and go ashore, as the muddy bank was very slippery and she was still in her yellow linen suit. It's a long walk up to the longhouse, but I was collecting Sandy [Evans] and an injured binturong (Arctictis binturong), also known as a bearcat. Sandy had also acquired a nice fat hen and seven chicks for us to take back to Base Camp. When I got back to the river some time later, I found that Gerry had changed into another outfit. She had disobeyed me and tried to teeter across the pole to the shore, fallen into deep mud and, much to the delight of the inevitable crowd of children, had to wash and change in the river.

FRI. 22. Arrived back at Base Camp to find little done as now there are no 9″ [23 cm] nails. Gerry says: 'Total shambles, great health hazards, must have latrine, no dogs, etc.' She swore she saw a turd floating down the river, although there is no one upstream of us and we have been happily drinking the river water. She now wants it all boiled. I am a bit worried but the scientists are cheerful and the binturong is eating fish, although its mouth is in bad order. Peter Wedlake is looking after it. Mike is full of tall stories and surrounded by many minute caterpillars, eggs and other specimens he has collected.

SAT. 23. Loading planks at Long Linei onto helicopter, which took four loads to sub-camps. Nigel & I in the jetboat, heavily loaded with stores, including a paraffin fridge which had been donated to us, collected Spurway [a Berawan] and 50 pieces of zinc, which were very muddy and tied on top of the boat, leaving little room for us. Had to stop once and blow through the carburettor. This meant we just failed to reach the rapids as darkness fell, heavy rain began and engine grew weaker so that it was mad to go on. On Spurway's recommendation we stopped at a small house on the bank belonging to Tama Puyang Wana, an old Berawan soldier, and had a wonderful night over goats and mad dogs, sleeping in wet clothes on a double mattress he provided and after an excellent big very late dinner. A poor old hen was killed and made tasty soup and meat. We were proudly shown Tama Puyang's medals: a Pacific Star and a War Medal 1939–1945.

SUN. 24. Made it up to Base Camp very early, arriving before 7 a.m. while everyone still slept. Mike and I visited the hot spring together, which we found on our own. Lovely hot water in which I soaked my hands for minutes and planned to make a spa. [It still has not been developed, 40 years later.] There was a Rajah Brooke's birdwing [a butterfly] guarding its territory, so said Mike. For last three days I have been on ampicillin for a septic foot. This has worked and stopped it blowing up, but it is painful nonetheless. Gerry operated once with a scalpel but couldn't reach the embedded object – too deep. Then 24 hrs later pus came, after which I could begin to put it to the ground again.

SAT. 30. Sandy and I left early and drove fast to Marudi. Much to do there very quickly. Flew to Miri and took a taxi to Piasau and on to Kuala Baram ([M$]17). Nigel and the Proctors [John and Sue Proctor, forest ecologists, who stayed for over a year with their daughter Katie] had gone up to Marudi on the 9.30 express, leaving the Land Rover for me. I drove to Brunei fast arriving to find Marika and Rupert [my six-year-old son] staying at the Hanburys' [my cousin Christopher was aide-de-camp to the sultan] and Lucy [my 17-year-old daughter] with the Lees. All okay but Marika had had a very bad time with her teeth and hospital check-ups. We all went out to a bbq given by John the sultan's blacksmith from Cirencester.

SUN. 31. Great day all together going to the regatta, where we sat just behind the sultan, his father and the high commissioner. Boat races for 15 to 30 paddles in very choppy water. Then to the yacht club for a press interview. Lunch with Hanburys. Swam in p.m. Fireworks in evening when we couldn't get to the yacht club, stood by river in crowd and had huge green rockets land on us. V. fine show. Dinner with John and Paddy Masterton [a vet from Jamaica and his wife].

MON. 1 AUGUST. Polo in afternoon, again close proximity to sultan, who played well. Dashing brother Prince Jeffry, only learned to ride last Nov. Everyone stood up when sultan got off between chukkas. Christopher introduced me to Mohamed the Wazir. Served in Irish Guards and is 'the brains of the family' [brother of the sultan, traditionally his 'eyes and ears'].

TUE. 2. Letter from Kuching saying 'No' to my human-ecology project. [They had cottoned on to my being chairman of Survival International and I was specifically forbidden to do any anthropological work.]

WED. 3. Rapids not bad but Marika fell through a raft and hurt her foot and was barely conscious. Saw doctor on arrival who pronounced it not broken but v. swollen and blue.

Long evening with many in camp and much to discuss. Heavy rain and roof still leaking, esp. my bilek. Rupert v. frightened of ants and flies and making a fuss, but Katie Proctor v. brave.

23   Marika treating her foot in the hot spring.

THUR. 4. Rupert much more cheerful. Lucy making friends with each of the scientists in turn.

FRI. 5. Return from L. Terawan a triumph with 20′ [6 m] python skin, killed while they were there, and a sweet little baby mouse deer which Sandy adopted. After lunch a huge scorpion walked across the floor by dining table. Most climbed onto their seats whilst Jo [Anderson] and I caught it and put a lead on it. Jo picked it up by tail much to horror of locals.

SUN. 7. Discussion with men about Sunday working. They want a day of rest with pay. I offered either no work with no pay or guaranteed light day's work with pay. They agreed to work on Sundays. I said I would pay them for that Sunday even though they hadn't worked. Also agreed that they should work 7 hours not 6 as they had slipped into 7–12 and 2–4.

MON. 8. Took Lucy to the Deer Cave in the morning. One hour out with Lucy going well and found without difficulty. Huge cavern, bigger than Niah, and enchanting views through the great opening into the sun and high white cliffs. Found way through to the far side for first time. A paradise where we lay in the sun and where the river flows into the top cave over gravel. Butterflies, no insects and a great open view of two sharp limestone peaks. Saw lots of 'big cat' footprints on the soft guano – clouded leopard? – some over 4′ [1.2 m] across and not on v. soft ground. A fantastic sight inside looking out to top cave through showers falling 150′ [46 m] from the roof – one regular as a sheet of zinc and falling from a round stalactite. Found better way back following a 'catwalk' along edge of cliff and over steep climb, but much shorter and easier than clambering over huge boulders. Most of river runs out underground but worth investigating again. Saw big fat white wild pig at small limestone rocks before last stretch to Deer Cave.

THUR. 11. Big party to the Deer Cave. Rosemary [Fullerton-Smith], Rupert, John Maidment [our Shell representative in Miri – Shell were extremely generous throughout the expedition with logistical help and fuel], James Barclay [an English friend working in Miri], Lucy (again), Rory Walsh, RH-T and Gerry. All did well, though Rupert had to be carried most of the way (by me). 'Sound of Music' trek over steep cliffs through cave and a good swim and picnic in 'Garden of Eden'. Brought back guano and Rupert on my back, which was exhausting. Also a bag brought by Lang [a senior Berawan, after whom one of the finest caves was later to be named], who came with us. No sign of clouded leopards but plenty of binturong tracks. A black snake seen by me disappearing into rocks on way in. Later M and I took jetboat down to L.T. to fetch Gathorne [Medway] and David Labang, but they didn't arrive. [David and Lian Labang were among five young Kelabit whom Tom Harrisson arranged to get trained in Kuching. They had their ears cut while in Kuching so as not to look different from the other students. Tom was cross, but they stood up to him and both worked at the Sarawak Museum for many years. David, who preferred to be called by his Kelabit name of Raban Bala, became a key member of the Mulu expedition team.] Drank borak and beer with Philip Ube [the Temenggong's agent], Uncle Melai, David Melai his son, and Usang plus father. They had just killed the water buffalo for the party – which the MD of Shell is donating – and it was in Philip's boat. Looked huge. We brought back the liver and heart and a drum of Super Shell, plus stores, etc. Sensational drive back up through the rapids with a glorious pink and blue sunset – one of the best I have ever seen – behind us downstream, and Benarat, Api and Mulu lit up orange against the dusk sky as we made it back just at darkness. Lovely being alone and happy together. Passed a large snake in the water – must get catching gear to keep in the boat. Long evening talking, playing backgammon and later fighting huge ants in the jamban [the 'long drop' we dug behind Base Camp]. There are apparently also rats.

FRI. 12. Sped down to L.T. Medway and David Labang arrived in the Forestry Office boat. Went up to Temenggong's house, took tea and collected three large pots for cooking the buffalo. This was already at Base Camp, green and stinking. Much fluent Malay chat from Gathorne. A good run back up, which I was pleased about, and back just as all 10 from Camp 5 arrived in the rubber boat and longboat. All in good form but had had colds. Lots of people at BC [Base Camp] and meat everywhere bubbling in pots and being cooked in our and their kitchens. Many decisions to be taken about labour, etc. now changing to new system and I must make a speech. Good to have David Labang back explaining Berawan ways and not being distrusted as I gather Manaf is. Endless talk until 2 a.m. – agreed to/offered [M$]10 per day. Drank Guinness. By and large good feeling from men. Much applauding. Kids swam and made a lot of noise.

SAT. 13. Day of party. [This was to celebrate the completion of our longhouse. Traditionally, a human head would be buried under one of the poles, but we were told that a buffalo being slaughtered and feasted on was the modern way.] Everyone with crises/problems. Radio packed up completely. Cooking buffalo. Temenggong arrived – agreed to name Long Pala, said appropriate as this is where men used to bury the heads after battles. His grandfather murdered 15 men from the Brunei government here, but one got away and gave the news. His grandfather was taken off to Kuching and kept there for a year by Rajah Brooke in 1910. His uncle, he says, killed 200 men. At 11.30 the Shell party arrived in their blue helicopter, 10 strong with 2 wives, led by Hans Brinkhorst [head of Shell, Miri] and his NZ No. 2, Graeme Brown. A cheerful bunch with lots of drink brought by them, and then I took them to the Deer Cave. Back rather late (5.30) just after the Forestry chartered helicopter had arrived with Abang Muas, Abang Kassam and Hajji Suleiman [from the Forestry Department] and Paul Chai [our scientific liaison officer with the Sarawak government]. Washing, etc. and then the party. Masses of food and drink and the locals mingled well, all sitting round on the balcony. Four groups really – us, Shell, Forestry and locals. 80 in all. Buffalo good. Head v. smelly brought in and hung over entrance, where it dripped. The Temenggong began to offer borak whilst Apa [an elderly Berawan famous for his singing]

24   Base Camp in the early days while still under construction.

sang toasting songs, 'lagu'. Then we danced Berawan and Western. Then speeches – first Temenggong, second Abang Muas, third me thanking Temenggong, Forestry officers, Shell and local people, and finally naming house Long Pala. A really successful party ending after 2 a.m. Started visitor's book. Cleared up.

SUN. 14. Bodies everywhere and warmed up fried rice for breakfast, but great enthusiasm from Shell people at our arrangements before the DO [district office] people left in their helicopter and then the Shell one arrived. The first flight took Temenggong and 1st 7 scientists while I took the Shell people for rides down the first rapid in the jetboat, which they enjoyed. Finished to find everyone had gone on second flight except me, so they laid on a third flight for me and 5 Shell personnel and I saw all round Api and Benarat without a camera and so able to look and absorb. They left before lunch with Nigel, who will be fetching stores, I hope. Hans offered Shell helicopter to bring things from Brunei, clearing customs at Lutong. Quiet afternoon catching up, clearing river and all talking in evening. Sunny all day. River only 3½ feet deep.

MON. 15. [...] Went down low rapids to fetch new arrivals, two Berawans and a prawn trap back to BC. On the way back up the rapids we saw 7 otters dive into the river. We stopped and heads popped up all round to look at us with startled expressions before diving again and eventually loping off in all directions up the banks.

THUR. 18. [...] That night Baby, the baby mouse deer, died very suddenly and sadly for Sandy, who had grown v. attached and whom it regarded as mother, running after him and sleeping next to or on him. Possible over-feeding with watermelon. Jo had a small snake he had caught in the river. I have a poisoned left foot – still keep getting septic cuts on just this one foot, but should be able to walk. Rupert in great form but still not swimming much. Forest ecologists worried to find their plots may have been worked over in last 200 years. [That afternoon Nyapun appeared.]

FRI. 19. Foot still v. swollen and looking angry red, but decided to set off early with Nyapun. We walked for 5 hours with one stop of 20 mins – best thing possible for my foot, though it began to ache by the end [...] Flat limestone country with humps and big trees. 2 p.m. Arrive Nyapun's sulaps. 3 big (6′ × 6′ [1.8 m × 1.8 m]) 1 small (4′ × 4′ [1.2 m × 1.2 m]). Paradise. Nyapun has 2 wives and 10 children (4 boys, 6 girls). All look healthy and cheerful. Ages seem to be 17 down to 1. The sulaps overlook the pretty Lutut River with high banks and a stony bed.

I bathed in the clear fresh water, changed dressing on my foot, and felt utterly content as only such contacts can achieve. They are all one family and have everything they need. I brought 1 kilo sugar, 1 tin Cerebos salt, a packet of tobacco and some beads. I said I had no food but wanted to share theirs. They produced delicious hot chunks of heart of palm in a soup. Sweetened brown sago looking, and tasting, like coarse brown sugar and flour. The eldest boy has a big scar on right shoulder/breast which was where the Miri doctor removed some huge 'sickness', so he has been there. Also, he and his ?15 y.o. brother have been to Limbang for work. But none of the rest have been to Marudi or anywhere outside (except Nyapun, who went there once). There are lots of pigs but none today. They stick to more or less this area – and who is to blame them? – it's v. nice jungle – circling round after wild sago. Will probably stay at this site 1 month. We nearly had a pig on the way, when N stalked it suddenly while I stood still. My jungle hammock caused interest and some admiration but no undue surprise. They are quite relaxed with me, which is wonderful. Probably not possible if there were more than one of me, so that we would have conversations in unfamiliar languages, excluding them. One baby cried a bit when I photographed, but stopped at once when I gave it a balloon. Their dogs are the fattest and healthiest I have seen, although small. There seem to be about 5. Nyapun's two wives, both fairly young with fine delicate faces, sit quietly weaving mats out of rattan, smoking the tobacco I brought and chatting peacefully. They say they eat about 1 babi [pig] each week throughout the year. Borne out so far by 2 jawbones killed over last 2 weeks. Little girl wearing monkey's teeth. Gave beads – half to each wife. Smoking minute quantities of tobacco in long tubes of atap leaf – rather like those Russian ones. Nyapun lights them for me and passes them over. Very charming little girl (Tagam) about 2 years old sat close staring up at me with big eyes and a shy smile. Of course in the end I produced a balloon and blew it up for her. They all played with it, gently tossing it up in the air with many warning about the 'poom' that would happen if it hit a thorn. Every now and then Tagam pointed out it was hers and had it given back. The boys all have shorts and the women and girls sarongs, bought I suppose from traders, but they really seem to have nothing else but a parang, blowpipe and a couple of cooking pots; and they seem to need nothing. Presents are nice and a bit of cash useful, I suppose, occasionally, but there seems to be no sense of need or deprivation. The children all have clear, round eyes, round but not bulging tummies, and are altogether a healthier lot than to be found at Long Terawan. Also no smell. Tinaw, the second boy, is now sitting by the fire hardening the points of a new set of blowpipe darts over the flame. Nyapun says they have no antidote to the poison if a proper wound is given, but gave me some leaves one can rub on for minor scratches. With a hard jab your throat closes up so you can't breathe or swallow and you die in about half an hour. King, the third boy, also has the same skin infection as his father. Their teeth are not very good. Lugoh, the eldest boy, is shaping the wads on the ends of the darts and eating some raw sago cooked in the fire. The camp is astonishingly uncluttered considering 13 people live here, mostly children. My very few possessions already make it look messy. There is a temptation to give them everything – to call Nyapun when the expedition leaves and hand over all surplus pots, mugs, cloths, nails, etc. but would he be any happier? And what is it that makes a very few people in the world still realise where happiness lies and refuse to come and settle in towns as the gov. would like them to? An added complication

1 Clive Jermy, a botanist and world expert on ferns at the Natural History Museum. He was our chief scientist and his diligence and wisdom were the key to the success of our work and the whole expedition's subsequent reputation.

2 Travel by longboat can be slow and hazardous.

3 Our jetboat, which could skim over rapids, was donated
by the New Zealand inventor Jon Hamilton.

4 A remote forest river in the Mulu Park. For me these are the most beautiful places in the world.

5   Buttress roots support giant trees on shallow soil.

6　Being greeted at the landing stage at Long Terawan. The longhouse is some way from the river. Note the slippery notched pole, off which Dr Gerry Mitton fell into the mud.

7　Nigel Winser and his team about to set off. From left to right: Paya Ding (Penan), Ipoi Jau, Tama Engan, Nigel, Danny Lawai.

8 Lusing, a nomadic Penan, sharpening a blowpipe dart.

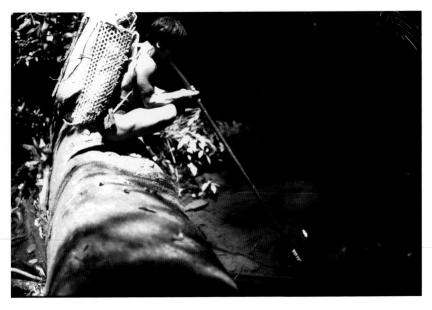

9   Nyapun drinking through his blowpipe.

10   Nyapun resting.

11 A Penan child from Long Liau, from where I made my first long journey through the Borneo rainforest.

is that the relatively recently settled people of Long Iman want to have a school but there are not enough children to justify a teacher, so they too are putting pressure on their nomadic relations to come and swell the numbers. However, Nyapun seems untroubled… Practising with the family's two blowpipes – one is old and short, the other long and new. Father and the two boys demonstrated sending darts far above the canopy through a hole in the foliage. I managed to hit a large tree at thirty paces. He reckons the range is about 50 paces, but it must be more if they can do the same straight up. Itang (no. 1 wife) is now strumming on a pagang, which someone recently called the world's most primitive instrument. Actually it makes a pleasant background, rhythmic and resonant. Both wives now playing in counterpoint, which must be a nice thing for a husband to watch. Nyapun seems unimpressed. When asked, Nyapun emphatically said he preferred the name Penan to Punan. Knew exactly what I was on about at once and was pleased I knew the difference. [These Penan thought Punan a pejorative name, although it is much used elsewhere in Sarawak.] Suddenly the children, on orders from father and mother, are doing a rapid little dance – v. like the twist – five little girls – side to side, arms and hands flapping at sides front and back, feet moving forward alternately. Rhythm goes 'there's a fly in my whisky'. Performance en plein air in the open jungle on dead leaves, v. rustic. Now Nyapun doing a more conventional longhouse dance with bird-like hands, little hops and cries, and considering the inaudibility of the music, a brave effort. Both wives now tuning their instruments and managing to sound like the Hallé warming up. The eldest boy danced – also graceful. Very well brought up obedient children who do what they are told but have lots of uninhibited fun as well. Coffee and a cheroot our only evening meal as dusk set in. What more could one ask for, accompanied by pagang played by one wife while the other dances gracefully, swinging her hips and gyrating energetically. Respectful audience. As the boys sorted their darts, discussing points, etc. the second wife danced as well, accompanied by the other. This, I think, was not just for my benefit.

Father in bark cawat only, and two boys in shirts and shorts, set off across the river with two blowpipes and one torch; a memorable sight.

The best is that they seem to be completely relaxed with me. Nyapun is playing with his youngest, walking her on his chest and crooning. The others find me quite interesting and sometimes remember to come and stare, but mostly they play together, fight, dance a bit, and carry on regardless like any other children. Yet they have never had an orang puteh [white man] to stay before, nor have any of the children, except the eldest two, seen one. How different from village or town people in the same situation. In the old days 'under the British' all the Penan from S. Ubong, S. Puah, S. Tapin, S. Melinau, etc. used to gather three times a year at L. Melinau to trade mats, baskets, etc. for clothes, pots, etc. Since Malaysian independence it doesn't happen any more (should we reinstigate?). Light, once dark falls, is provided for us by a large taper of damar which flames between the end sulap and my hammock.

25 A damar gum light at Nyapun's camp.

SAT. 20. Squatting at first light round the fire at the edge of the sulap where sago is being roasted and Nyapun is boiling water for coffee. The wives seem to have their own families around them and to be cooking quite separately. Very sweet little girl, sitting staring/ smiling at me, suddenly yawns widely and in the most ladylike way covers her mouth with the back of her hand. A universal polite gesture? The absence of material possessions still strikes me. Apart from the metal for their spears and parangs, which they make themselves anyway, and, I am told, used to mine the metal for, they have two cooking pans, a bowl, one enamel plate and two ladles. The rest is all home-made. Sheaths for parangs and darts of course; blowpipes, tongs for cooking and lifting food from pans, several baskets, bamboo tubes for holding water, atap as well as rattan mats for sleeping on, wooden spoons. The design of the two main shelters is the same; a platform of sticks about 18″ [45 cm] from the ground covered by a lean-to atap roof, reaching from 3′ to 6′ [1–2 m] and facing the river. At the front the fire with over it a shelf on which wood for burning dries, with a few things stored on top or hung from the beam. A small screen slopes down from the high point of the eave to protect this area. The set-up here approaches closely to my concept of a control or model for the alternative for all that progress has to offer. The proofs that it works are the healthy children and the atmosphere of peace and contentment. The absence of need is something that we, and almost all 20th-century people wherever, find hard to grasp. Monks in their monasteries have retreated from life in order to come closer to God. Nomadic hunter-gatherers have evolved and retained a way of life which could hardly be retreated from – except the domesticity! – and so are as close as man can be to nature and so to God. It is, of course, a subject impossible to discuss without being accused of romanticism and worse, but what has life really to offer more than this? The great heights of human achievement are all products of man's changing view of the world and his own ideas growing together to produce a new concept of grandeur or beauty. Beethoven would be a cacophony to the Penan; Rembrandt, to say nothing of Picasso, meaningless; the Acropolis and the Taj Mahal impressive but pointless – indeed, even the scale would not amaze them much, since nature has built greater structures from trees and rocks all round them. Jesus would have loved these people. There is no cant, bigotry or hypocrisy about them, the human faults which angered Him most. He would not have wished to change them, I am sure. What has been done in the name of religion, and esp. Christianity, is very terrible, both in instilling needs and aspirations which the simultaneous work ethic can never satisfy; but also in subverting the original virtue in which I profoundly believe, and replacing it with guilt and shame and original sin. These Penan are not ashamed, nor are they proud. They simply are. They are not so shy as people think, yet there is no aggression. They are, to a quite shattering degree, self-sufficient, and that is something a modern mind finds almost impossible to grasp. Surely they must want something from me. The sugar, salt and tobacco were most welcome, it is true, but they have used them generously to entertain me, and will, I feel, not miss them when they are gone, having substitutes. The balloons gave the children passing fun, but are now forgotten and have left no need. The torch batteries I gave the boys last night when they went pig-hunting (unsuccessfully), they do need replacing. I forgot to mention they have a torch. Perhaps the need for torch batteries will be what will at last bring the Penan in from the cold to settle in poverty on the overworked Baram and scratch a living from the soil, 'like all progressive people ought to do'. I gave them a cord to tie a knot in each day and to attach jawbones of all animals killed. [This was part of a study the zoologists were doing.] Also left letter for next scientist to visit here. We left the camp rather casually and all together at 10.30 and started walking back along the faint Penan track. Everybody came along and at first I thought they were setting off to gather sago, or hunt. But after the three eldest boys had peeled off with the blowpipes and most of the hunting dogs (seven in all, in fact), the small girls hoisted the smaller ones onto their shoulders and started trudging determinedly along in single file. They were v. sweet and brave and cheerful and we went almost as fast as the day before. It was a tremendous feeling to be walking as part of a whole Penan group, and at last I realised that they were all coming home

26   Lucy setting out to climb Mt Mulu. Note the leech guards!

with me. Got some nice photographs of them trooping across narrow
log bridges, and squatting to have a rest. At one stop I shared out my
only orange – one pig each – then King, the remaining boy, aged
about 11, and I started pulling ahead and we finally arrived back
ahead of the rest. Simultaneously, as it happened, with Lucy and the
first of the Mulu party.

Lucy had done well on the climb and become the first woman to
climb Mulu, 10 mins ahead of Rosemary. Found everyone had been paid
by Nigel and including the difference to bring them up to [M$]10 per
day for the whole time they had worked for us. As a result everyone in
good form and rather tight. Sabang [one of our best Berawan workers,
but a bit prone to drink] had spent nearly all his pay on drink. Later
in the evening the Penan came and danced for us and then, of course,
we all had to as well.

THUR. 25. Rat traps were set in the kitchen and in the night there
was suddenly a fearful racket when one got caught and squealed in
fury. I moved it outside and it shut up. In the morning I drowned it

in the river since the girls wouldn't let me keep it in the fridge. Later Gathorne said he would have liked me to keep it after all. M[arika], L[ucy], R[upert] and I went to the hot spring and sat in a row on a log soaking our feet in the water. A good family outing. In the afternoon it began to rain, signalling, as it turned out, the end of the long dry spell. The river began to rise and we saw no more of the nice sandy bottom which was excellent for swimming on.

SAT. 27. [...] We went and called on the Southwells in Marudi in the evening and had coffee and ice cream. A very interesting man and knowledgeable about Sarawak, but too much of the usual evangelical stuff. [Hudson Southwell was an Australian missionary who founded the Borneo Evangelical Mission in 1928. He travelled energetically and proselytised successfully, stopping the people he converted from drinking and practising many of their traditions. It would be hard to find anyone more different from Bishop Galvin, who was deeply respectful of Kenyah culture. Southwell had been interned by the Japanese during the war. In 1947 he and his wife first visited Bario and brought Christianity to the Kelabit. They were helped by Tom Harrisson, although their attitudes were chalk and cheese – and he found them humourless. Later they were to be invited by the Kelabit to come and teach them, which resulted in their lifestyle changing utterly – mainly because they stopped drinking. Even years later, when most had been converted into being devout Christians, the Kelabit would assert that Tom had done more for them than the Southwells.]

MON. 29. It rained hard all day and the river came right up to the top steps of the rest-house side. We all thought it might flood over, and so stores were moved up from under the rest house and contingency plans made for the longhouse, but it stopped after coming up about 10′ [3 m] from low water level. In the evening Marjorie [Sweeting] gave us a talk on her geomorphology work.

WED. 31. Started new rubbish pit and covered over old one. In evening went in JB [jetboat] plus M, L, R and Sara and Arun to Long Iman to collect the v. pretty bead bracelet they had made for Lucy from beads we gave them. Took two kilos of sugar as a present. Took some photographs of pretty girl pounding rice. Also M doing the same. Sat with children and women for some time in nice peaceful atmosphere. One baby girl had spots on face and in ears which looked nasty, and they were worried about it, so we brought her and mother and brothers and sisters all back to BC – 15 in the jetboat. Not v. serious, but whilst Gerry was treating them a boatload of people arrived from Long T[erawan] with a v. sick boy who had pneumonia. Lots of others wanted treatment too and in the middle Sandy poured petrol over his balls and burned them quite badly. Lucy's last night and dramas over her ticket to NZ. Gerry made fudge which made us all feel sick but was v. good.

THUR. 1 SEPTEMBER. V. few in camp after big JB departure in the morning. Worked on my water tank again which leaked after rain. Talked to Julian [Dring] about his frog programme and worked on the raft which is cluttered with driftwood so that the ladies' wash house is not private any more. Complaints. Poor Rupert, who was in great form, was hysterical about washing on the raft, and then had a dreadful screamy time while I held him and toothpaste-tube quantities of pus were removed from a boil on his bottom. Big ants back in the jamban – my own private horror – makes me sympathetic about other things I don't notice so much.

FRI. 2. Went and fetched gravel from the mouth of the Melinau, plus Rory [Walsh] and M, to try and fix the sullage pit. We went in the rubber boat which was slow but pleasant, and stopped on the way back to visit the hot spring where the Rajah Brooke's birdwing was aggressive and ravishing and I took lots of photographs of M. Rupert was off colour all day, but in the evening whilst having his dressings changed by Gerry, got hysterical at the prospect of another boil being lanced and when I held him down he passed out and had a convulsion which was v. frightening. Gerry ready to give mouth to mouth, but he came round and was quite cheerful but v. weak and had a headache. Gerry says he is highly intelligent and highly strung and we must try not to let him get hysterical.

MON. 5. Up early to boil tea and fetch water from the rest house. A good feeling being up before anyone else and getting things done quietly. Work on raft and boats. V. hot a.m. Men digging their own jamban. Sue went up to Camp 5 with Engan leaving Katie, who behaved impeccably all day, and I got some nice pictures of the Mulu mother's helps, Nigel and Sandy, playing on the beach with Rupert and Katie – like the seaside. Rory and Bob [Hoskins, a teacher from Brunei] set off up the mountain with loads of rain gauges. Badly need rain – fetching water twice in one day is ridiculous, and anyway I am sure the river water is cleaner but Gerry and Sue think they saw a turd.

27   Rupert with Bob Hoskins, a teacher from Brunei.

WED. 7. [...] I drove like an angel down v. shallow rapids until just below Long Abang where I hit a log and catapulted Nigel into the river. Long drinking evening at Long T. in open shed at back. Philip Ube, Usang hosts. Drank 15 tumblers of borak 'gin and Marmite'. Very very ill. Nearly died. So did Rosemary. Everyone curled up by 3 a.m. like puppies.

THUR. 8. Woke everyone at 5 a.m. feeling surprisingly alive myself but others mostly comatose on drive down to Marudi. Nigel heaving over the side. All rather tight and singing on arrival 'Johnny's got a jamban' – seemed v. funny. Coffee and endless 7 Ups helped shopping, etc.

FRI. 9. Marika's birthday and a million things to do, suddenly inter-rupted at 10 a.m. by an urgent radio call from BC saying Sandy's con-dition deteriorating and he must be got out. Started flying-doctor alert but they had not found the helicopter by 3 p.m. by which time – after repeated telephone and radio calls – I was about to charter a Borneo Skyways helicopter when I heard that the FD [flying doctor] was on the way. Sandy arrived with Nigel holding him and the drip up at the hospital at 5.20 and we carried him in, barely conscious.

SAT. 10. Cleared the Kraft cheese through customs with difficulty and seconds to spare. Also bought tinned meat and gas cylinders and sent all, plus Nigel, plus my remaining things from John Maidment's house, up in a chartered Borneo Skyways helicopter, since BC was badly unmanned. Plans to take family to Niah Caves next day but M broke off her front tooth.

SUN. 11. Morning spent with her at Dr Yie who did a fantastic job sticking a new one on to her plate, seeing Sandy – still more or less in coma – and at the Miri Club. Went shooting snipe in p.m. with HB [Hans Brinkhorst]. Automatic single-barrelled shotgun, not really my thing, but only four snipe there, one of which was close but I missed. Marvellous approach by old railway to pumping station.

THUR. 15. [...] Gathorne in v.g. form: one rat (giant) new to Sarawak. One monkey, new to Mulu (female hose [Hose's langur]). One bat, new to Borneo ('if it's new to me it's new to Borneo').

FRI. 16. End of Ramadan. Thanks to Christopher I was going in advance of the madding hordes to greet the sultan and M[arika] to greet the Rajah Isteri [his senior wife]. We waited in great state in private reception room, then I and Mr Laurie (surgeon) stood on stairs in front of massed officers of Gurkhas, before being the very first two to wish first the sultan, then Sir Omar [Omar Ali Saifuddien III, the sultan's father], then three brothers and four brothers-in-law 'Salamit Hari Raya' ['Happy Eid']. I brought greetings from Lord Boyd, telling about his broken leg and getting a good response from Sir Omar, who said he would write condolences – and also from Malcolm MacDonald [former governor general of Malaya] and Lord Colyton [Marika's uncle]. A sad day of send-offs. M delayed but promised first-class passage all the way. Rupert in the evening, unaccompanied, on BA [British Airways] but full of beans and quite unafraid. Then Gathorne with animals folded between his clothes. In the afternoon I had acupuncture for my back, which was a bit like going to the dentist. Painful massage, quite noticeable pricks into the muscles, and electric shocks – terminals attached to needles for 10 mins. Really left it rather worse, but we shall see.

SAT. 24. [...] The Iban tree-climbers from Kuching caught lots of fish and giant prawns with spearguns.

TUE. 27. [...] Nigel had swollen eye from bite. Barry [Bolton, described recently by the entomologist E. O. Wilson as 'one of the finest myrmecologists in the world'] returned at midday ecstatic over finding '2 species belonging to an entire tribe which shouldn't be here. Amazing broad flat head – and great mandibles – no idea what it does.' 4½ hours on his hands and knees and the poor chap lost his glasses over the side. In p.m. a whole family of Penan arrived, brought up by a Berawan, with one v. sick young man (25 y.o.?) who was dehydrated and had been v. sick for 7 days. Carried in today from some inland group on the Tutoh. Name Lisang. Got flying doctor on radio. Helicopter arrived at 5.45 having got lost on the way, with 2 on board. Sent letters from Gerry to Miri doctor and to John Maidment asking him to look after the friend Nyiling who had not been to Miri before and was frightened. I gave him [M$]30. Lovely family whom I must go and visit soon – 4 houses. Usang says he knows the names, etc. They left in evening after scrounging some petrol – almost our last. I offered to buy the boat – v. big longboat. At 6.25 great cloud of bats came over high and Sue got v. excited to see at least 3 bat hawks hunting them. They looked exquisite through the field glasses, russet in the setting sun with scimitar wings. Seemed to go for isolated bats and miss a lot.

28   Bats leaving Deer Cave. One of the great Mulu sights.

WED. 28. Early p.m. John [later Field Marshal] and Annabel Chapple and Miles [later Prince Philip's private secretary] and Gay Hunt-Davis arrived with Nigel after interesting journey stopping at L. Panai and Long T., talking to Temenggong, etc. Went straight to Deer Cave at 3.30 just the 4 of them and me. They thought I walked v. fast. Didn't go through, but a good visit. Very bright yellow luminous moss/fungus at entrance.

THUR. 29. After some work and chores in a.m. the 4 visitors + Nigel, Rosemary, Gerry and Usang went for a picnic in U's longboat. A really good day. First to Cave of the Winds, which we went into. Saw what might have been eagle owls in sinkhole. Then picnic at the mouth of Clearwater and v.g. swim. Excellent site. Then to new cave. Named it Clearwater Cave about 8 mins walk in. A nice cave, not deep but with good stalagmites/tites and a very nice site for sleeping. I went a long way up a v. small tunnel/watercourse/cave which meandered into the cliff but didn't open. Nigel tried to catch eel-like fish. I poled back in front – river low, in and out of water – v. hard work, but tremendous. Great guests and a v. happy day.

SAT. 1 OCTOBER. Climbed the batu + Ken [Scriven, director of WWF Malaysia] before breakfast and listened for birds. Can now identify the plain babbler and the yellow-crowned bulbul.

SUN. 2. Got up at 5 to make N[yapun] tea before he set off to Marudi at 5.30. Rained v. heavily in the night – about 1 inch [2.5 cm]. Worked on 100-day report. Later went fishing with Ken who caught 3 big ones with my spinning rod and a No. 3 Mepp. As usual I had no luck. The Deer Cave party arrived back tired but stimulated. Sandra [Leche] had never been anywhere tropical before and apparently didn't sleep at all for worry about insects, etc. Main event of the day was cutting down the big tree as several were worried it would fall on the longhouse.

Final straw was Barry Bolton finding a termite nest and saying it was probably hollow – it wasn't. It fell a surprisingly short way across the river, held by 2 tight ropes. The canopy fell conveniently across the log and I floundered about in the water catching ants, grasshoppers, caterpillars, urged on by scientists. Best were a skink and 2 bewitching dracos [lizards], probably a pair – one with yellow and green, the other red and brown tops to wings and both with lovely turquoise tummies.

MON. 3. Manaf set off to cut his trail. Photograph of cheque-handing-over ceremony by Ken to me (M$5,000) and promising news about the rest coming through. Ken and I then went off to the Deer Cave, walked through and had a picnic lunch in Garden of Eden. V. interesting walking with him. Found strange large pile of dung – some fresh – inside cave on ridge. He took a sample back to have it identified. Thought it might be goat, but they don't exist. Then across G. of E. and it really is Rousseauish. I left K and climbed up the Osmastons' trail to cave under cliff, but too steep and the wrong entrance to the Green Cave they discovered. [Henry and Nigel Osmaston, father and son, were both geomorphologists.] Got back to find Nyapun had arrived. Really very moving to see him again and he clearly felt the same and clung to me.

FRI. 7. Decided to go + Usang and Spurway in boat to Camp 1 to make sure men came back, as much to do next day resupplying Camp 5. Melinau Paku [a tributary of the Melinau] attractive and easy travelling as there had been a lot of rain and it was v. high. Usang brilliant at driving his longboat fast over logs across river, up to 9 inches [23cm] out of the water. V.g. driver. Saw Hose's monkeys [Hose's langurs] and long-tailed macaques on way. Reached Camp 1 in 1½ hrs where they had cleared the dangerous trees and dug a latrine. As Kevin [McCormick] and Mark [Collins] out, I hurried to Camp 2 (25 mins unloaded) but [John] Dransfield and co. also out, so left their letters and a note and hurried down (20 mins). Saw 3 gorgeous red wood partridges.

SAT. 8. [...] Ten of us invited to party, sleeping in Temenggong's house. Party in his room. Drank lots of coffee first and ate biscuits in desperation – also heavy bread sandwiches in boat. Then Betty [Malang, Temenggong's niece] kept her promise and gave me Milo [a chocolate drink popular in Malaysia then and helpful at counteracting the effect of too much borak] before the drinking began, but that was as bad as ever – except that antacid tablets sucked continuously absolutely kept me from feeling sick all night. Gerry and I had our names changed in a speech by the T. Hers had already been made into Lalang by the Kayans. Now she was given Bungan by the Berawans. I only had been told that mine would probably be the T's grandfather or father but in the end it was Oyau Abeng, which means, loosely, 'Prince of the Mountain' and is a legendary hero. He appears in Bishop Galvin's book several times and seems to be the senior heroic figure in Baram mythology. A bit like being called George Washington, but more of an honour as name is bestowed. Bungan was a lady who lived in a cave on the mountains and was much sought after. Then a long night – till 4 a.m. – dancing wildly – I got blisters on my feet.

MON. 10. A small pretty snake fell on Sue's shoulder in her room and Barry and I caught it; he pronounced it non-poisonous and released it – about 1 ft [30 cm] long.

TUE. 11. Gerry and I went down again to see Lusing [a Penan]. Much improved, but squalor at camp really getting a bit much even for my stomach. Worry about 15 more sick people at timber camp downriver. Radioed DMO [district medical officer] to inform him, as outside our jurisdiction. V. hot day. Read Animal Farm, which successfully put problems in perspective.

Penan girls driving Gerry mad, but she has turned out to be one of the best. Always ready to take on any chore or extra job – not easy in the tropics – doctoring v. hard and well, doing all cooking and cheerful at all times. I would not have believed that the person who arrived full of distaste for the 'utter chaos' of Base Camp could have become such a willing and able member. I think it's all done her a lot of good and got rid of a lot of the hang-ups she arrived with. Good for the expedition!

After more abortive radio attempts, David [Labang] did arrive, having broken down and changed boats three times on the way. He came with his brother Lian from the [Sarawak] Museum, and Philip Ube. Also brought up Lusing's wife and 4 children from the timber camp – some of the sick 15 – so Gerry had to cope with that as well. They responded v. well to antibiotics and were unrecognisable next morning.

Lots of packing, rearranging everyone's lives, writing letters, doing wages until after midnight.

EARLY RECCE ACROSS THE PARK, TO THE LIMBANG RIVER AND BACK FROM BASE CAMP, WITH DAVID AND LIAN LABANG

WED. 12. [...] Walked to Melinau Gorge in 2 hours, easy going. Good view of gorge from Melinau crossing. Arrived in rain to find only Barry and some men of Paul Chai's in camp. Sandra and Gwilym [Lewis] came in soaked later, having been lost with Ding the Kayan, whom everyone is now against. Trouble brewing, so made contingency plans. Letter from John D[ransfield] who had gone up to Bukit Buda with Paul. Looked longingly at the Tiger Cave which Usang climbed up to when he was 16. Big cave inside and not difficult but no time now for Mark. Nyapun went off to fetch a brother, Ta'ee, who, with 2 other families, is not far away up the Melinau. Hugged me and introduced me as his father when he got back. Sited the jamban, which has not yet been built. Set up my hammock, much to Usang's consternation, as he said I would be cold. It seemed to be keeping the rain out. Long evening in camp. Talked with David, Lian and Usang about walking to Long Seridan (6 days and nights, crossing 3 main rivers). Lian came down the Tutoh 6 years ago. He also went with Tom Harrisson across my route to the Belaga. No way through the gorge to Long Seridan – only the escaped prisoner Lawai did this – but easier way is round by Medalam River. Should do circuit of the park. Nagan and Lawai (after 2 shots with David's double-barrelled shotgun) came back with a mouse deer. No comment. Off to my hammock. Talk of numbers of Penan increasing in the park. Most arrived 20 years ago – Nyapun, etc. – following the wild sago and the migrating pigs, stayed, and more have arrived since. If we find that the population really is around 500, then it will pose a severe strain on the park and measures will have to be taken. The brother of Nyapun, Ta'ee, had a brand-new Aguirre Spanish shotgun (3 months old) belonging to Lusing. Well looked after, single-barrelled with shiny clean inside. Maybe there could be a rule about nomads being allowed to use only blowpipes, but hard to enforce.

[This was a time when the idea of tribal people owning and managing their own land was still in its infancy. Since then much has changed in many parts of the world. In Brazil and elsewhere in South America vast areas traditionally occupied by Indian tribes have been legally recognised as theirs, and these are often the only environments still being protected from exploitation. Satellite imagery can reveal this in a very powerful way. For example, there is a part of central Brazil which I first visited in 1958 into which only a handful of pioneering settlers had then penetrated. In 1961 a national park the size of Belgium was created for the 6,000 or so Indians, from 17 tribes, who lived on the Xingu River. A 1995 map shows settlement, in red, approaching from the east, but most of the land is still green. Twenty years later the straight lines demarcating the edges of the park are completely surrounded by red and only the park itself has been preserved – by the Indians, who have fought to prevent encroachment. I was there again in 2016 and, although there is pollution coming down the rivers into the park from the soya plantations upstream, the environment of the park itself is healthy and the forests are intact. There are many other examples of how tribal peoples are better at looking after their environments than anyone else – after all, they have been dependent on and managed them for millennia. And the same story can be told all over the world. A 2015 study by the Center for International Forestry Research (CIFOR) found that in national parks created a decade ago in three Papuan territories, from which the people were not removed, communities maintain their traditional land claims, customs and tribal systems, as well as continuing to hunt, fish and use forest resources, but have a recognised responsibility for protecting key resource-rich areas. Another CIFOR study, from 2012, found that 'community managed forests presented lower and less variable annual deforestation rates than protected forests'. The World Wide Fund for Nature (WWF) has revealed that 80 per cent of the world's biodiversity is found on the lands of tribal peoples and that the vast majority of the 200 most biodiverse places on earth are tribal peoples' territories. I wish that evidence had been available in 1977, but back in those days we were preoccupied with creating a national park and protecting it. Now, having seen how often environmental enthusiasm has destroyed the way of life of tribal people living in areas rich in wildlife, often to the detriment of both, I would approach the problem quite differently, recommending that the Penan be granted ownership of their land and the right to manage it, which I believe they are better able to do than anyone else; but if I had suggested such a thing then we would almost certainly have been thrown out of the country.]

THUR. 13. Slept well in hammock, but needed a pillow. Very dry and warm inside sleeping bag. Bathed in Melinau at 6 – more refreshing than Base Camp – actually colder. Waded river and walked quickly to Sungai Terikan above Lobang China [a cave in the limestone], where we caught up David and co., who had set out earlier. Penans rather slow with heavy loads. Talk of how the Ibans come up regularly and use tuba [poison extracted from the plant of the same name] in the river to catch fish. No one ever yet prosecuted for this – a good place to catch them. Just upstream, stopped again to put nets across the cave where the Terikan comes out of the cliff. Several of us inc. David and Lian then swam inside with poles and rocks and noise to drive fish out, but none there. Doesn't look much like St John's drawing [Spenser St John, then British consul in Brunei, reached this point in 1857] so probably water flowing in to Lobang China. On along edge of Benarat through more kerangas, where the argus pheasant called, to a couple of Penan camps under the high peak at the end. Counted poles and measured with David. Found Paul's [Chai] camp soon after on one of the islands in the Medalam and had an hour or so to dry clothes on the rocks. A stunning wide clean river coming from a broad valley leading into the hilly country behind, whence came some of the Penan. Nyapun said he didn't know who they were. Put my hammock up and then it began to rain very hard indeed. Seemed to get in everywhere, even our now long and well-made camp sheets. David made a good fire in the buttress roots of a large tree and Usang ministered to me. Paul, John D. and men arrived back very wet after an hour of rain. We thought they were probably lost, but not. The day before they had been within sight of the top of Buda – climbable, they say. [As far as I know, it still hasn't been climbed.] During early-afternoon makan, soon after arrival, sudden hiss from Nyapun pointed out a pig on stones opposite. Usang grabbed D's shotgun and hurried off. Fired a shot and I saw a huge red boar run off. Nyapun later went in pursuit, but returned empty-handed. Walking is no trouble – in fact I find it rather slow and the rests too long. Feet bearing up well but shoulder and back stiff (from damp?) although I am only carrying a small load. A long, damp, dripping evening by

29   A Mulu stream. This is one of my favourite images of Mulu.

candlelight. Paul and co. have a tilly lamp their end. I find the simple food of rice – sometimes hot, tonight cold – pusu (little salted fish a bit like yellow flat whitebait) and sometimes a tin of meat or some pickled greens, plenty and satisfying. I wonder how long it will take to pall. [I wrote a poem titled 'The River' on this night. See Appendix 1.]

Buda only 1,000 m – v. low montane forest, possibly the lowest in Sarawak – reason for including in park. [Gunung Buda is the third large limestone mountain after Api and Benarat, both of which were already included in the Mulu National Park. All this area was logged, disgracefully, before the largely cleared land was included in the park. One of my biggest and saddest shocks on my first return to Mulu 20 years after this was to see from the aeroplane how much of that immaculate forest with its clear rivers had been brutally felled.]

FRI. 14. Left at 7.30, sleeping bag sodden mass because I left it in the hammock during the heavy evening rain and a sizeable trickle got in. Walked first along the vaguest of Penan paths keeping more or less to the true right bank of the Medalam, hence outside the park. Reached Kuala Buda in 1½ hrs and stopped for a bit. Then stopped to eat ½ way to S. Assam. Shortly after starting, Ajang the young Penan got lost and we stayed (rightly) where we were and called, hooted, blew through the gun, blew my whistle, etc. for 1 hour before he answered. He had, blast him, as expected carried on to the Assam and returned, but no good taking chances. Saw a large frogmouth still in a tree 30 ft up and tried to photograph as David said it was very rare. 4 clearly marked white-edged feathers on each side of tail and white spots on folded wings. Big wide froglike beak. Flew off at last like an owl. [It was probably a Dulit frogmouth (*Batrachostomus harterti*). Only eight museum specimens are known.] S. Assam deep and only crossed with difficulty on sunken fallen tree. David made a handrail of lianas. Then a long and quite hard, but slow, walk over a couple of hills and doubtful of whether we were heading right. A glimpse of G. Benarat to the south from one of the hills. Out of earshot of the river all the time. Hit S. Terikan dead on – v.g. navigating by Nyapun. Faith in Penan restored. A lovely spot.

River clear, black water [clear as opposed to cloudy]. Bathed at once and spread everything out on rocks to catch the last of the sun before inevitable rain. Saw that Nyapun had a good scrub too and put on his ointment afterwards. His skin infection seems to be getting a bit better. Remains of Iban shelter at Kuala T. so erected camp sheets there, while still waiting and hoping for boat downriver. No boat, so put up 2 camp sheets – some rain. V. nice campsite. D[avid] & N[yapun] went off and shot a game cock (crested fireback pheasant). Only bamboo around campsite, so no platform to sleep on. Palm leaves for me and Penan. D[avid] & L[ian] made poles for their 'hammocks'. Nowhere for me to sling mine close. Luminous fungus at base of 2 or 3 bamboos. Very bright white light in steps an inch or so apart.

Much talk with David and others about when Japanese were hunted through here – ambushed on the Medalam by 2 Australian officers (Tuan Sandy). Temenggong still has the ceremonial sword of the Japanese officer his father killed. Southwell was caught here and put in prison. Others, e.g. the DO [district officer] in Marudi, were killed by Ibans, not for the Japs but for his gun. D very keen on Kelabit culture. Believes it is important it should be recorded and preserved. Wants Kelabit tools collected and a model of a warrior for the museum. Has written a lot about his people's customs and history. Mention of Orang Ulu ['people of the interior'] Society which he and Lian joined some 10 years ago. Now rather too political, I gather, for their taste.

SAT. 15. I slept rather badly on the sloping ground – give me a hammock, even a wet one, any day. No boat, so plans to be made. 'Let's build a raft.' At first Usang horrified. Two bad gorges and many people lost there, drowned, he said. But once persuaded, he and D & L and the 2 Penan set to and began to make a great raft out of bamboo. I helped to begin with but found that (a) they were so much better I tended to be in the way and (b) the bamboo, covered in fine stings, irritated my skin and sliced bits off, so that I was soon pouring blood. Decided they were better on their own and went and washed my clothes, dried out hammock, etc. Raft said to need 20 bamboos per man. 4 of us going.

1st made 4 pontoons of bundles of 12 bamboos, then a platform of another 30 which + crosspieces makes 80. Raft finished by midday, when Usang and Nyapun went hunting. Talked to D rather ramblingly about politics and crocodiles. D wants to conduct a study to find out how many there are still in Sarawak, how threatened, etc. To this end he accompanied during his leave one Tommy Chin, a crocodile hunter from Singapore. Result of study: Sarawak could earn [M$]5,000,000 in revenue from the sale of crocodiles. IUCN [International Union for Conservation of Nature] has them as an endangered species so they say none should be shot. D is a realist, says they are not protected in Sarawak and the best way is to control hunting by involving Nat. Park and Wildlife Office so that if numbers are being reduced they can prove it and have them protected.

Ajang meanwhile making nose flutes out of bamboo. Only the Penan play these. About 18 ins [45 cm] long, hollow, small hole at one end (in end) and 2 slots near the other end one side, one slot other side. Small-hole end inserted across septum into far nostril and blown across. I tried, but suspect my nose the wrong shape. They made a soft warbling repetitive up and down the scale. Lots of notes and half-notes. Tone achieved by trimming very small slivers off big end of pipe.

Nyapun and Usang returned with a black leaf monkey, neatly wrapped in leaves, which they had shot. I photographed U stuffing meat into bamboo tubes with the head, skinned but eyes still in, sitting among remains on the raft. Lian and Ajang went hunting. Came back with a long-tailed macaque. Had the leaf monkey for dinner. Tough red meat, hard on teeth – I have a disintegrating molar – but v.g. soup. Meat itself rather tasteless, like tough beef. Talk of crocodiles by candle-light. D has done surveys of where they breed – an area of swamp in 1st/2nd Division, now to be drained and sago planted. Someone was killed by a crocodile in the pool below Lang's house last year, 1976. Old man. Croc. took the man away, but the charmer was called and the body was 'returned', floated to the surface three days later. By the rocks above Long Terawan it seems is where the pool is. Several people taken over the years. Crocodiles hard to protect as no one likes them. But they will go v. soon if not protected. See what happened in Brazil.

Nyapun says there are a lot of crocodiles in the Medalam – Usang agrees. Talk of birds and snakes. Hornbills seen or heard in Mulu so far seem to be: rhinoceros, helmeted, pied, black, bushy-crested (Andrew [Mitchell]), wreathed.

SUN. 16. Excellent night in hammock. Set off at 8 on the raft. Medalam a much more attractive river than the Melinau or Tutoh, big and clear and fast-flowing, rocky. Rather like the Tutoh Gorge without such rapids. A lot of shallow drops but only one at all alarming, down which we planned to lower the raft on 2 lianas but in the end rode through without trouble. Poling and paddling with the bamboo poles we reached Kuala Mentawai at 9.30. Lovely way of travelling. L[ian] always made me sit in the rapids, which was wise, but demeaning. Otherwise I worked, if anything harder than them. Saw a huge monitor lizard draped over a log at the water's edge. No photographs, of course, as the camera was well stowed. At 11 we heard motors round the next corner and came on 2 Iban longboats just completed negotiating a rapid and stopped as we arrived. A third boat arrived soon after. 12 men in all. D took their names. Different, piratical faces of Ibans – always a jolly, energetic lot. Probably up to no good. Soon arrived after whizzing down shallows at Long Nanga. Shabby-looking place at first sight – 6 rooms, all open into each other – only been here 6 months. Small, low and cluttered house on stilts with open-air platform in front à la Iban. Masses of large but beaten-up dogs and chickens everywhere. No women on arrival – 3 men and 4 children. Not really a longhouse. Speedily fed us rice (ours) and two sorts of wild pig. One cooked in bamboo with leaves and rather strong-tasting; one boiled and for once not overcooked. Probably more dangerous but tender and succulent and not a worry for teeth. Ate with hands, which D[avid] & L[ian] seem to prefer anyway and which is actually better than using one rather grubby spoon which was belatedly produced. Trick is to roll rice onto outside of first two fingers and flick it to the mouth with thumbnail. Then down in new boat, faster, excellent driver. Past many settlements and clearings. Stopped to talk to Iban pengulu Jarum. Then on to Long Belaban, a sudden huge 3-storey, 34-door Iban longhouse. Quite unlike any I have seen before. Outside gallery, inside gallery and houses facing this having glass windows. Crowds of children and young men came to have a look at us. Attractive people. Different. Then on to the main Murut longhouse at Long Medalam. Pleasant wide gravelly junction of the two rivers. Coconut trees and the remains of an old longhouse opposite – true right bank of the Limbang. Behind it, across an open meadow with cows, pigs and chickens crossed by a low bridge over a muddy pool, was another imposing building. About 20 doors. Different from Iban, enclosed along the front, gallery inside just the same and three rooms deep behind. Not as smart and prosperous-looking as the Iban one. Met Pengulu Madang, who knew Usang of old but had not met D & L. Sat and talked. Were taken into back room to be fed where on the wall was the stretched skin of a clouded leopard. Five months old, they had killed it in the padi fields. D says he will confiscate and take to Kuching as it is of course a protected animal. Awkward when receiving their hospitality but must set an example. Skin in bad shape anyway. Talked with D about urgency of getting warden's house built soon at Long Mentawai. Amazing religious posters on the outside wall of the pengulu's bilek. Rather impressive primitive art, reminiscent of Bosch and Disney, showing devils tempting – green, armed with tridents and wearing briefs – while the goodies are all in shirts, jackets and long trousers or dresses. Most unlikely symbolism really with jolly-looking snakes being overcome by wet-looking boy with sickly grin. Food rather hard to take. A salted fish like sour and off soused herring, a very nasty pickled vegetable, tough unidentified meat. Teeth really suffer from that sort of meal. Usang makes me cheroots out of tobacco rolled in atap leaves – count as cigars, as I'm running out.

David interviewing people about numbers and guns, etc. The 12 men we saw upriver had 6 guns. Seem to be (are) far more Iban up the Medalam than anyone expected. Maybe 500. Long Medalam a mixed house Murut/Iban. Pengulu Madang is a strong middle-aged man with a bit of a grey moustache and a few hairs of a beard. He has Iban tattoos on shoulders and arms but not neck or back.

Rural scene outside longhouse. Ladies with wide coolie hats and round baskets on their backs return across the bridge leading children by the hand. A well-muscled young man with slender wand drives home 5 white ducks. The cows, sort of Guernsey type but with drooping ears and other hints of Brahmin or something tropical, suckle their calves. Pigs, large and white, smaller and black, piglets all colours, mill about. A man in sarong + paddle runs off across the bridge in a hurry. The wind is up, the sky darkens and it is going to rain soon. A horde of noisy children scream, and shout, play games with sticks, organise like kids anywhere. A brief Turner sky over the sunset. They keep a lot of fine cocks here, tied up individually and carried about. There is one tied inside the gallery outside the door of each bilek – for fighting, of course. My towel blows off the shutter I have hung it over and I just catch it in mid-air before if falls on down into the liquid manure below. Happiness is not having a filthy towel.

A meeting finally took place at 10 p.m. in the longhouse, at which all those resident sat round in a circle and David and I addressed them. I first, apologising for not doing so in Malay or Lun Daya [the local language], thanking the pengulu and everyone for everything. David translating excellently in spite of distractions from dogs roaming about, scratching, and other diversions. Usang fell asleep in the middle and started snoring loudly. Refused either to wake up or lie down. He had been drinking with friends. Pengulu and Tua Rumah of next longhouse upstream answered. Pengulu claimed to know nothing about the nat. park. Never informed by Limbang! I explained my position and D then had to do a lot of fast talking while I sat and tried to avoid a flea-bitten scratching dog that thought I was the best place in the whole longhouse to sit on. D talked for another two hours, but I slept where I sat – or lay – until moved at midnight into a back room where we all slept in a row on the floor.

MON. 17. Wrote in pengulu's visitors' book and had breakfast before leaving. Huge breakfast but I stuck to coffee and rice. D failed to secure the clouded leopard skin, but got a promise not to sell. The Limbang in flood, but Medalam same as yesterday. Pengulu also setting off for somewhere. Somehow couldn't get close to Madang. May be that it's difficult with D & L speaking all known languages so no need for me to converse at all except when I have something to say through interpreter. Better for me when alone, but better for what we are doing this way as D obviously an excellent ambassador.

9 a.m. arrived at Long Belaban where Pengulu Jarum, head of the Ibans here, met us. Good-looking youngish man with a lot of tattoos on arms and back. Speaks English, but David explained about NP [national park] in Malay. Jarum answered that there should be a pamphlet explaining all this sent to the longhouse and telling the people what they can and can't shoot. Then they should all sign that they agree and all would be well. Such a pamphlet, D says, exists, but the people in Limbang never sent it up. Really very bad organisation that after about 2 years we should bring the very first news of the existence of the park to these people. A PR campaign is essential if the people are not to be alienated. Best thing would be park warden's house at S. Mentawai with literature and clear powers.

[It was disgraceful that so few people had been consulted about their traditional hunting areas, let alone about the forests in which they had always lived, in the case of the Penan, being turned into a national park. The Berawan had been informed and I understood that there had been some discussion of hunting and gathering rights. The Temenggong had raised objections and some of the proposed park had been excised, but there is still resentment today at the way they were treated. Local people played no part in the planning and running of the park, which was entirely in the hands of the Forestry Department.]

Jarum seems a nice intelligent man and I feel much easier with him than with Madang. He agrees that if something isn't done all game and fish will be gone in a few years – as it already has in 1st Division and soon will be in 2nd. We all signed his visitors' book. Then on to Nanga Sepua. Stopped at Kuala Mentawai to inspect the site for the park warden's house. Excellent spot on a high bank with views. Usang shinned up a tree and collected lots of langsats which shouldn't be ripe at this time of year but were and we all got sticky eating them.

TUE. 18. Good night, some heavy rain. Skipped breakfast this morning. Couldn't face rice and cold mouse deer for once. Usang and Ajang had got back last night with one on which we all feasted after sleeping first. Strange feeling – midnight feast. Nice walking alone for a change. Stimulating. Saw an argus pheasant stamping ground and heard several. Also heard gibbons a couple of times. It began to threaten rain with wild howling winds passing overhead, sounding like flocks of giant bats. Some danger of falling trees. Feeling incredibly fit – feet perfect – and ran most of the way. Halfway rain began and then teemed down. Took a few falls but kept running. Found Paul Chai and John Dransfield and their party at Camp 5. Long talk with Paul. Promised list of scientists taking part with what each has done.

WED. 19. Went up to see sick Penan, ½ hr walk up steep ridge through gorge on right. Ta'ee said it would only take 2–3 days to climb Mulu by the E. ridge. Found the Penan looking very lethargic and rough. Several with high fevers, most with puffy eyes and all coughing and looking miserable. Able to do nothing but put drops in all eyes, which Gerry later said all wrong (Betnovate-N) and later sent up Strepsil lozenges for sore throats. Took all names and photographs. Decided not to go to Tiger Cave with D and Paul as better leave for Base Camp soon. Later turned out they had found a fabulous cave with great vault and stalagmites. Then Robb [Anderson] arrived and we talked, so didn't set out at last until 11.45. Walked v. fast, overtaking others and eventually leaving Usang behind, so that I reach BC just as rain was beginning at 4.15. 4½ hrs Camp 5 to BC not bad. Feet sore, but bearing up.

THUR. 20. Everything happened today. Jamban full of maggots, so drained both generators and put oil down. Took time. Had sent some medicines up early to Camp 5 Penan, but later radioed flying doctor to ask for helicopter, either with a doctor or to lift Gerry up next day. Then Nyapun came back to say Nyaling [his younger brother] was v. v. ill on Tutoh. Radioed again to ask for diagnosis from lab on Lusing. Came back loud and clear cholera. Not possible, says Gerry.

FRI. 21. More radio calls from flying doctor. Gerry and Nigel went and fetched Nyaling from Tutoh camp. I went on radioing. At last heard heli was coming. Hurried across rope in time to be there when it landed. Helped Nyaling on board and sat holding his hand on flight. Glorious clear day and good views of Api, etc. and Batu Birar. [Flew to Miri hospital.]

THUR. 27. To Miri hospital to take Nyaling fruit and sweets and to see district medical officer… he said there was a measles epidemic on the whole Baram River and they could not cope with the Penan. However, we might treat them and could have as much medicine as we required. [Nyaling recovered.]

MON. 31. [Back in Base Camp.] Lian showed me the things he brought back from the Batu Birar cave last week. They are v. nice and it is clearly an important site. Also a magnificent cave, they all say. Things include: 1. large Chinese (Ming?) bowl, blue and whitish pattern. 11½ ins [29 cm] across. 2. A dozen? copper bracelets. 3. Small length of chain. 4. Shell ornaments. 5. ½ dozen knives and a strange metal tool. 6. A lot of bones (human), skull, big leg bones, jaw, etc.

Day preparing for departure for Long Seridan next a.m. Cold coming on – sore throat, cough, etc. A lot of it about, but walking for 10 days should drive it away. Nigel arrived back at 5.15 which was good, with Nicola ['Hokey' Ingram, now Bennett-Jones, our best nurse, who went on to become a leading light in the RGS], who seems quite calm about being in charge without a doctor.

FIRST (PERHAPS ONLY) CIRCUIT OF
GUNUNG MULU NATIONAL PARK

TUE. 1 NOVEMBER. Shane [Wesley-Smith, now Winser, our indispensable head of admin] cooked scrambled eggs – 1st time and a great treat. Set off in overloaded jetboat at 7.30. Party consisting of RH-T, Raban Bala (David Labang), Lian Labang, Engan, Lang, Ajang, Usang, Padan, Tu Au. Went up to below last rapid but one before S. Tapin. I fell and cracked my shin which is a good start – goes with my ankle blisters from Deer Cave walk. We all scrambled along the true right bank of the Tutoh along a track Lang had prepared while we were waiting. Not long to S. Tapin, but then had to cross it. First Lian swam across, holding end of a fish net. We could see remains of large camp on far side. Then going a little way upstream we all stripped off and carried the barang across bit by bit. The camp was partly Penan, but mostly had been made by Land & Survey Dept. expedition who came up the Tutoh by boat earlier in the year. They were apparently

30   Padan, Tu Au, me, Ingan, Lian Labang, Ajang and Usang
setting off to walk right round the park boundary. Taken
by David Labang, the eighth member of our group.

surveying the large forest reserve across the Tutoh for logging. This means that if the timber is any good it will all be logged in due course. True left bank of the Tutoh should at least be protected.

We put up 2 camp sheets and my hammock. Sunny for a bit, then rain almost solidly through evening and night. I decided to stay under the camp sheet and this was just as well as my hammock was full of water next morning. It's a long, long night, especially when it rains a lot.

WED. 2. Long Tapir. Up, tea and off in pouring rain by 7. Lian's ankle v. bad after his fall yesterday and only able to hobble along slowly without barang. Tried to persuade him to go home + 1 or 2 but wouldn't. Steep climb to begin with, then long easy climbing up and along ridge for 1½ hrs heading east. Stopped near old rhinoceros wallow for makan – rice and babi (still excellent) as no fish caught last night. Still raining – pity about the views. Shortly afterwards came to the junction with the path to S. Langsat and Melinau, which we would have been coming along if we had not come up in the jetboat. Said to be 1 day and 1 night away from that point, so not much gained except a day's rest actually. We continued along easy ridge following at times a broad trail like a highway, at others cutting across steep hillsides on almost invisible tracks. At last we left ridge for good – the track along it was, said Ajang, much harder and longer. We cut down v. steeply towards the Tutoh (still not far away on our right). At the bottom (maybe 1,000 feet [300 m] down) we crossed 3 smallish streams in succession before climbing again v. steeply for 1 hour to top. Left others far behind (Engan, Ajang and me). Feet sore and bruised and aching, but standing up well under strain considering I am wearing my new Robert Lawrie boots for the first time properly, except for the Deer Cave last Sunday. Amazingly no trouble with toes, but ankles and esp. tendons sore and left foot blistered. Also heels sore. Passed 3 more rhino wallows – all old, but able to see on one, which I photographed, where he slid down a ramp and worked the pit larger playing with his horn. Now only signs of pig using them. 2.15 others arrive up the ridge (½ hour after us). Another ¾ hrs walking and signs of human habitation suddenly everywhere. Sago trees along ridge cut and cleared. Many cut trees. Then sago preparation. First a bamboo tray and pulp in the stream. Then nearby bark boards like a platform and a sort of gutter of wood. Smell of rancid vinegar. Up the hill a bit and arrival with Ajang's family. Only his sister and 2 small sons and his mother there at first. Beautiful smiles of pure delight from the sister, who is not v. shy. Mother very, making her look cross. Both shook hands. When others arrived I dashed off to photograph the sago then back for shots of family. Sister's husband arrived in the middle. Strong straight-looking man. Long hair, loincloth, v. muscular. V. smiling. Pleased to see us. Our lot all got v. busy putting our camp up in the middle of their 'village' – only 3 huts, one for father and mother, one for daughter and son-in-law and one tiny guest hut. Meanwhile Lian bled his swollen ankle by cutting it with a scalpel and putting on rubber snake-venom extractors. I tried to get leeches to suck the right place (where blue bruising and swelling showed) but couldn't – he said they wouldn't. How did Victorian doctors do it? Have just slipped quietly over to Ajang's sister's house where she, husband, Ajang and 2 sons are sitting cooking sago. Gave husband two packets of tobacco. Very self-possessed, polite man, he seems. Then began to blow up a balloon for alarmed-looking small boy. Father said, 'How kind, it's OK, don't be afraid,' or words to that effect and son bravely took it and began to play. Successful brief visit. After supper, with delicious addition of some small pieces of meat from a giant squirrel the Penan had killed (illegally, incidentally, being in the park) [obviously the Penan didn't view this as illegal; it was just them hunting what they'd always hunted before people turned up and told them they shouldn't!] – tender and sweet red meat, like but better than mouse deer – we interviewed Ajang and his brother-in-law Asik and compiled a genealogy of their relatives. Rather more complicated than the Pejomans [Nyapun's family] as each of the old couple had been married before and had children, while having none together. Asik has nice smiling eager face with grin creases at the side of his mouth. It's a very attractive set-up here. The houses are mostly covered with palm leaves with only one mat on each as well. Everything seemed clean and healthy on arrival, although they said the reason they had not gone to Long Iman with Ajang was because they were sick. The old man Kulung, when he came back later with a selabit full of firewood, had a pleasing face. Longish pierced ears, lots of beads and a nice if rather henpecked face. His wife has more bracelets than any Penan I have yet seen. Wrought silver ones as well as wooden ones. Kulung has quite heavy copper bangles through his ears. All have good teeth. Ajang and Padan are both very handsome almond-eyed boys. All the people here seem to have only very slight epicanthic folds.

7. p.m. and a strange scene. Lian, Raban [David Labang], Robin [me], Engan, Lang, Usang – in that order from right to left – are sitting or lying on their stretched hammock beds by the light of one candle stuck on the end of mine. Grouped in half-darkness at the ends of our beds are all the Penan, crouched so their heads are on a level with ours and all answering questions about some other family tree which Raban is compiling. The faces in the candlelight are immensely moving and I wish I could do something for them now other than probably give them my cold. Asik has a small thin moustache and a tiny spot of beard below lower lip, but the rest are completely hairless on face. Their eyes all seem to be brown. Hair always black – seems to be thinning on older men, but no real baldness. Most interesting discussion taking place about settling. Some want to settle now, but are having trouble doing so at L. Seridan, as they started to farm land already belonging to Long S. people who stopped them and told them to clear virgin forest, which is too hard for them. Meanwhile Tu Au and Long Iman people want more to settle there, so they will get a school, etc. – at least so they are told. Raban says not to listen to anyone who tells them what to do, but to do what they want to do. I have put forward a few ideas for R to put across:

They are important people because their knowledge of plants, medicines, etc. is unrivalled and has already proved useful to our scientists. Also, they know the park best and already there are signs that the L. Terawan people don't know their way about.

Any change is not going to be easy and they should never believe that it will be.

Asik is an intelligent man and already knows most of the problems. We want to help him do whatever he decides is best.

They talk eagerly and laughingly about how they can't change and be like Usang [Berawan] but the children can be trained to live a different life, if they live at Long Iman. They seem to think this is a good idea and suggest they might spend a week or two there – in their own house – and a week or two back in the ulu. They have just asked me to say what I think about settlement. Is it good or not? My answer: I have come to see them and visit them because I am interested in and respect their way of life. But I have always lived in a house with electricity, etc. and would find it very difficult to change to a nomadic life. In just the same way they may go and see and be interested in longhouse life, Marudi, etc., but it will be just as hard for them to settle as it would be for me to become nomadic. Asik is a wise man and knows the problems. He must make decisions and we will help him. Finally, whatever they do they should do slowly and take their own counsel – not listen to anyone else who tells them what is right and what is wrong. Then I told them I had seen a lot of other people like them and facing the same problems in other parts of the world – and it's always difficult – most are worse off to begin with. Government officials never understand their problems but at least in Sarawak there is goodwill towards them and a desire to help. An agonising and thrilling position to be in – advising articulate and aware nomads about whether to settle or not – very hard to give sound, unbiased advice and the pressure increased by translating through Raban, who knows the problem better than I do, locally at least. They say that what I have said makes sense. They have heard things before from people, but they didn't understand – had never been to see for themselves. We have come and understand – oh that it were as simple as that! In answer to a question from Lian, they say the game is getting less and less. But as they have no calendar this may be a stock response and there are plentiful and lean times. Incidentally, it has just come out that we are the first ever to tackle this route. By the river, yes. From Apo to Long S[eridan], yes. But never this way before, except Penan.

THUR. 3. 'How things can suddenly all go wrong at once when everything seemed perfect'. At the end of a long day's walking – 7 a.m. to 3.15 p.m. with only brief stops – we finally reached the river we were heading for – name later when I can unpack the map. I had been leading (behind Ajang, our Penan guide) all day because that's how I like it best. I walk faster knowing there's no one in front and never have the worries of either being left behind or having to wait for someone else to get a move on. All had gone very well. My new boots were settling in nicely and no serious wounds or aches developing. Incredible quantities of leeches – at times literally growing on the forest floor like flowers – but now I crush them between finger and thumb – tough! Reached the river, beyond which we were to camp. I stripped off, waded waist deep across the river with rucksack on bare back and boots hung on it, and then climbed the farther hill not sure whether I felt like Tarzan or a Penan. A spot was chosen to make camp, a moment when I tend to sit down and let everyone else get on with it as they are so much better at cutting poles and tying them together than I will ever be. I decided to sort out my things. Needed a peg to hang camera and boots on – none naturally on nearby trees so tried sticking parang in tree. When vertical it just bent down and would support no weight. So tried hard, 2-handed horizontally. The rattan woven guard on the handle slipped down over the blade with my right hand over it and the blade sliced between my thumb and forefinger. Impossible to tell how deep and reluctant to find out, so wrapped it in a towel and cursed a bit. Not to be defeated, I jabbed the little Penan dagger into the tree – also horizontally. Tested to see if it would hold – and the blade broke, cutting me.

Otherwise a good day all round. Should be halfway to the Ubong [River] now and so should reach it tomorrow. Passed (and counted building materials) 4 or 5 abandoned Penan sulaps – all connected with Ajang's family. Also lots of sago palms, mostly with signs of being used for food. At one point 2 large trees felled by the Penan for their fruit – oh dear... [However, it is an interesting thought that the truly sustainable main diet of the Penan, the repeatedly harvested wild sago palm (*Metroxylon sagu*), is now being replaced all over the island of

Borneo by the commercially valuable but ecologically disastrous oil palm (*Elaeis guineensis*) from Africa.]

Once while resting we heard a troop of silvered leaf monkeys (Presbytis cristata) making a racket nearby. The two Penan boys dashed off with Raban's gun – although we are, of course, still in the nat. park. As so often happens, they went too far, but the big black male came right up to where we sat making a very loud hornbill-like growling cry and chasing off an intruder on his territory, who ran off. The most surprising part was the speed with which he moved through the forest and almost silently except for the loud grunting.

Evenings are long-drawn-out things in the West. Drinks, dinner, television, parties, etc. Here they hardly seem to exist. One moment one is still sorting out a few possessions so that they will be handy if needed in the night, then rice and pork in salty water with a few bits of onion and ginger appear. Then suddenly everyone is curled up inside their bedding and asleep by 7.30 or 8 p.m. The night seems an awfully long period of inactivity ahead until dawn. But in fact, whether I read by candlelight until quite late or curl up with the rest, I sleep through it, except for the inevitable interruptions when it rains.

FRI. 4. S. Sepugin. A good early start, rain just stopping. Fast walking for first two hours up and down very steep hills and once along a ridge. No big rivers to cross but 3 sizeable streams. Heard Argus pheasants calling. Later walked into a troop of macaques. Padan, who was leading with the 12-bore, would have shot one. He tried 3 times but didn't know how to work the safety catch. Raban says we need specimens under my exceptions [I had permission from the Sarawak government to allow animals to be killed in the interests of science], as they have never been collected in this area. Also we need meat... Stopped at 9.45 by another old rhinoceros wallow – there have been a lot along the way – but all old. Also passed 3 more abandoned Penan villages on way. At one Raban collected some bones from a v. big python they had eaten.

The tree above my head is noisy with coppersmith barbets eating the figs, and a huge rhinoceros hornbill has just landed noisily and fussily to eat. He moved with great whirrings from place to place, calling occasionally, before suddenly spotting us all sitting below preparing makan, when he took off with a great rush. Ate the usual – rice, meat (v. small pieces now), etc. I really feel the need of nothing else, but whether that's because we are so tired and hungry when we stop that anything would taste good or whether it's just me I'm not sure. Then down a long steep ridge a first glimpse of the Ubong, not far upstream from its mouth. A rushy mighty white river which looks quite unnavigable but up which Lang has been collecting illegal timber, which he then floated down to waiting colleagues at Long T[erawan]. Crossed a small river, another ridge and yet another larger tributary before coming to some relatively flat land with bits of marsh and some regular slopes (something I realise now I haven't seen for 4 days – only steep, almost sheer slopes and ridges). At 1 we reached the Ubong crossing point and Lian says we must camp on the far bank as there is no water after that up the ridge. I suspect he is being lazy or wants to stop because of his ankle, which seems to have improved greatly, but cannot argue with him. So I have a good bathe in the ice-cold Ubong, wash all my filthy clothes, treat cuts and sores on feet and hands, give my boots a really good polish and oiling and am just about ready to climb into my hammock bed when the camp is ready. Nice to have time to sort oneself out for once – and even better to have others make the camp, cook, etc. Said to be 2 more days to Long S[eridan]. A long restful evening and night lying and reading and sleeping, while the rain falls outside and the camp sheet for once doesn't leak.

Sat. 5. S. Ubong. Getting more efficient at knowing where everything is and being ready quickly in the morning. Order of events. Sit up. Engan (Tama Bulan) brings me tea in bed. Shave with electric razor. Pack sarong, tablecloth, sweater and sleeping bag in dry. Dress in wet clothes from yesterday. Oil feet with talc. Put on boots. Ready. 6.45 off. Raban leads prayers.

Long steep climb up to the ridge where we are rewarded with a tremendous view of Mulu in the morning sunlight. Looks close enough to touch and the colours at the top are soft like a Tuscan landscape. Can almost see the trig point. Compass bearing 345° – almost due north. The long ridge towards Long Seridan is clear and it looks a relatively easy walk. Argus pheasants calling and we pass one display ground. Outside the park now. Pass 2 Penan sulaps on the way up ridge and stop at 8.30 at another one. Running v. low on food now. Just rice and what we can gather. Some heart of palm and the delicious core of a rattan – bitter taste just like a strong tea leaf. There are two very similar rattans apparently. One is called mati ratus because it is v. poisonous and once 100 men died when they ate it when on a headhunting campaign. They assure me this is the other one – they think... On the way again by 10 somewhat nourished and now I think the hardest day so far. V. long steep ridges and slopes up and down. A few rests and some slow going while Raban goes ahead with the gun looking for game, but it's 3 p.m. before we reach S. Siwan where we will camp and all are tired after 8 hours' walking. A bit of rain on the way, but dry on arrival and time for a good swim and wash while the others put up camp. I actually feel quite peckish! Padan shinned up a tree and said he could see the farms of Long S. Should arrive midday tomorrow. No fireworks for me tonight.

S u n. 6. S. Siwan. Good early start from clean camp right by river. Put on clean shirt and trousers because old ones have got so sweat-soaked and torn and because I felt like it. Off 6.45 a.m. Two stops before makan and passed two Penan settlements (abandoned). Seems to be a little more game here.

9.15. Stopped for makan. No food so they all went fishing with goggles and speargun but I am not optimistic. Anyway, rice and heart of palm is OK. Added to our normal rations were 2 small turtles and 6 small bony fish. Turtle meat delicious, tender and sweet but very little of it – and the sadness of those little claws! Refreshed we set off again thinking it would not be far now. Consequently it was a frustrating time as for another 4 hours we struggled up and down ridges and along stream beds as slippery and exhausting as anything we had been through during the last 6 days. Then at 2 we broke out into bright sunshine on the cleared and cultivated hill padi fields. Extraordinary feeling – almost agoraphobic – being out in the open under the scorching sun after weeks in the jungle with only open spaces being occasional rivers – not the same as hot fields. A tree at the edge had a hole torn open leaving big shreds of bark up and down. This was done by a bear to get at honey. Sat for a while under field hut, then trudged fast along a real path with little wood-pole bridges and open between scrub sides. Felt so civilised. After some 15 mins came over a ridge and saw – joy – the buildings of Long Seridan and the airfield spread out below.

There is a big new blue school being built a little way to the right, but the main centre consists of 2 opposing longhouses facing each other across the end of the runway. About 12 doors each and typical Kelabit design which is rather shut-in like Murut, but has good wide gallery inside, big single rooms in bileks and lots of kitchen and wash areas out back. There are quite a few odd houses set on the hill behind and a riverbank below, including the old school building and a 'rest house' (hovel) for Penan children at the school. The Magoh River is

31 First sight of Long Seridan.

deep and fast and dangerous at this point – a great rushing sound of rapids always in the ears. So we had to sit and wait for ½ hour while the two Penan boys swam up the near bank like otters under the over-hanging undergrowth before crawling fast across and going to fetch a boat. Raban also swam straight across after a while. Taken over, we strode down the runway towards the houses, apparently being ignored. But friendly reception on arrival and of course Lian and Raban being Kelabits and known to many, so no problems. I talked to one Herbert (Madang), a nephew of Betty's from Long Terawan, who had flown in that a.m. by MAS [Malaysia Airlines], having finished 2 years' teacher-training in Sibu. [Many of the Berawan (but none of the Penan), like Herbert, had Western names.] He is married to the Tua Kampong's daughter and will be the teacher here in a year. He had seen Nigel in Marudi before leaving and N had said he would give him a message for me, but had failed to do so. Different-looking people, many with pudding-basin haircuts, round faces and muscular bodies. The Tua Kampong especially seems a giant. Herbert took me round the place to take some photographs, had a good bathe in the river with Lian and time for a short rest and read before The Meeting. Had to make a speech, as usual, about the expedition (rolls off easily now) and then sit interminably while Raban and then everyone else talked. About 80 people to begin with, sitting up and down the gallery with backs to the walls and listening rapt. All, of course, in shirts and trousers, except for 3 Penan straight out of an American Indian print. Sitting in among everyone else without apparently fear of favour, they were stunning. Dark interesting clear faces, long hair, only loincloths and many beads – also silver bracelets – wild alive faces. Most Kelabit men have pierced and many stretched ears. Several small children also have the heavy brass earrings. No one in Long Seridan smokes. They sat up until the small hours talking, but I went to bed – or rather hard wooden floor. A bit stiff next am.

MON. 7. Long Seridan. Went for some breakfast with old Tua Rumah – now deputy pengulu – with whom Raban was staying.

Apparently much talk last night was of the Penan problem and the Penan themselves, including their local headman – responsible for some 6 or 7 families – were quite outspoken. About 2 years ago there were 40 Penan pupils at the school here. But the parents took about 10 away – most of the rest followed soon after and now there are only 3, who I saw setting off for home as hols began this weekend. There are some 42 Penan families at Long Layun, between Magoh and Ubong on the far bank of the Tutoh on the old route to the Apo River from Long Seridan. They are like the Long Iman people, semi-settled – do they have rights in the park? Much talk of Penan problems – for and against settlement. My advice – do it slowly and with the best possible people and help. There are so many factors on both sides: Benefits of being settled:

Education. Children can go to school.

Health. Easier to treat.

Agriculture. Learn settled padi farming (?advantage).

Less hunting in nat. park.

They say they want to settle now – quite urgently – but sensibly add that they must have proper government help to do so. Those at Long Iman e.g. appear to have received none. Govt says if 20+ families settle at once they will do something, but Penan say this is not possible to arrange – and anyway it would be a big risk.

Advantages of remaining nomadic:

No settlement scheme has ever worked well. They are certain to be worse off before things get better, even if they ever do.

Education can work with nomadism, but as experience at Long Iman has shown (and elsewhere) it isn't easy, as they run away.

Health also possible if good clinics to visit. In fact, except for epidemics, health better under nomadic conditions.

Agriculture. What's so special about settled agriculture, many would argue? They are using food sources not needed or used by anyone else – wild sago, pig, etc.

Immeasurable loss of knowledge if they settle. Knowledge of foods, medicines, trails, etc. This at least should be learned during settling process, otherwise terrible waste.

Answer proposed by Raban. Help those already settled – Long Iman, Long Layun, Long Seridan, etc. – and this will encourage others to come in, if it works. Good idea, it seems here.

[On the whole, the experience of the last 40 years has shown that it hasn't worked. Most Penan will say that life was better when they were nomadic, but they settled voluntarily because the government promised them services, most of which have never been provided. Even today, when there are many examples worldwide of how benefits, such as education, can be provided to nomadic people, it is depressing that the Sarawak government is still desperate to settle them and turn them into agriculturalists, but continues to break its promises at every turn.]

Each time I spend a day or part of one in a longhouse, I am amazed at how noisy it is. It's all very well to romanticise about community living, but one must remember that there are certain prices one has to pay in terms of privacy and peace. Take now, for instance – 10 a.m. Monday, Long Seridan. A small child is screaming deafeningly and apparently ignored by all. Bad temper, it sounds like, and probably best ignored, but hard to read to. Nice stunning background as two or three young people, including my hostess, the Tua Rumah's daughter, Herbert's wife, practise on their guitars and sing a little, softly. Under the house a dog suddenly starts screaming, howling as only dogs can when it sounds as though their entrails are being slowly removed. No one pays any attention, except the other dogs who all bark. Cocks crow regularly and every now and then a hen looses off an explosion of post-egg-laying cackles. Small boys stamp importantly the length of the gallery shaking everything because of the loose floorboards. Much more background noise – the river rushing, distant voices, a pig squealing, someone hammering – if one cares to listen that far, but no need. Just went out and photographed Herbert and family playing guitars under my drying hammock. Peaceful happy scene (in spite of background noise). Reading 'Akenfield' [*Akenfield: Portrait of an English Village* (1969) by Ronald Blythe, an account of rural Suffolk life over the course of the twentieth century] – v. suitable. Later in p.m. I walked to see the Penan living near Long Seridan. About 5 families here and more about an hour further on. Men very fine pure-looking. Women smart in sarongs and bras (only to be expected near Long S.). Children rather scruffy and dirty. Took down lots of names from helpful eldest boy, Darion, who spoke quite good English and was at the school. He said he didn't like school much as there were no books but it would be better when they came. Some sickness – and one child with spots – could be measles starting. Got caught by the rain and had to hurry back. Deafening on the longhouse roof when heavy. At least drowns all other noise.

TUE. 8. Long Seridan–Long Napir. Left in 2 boats. The Seridan's a pretty river, full of rapids and we made good time. Saw pigs and monkeys but failed to shoot. Reached point above L. Terap where trail to L. Napir and the outside world begins. Stopped and ate there at 10.15. Then at 10.45 began the longest walk so far and one of the hardest I can ever remember. We climbed for 4 hours reaching the top of the last ridge shortly before 3. There we stopped and had cold rice and sugar, which was rather good. Then 2 hours down to the Madihit River when I thought we'd arrived, but there was another, often hard and frustrating hour, fording a tributary waist deep and then along the riverbank. Arrived at 6. Passed 6 or 7 Penan sulaps on the way but saw none. Only interest was glimpse of a mongoose and a v. pretty beetle I caught. Long Napir is rather scruffy and seems run down, a mixture of Kelabit and Murut. Open grassland round – a Swiss feel to it! Endless sitting about on arrival. Lots of noisy/attentive by turns children and a few pretty girls in the background with big brass earrings and long ears. There is a Penan longhouse here. Going on for 8.30 and we have been fed, but the almost inevitable vegetarian meal again. (We did have chicken, pork and mouse deer, even, once in Long Seridan.) Bowls of rice – 2 sorts admittedly but of little account to me – 2 little bowls of spinachy stuff in a bit of liquid (green) and one extra bowl – blatcha or something equally hot and nasty. Today a pleasant smallish plate of bland green veg. which I liked. Now all I want to do is drop, but have to stay sitting up on a hard floor and occasionally looking interested.

Nothing to do but long for bed – or just to be horizontal. Really quite tired physically tonight.

WED. 9. Fairly slow start in a.m., so I peeled off to go and look at the Penan longhouse. A depressing place, 7 doors and soulless like a cattle shed on stilts. Bare and bleak inside and only a couple of men there who told me that 70 people lived there. Shot a succession of rapids before the Madihit met the Limbang. Then the river continued much the same – brown and rapidy and often rough, but never really dangerous all the way down to Long Medalam. Should be a good jetboat river. Moored below the school there were a whole lot of boats and I counted over 20 outboards all looking new and fresh. Those Ibans! Turned out there was 2-day cockfighting festival on [described in Chapter 2].

THUR. 10. A day mostly of frustrations. First the nightmare of sleeping at Long Medalam with all the fighting cocks... We stopped to call on Pengulu Jarum, who is nice (the Iban one), and eventually, after stopping to eat, reached the Terikan [River] at 3. No point in going on so camped there. A v. nice site where the path to Long Birar begins – on the river. Good for bathing.

FRI. 11. A very long walk to L. Birar. The path is reasonably clear and obviously has been used by more than Penan, but a guide is still essential in its present condition. It should be opened in due course and paint marked and side tracks made to L. Mentawai and perhaps across to Melinau Gorge. We took 6½ hours and were glad on arrival at Long Birar to find a boat and motor waiting. With this we were able to reach BC by 3.30 and it was good to get back again. Found everyone in high spirits. Philip Leworthy had just arrived in the Forestry 'speedboat' [in fact a longboat that was far from speedy!] and Colin Bertram, Wilfred Thesiger [the famous explorer], Hilary Fry and Katherine Clark had come up + [N]igel in JB. the evening before. Shane and Nicola coping well with their respective roles, but a welter of problems, especially in letters from home, RGS, etc. Being away has given me a good perspective on life and I really cannot find any of them as grave as everyone else seems to. Glorious, after long talks until 1 a.m. with Nigel, to flop into my hammock, but an insect (baby centipede?) in my T-shirt bit me!

SAT. 12. Sent Wilfred off up mountain with Vincent [a Berawan]. Nyapun, looking 20 years older and almost making me weep, arrived + small daughter to say all his family were v. sick and had no food. Sent food, etc. back with him and he will fetch us again tomorrow a.m. so that Nicola can visit. Long talk with Colin Bertram about expedition and future of RGS. Big plans for an advisory section for expeditions which would require a young experienced dynamic director. Obvious choice NW [Nigel Winser]. CB agreed.

[Soon after our return, the Expedition Advisory Centre was established at the RGS, with Nigel as its director. Hugely successful and popular, it has advised innumerable school, university and private expeditions over the years and is often referred to as the jewel in the RGS's crown. When Nigel became deputy director of the RGS, his wife Shane took over and she is still running it brilliantly under the new name of Geography Outdoors.]

SUN. 13. Nicola and I walked with Nyapun to his family's camp about an hour N of BC. They have all been v. ill but most now a little better, except for elder wife who N[yapun] said had collapsed and should be medevacked out. She said she didn't want to go to Miri hospital, so given penicillin injection and decision postponed until next day. Also eldest boy sick – injection. Other children with pneumonia given penicillin tablets. Camp very squalid and smell of faeces and their dogs. Gave them food as they are hungry. Hard walk through swamp to get there and back. Mark [Collins] and George [Argent] arrived back on foot having failed to climb Api. John [Proctor] & co. coming down by raft.

TUE. 15. Time spent on smoking pigs, etc. Main drama the arrival in the evening of Paul Chai with the Temenggong, John Madang, his nephew, Lawai and Usang. The story is an extraordinary one. In September Medway discovered a cave with burial artefacts on the Melinau downstream of BC and duly (and fully) reported it to the museum. This is what we had been instructed to do before arrival. In October Paul Chai discovered a burial cave on Batu Birar and reported to museum. On 11 Oct. David and Lian Labang arrived, Lian being from the museum. On Friday 28 Oct. [I was in Marudi collecting stores and scientists] David & Lian, Betty (Temenggong's niece), Colin Crewe [a visiting friend] and Wit Trego (Nat. Parks – Miri), went and stayed at Long Birar and visited a cave (¾ hr walk away) discovered by Paul Chai. Said to be v. attractive, with stalagmites and stalactites and lots of burial things – urns, plates, bones, brass rings, etc. Lian collected a fair bit of stuff in plastic bags for the museum (Colin was rather shocked by the way he did this, but was in no position to question it). Meanwhile Betty rushed round and took lots of things too. They came back and Lian showed me what he had, including a skull.

Two weeks later (11 Nov.), I returned with David & Lian from the Long Seridan walk to find a strong memo from Forestry saying serious business raised by Temenggong who was very angry about the expedition robbing graves and doing excavations. Had been to dep. chief minister and we were to put everything back and not argue. Paul Chai and the Temenggong and co. arrived today and it was much worse than I had thought. The penalty for what it is suggested we did is death. But Temenggong is letting us off lightly because 'he knows Robin and David and Lucas Chin [Director of the Sarawak Museum]' and because Lucas agreed to all his demands at once, realising that any quarrel would inevitably be lost in present govt climate resulting in D[avid] & L[ian] losing their jobs and the expedition being kicked out. The fine agreed is a gong (£200), a pig, a parang, 10 gantangs [a Malay measure equivalent to 2 kg] of rice, food, drink, etc. from each person who went into the caves. It's been agreed that the govt people will all come under one fine, but they're still expecting us to pay two. I shall discuss this later with the T. Will Betty pay a fine? The whole thing is grossly unfair and I suspect more than somewhat a rip-off on the T.'s part, but there is nothing we can do and no appeal. In future certain caves will be declared out of bounds and any we go into we will have to be very careful and NOT TOUCH. The fine for looking only is 1 parang and 1 chicken. The speleologists will have to work out their programme v. carefully.

[Just to make this incident clear, no member of our expedition took anything from any of the caves visited. Material was only collected by people from the Sarawak Museum, who were visiting us and over whom we had no control, as they were government officials. But, of course, we had to take the blame!]

WED. 16. Coming back from Long Terawan alone was breathtaking – boat going well and v. fast (40 mins LT–BC). The mountains were etched clear in the late-evening sky rising above soft misty clouds in the valleys and lowlands, while the trees stood ghostly in the mist. Very Chinese silk painting. Philip [Leworthy] had dropped one of the outboards in the river, but rescued it.

THUR. 17. Lit newly repaired bread oven. Lusing and Nyapun arrived + some of family. N looking terribly ill and barely able to walk. Decided to take him to Marudi today. Set off 1 [p.m.] in JB + Paul Chai, Nyapun and Phil and Wilfred Thesiger. [Wilfred had climbed Mount Mulu and thoroughly enjoyed himself, but he did say he preferred deserts to rainforests!]

Phil drove the whole way v. well – no trouble and boat going well. Dropped Wilfred at rest house, tied up at Shell, left Phil to fuel boat, drove Nyapun to the hospital and checked him in. Talked to nurses. Shopping lists to Johnny [shopkeeper in Marudi], masses of post, tied up boat for the night, beer + Paul and back to rest house for wash. Excellent dinner in market with Wilfred, who paid, generously. He was in very good spirits and we sat up late over tea in the rest house, talking of the Sahara, publishers, travels, boats, Kashmir, etc. He agreed to send a cheque for £50 to RGS soon to cover his stay.

32   Wilfred Thesiger at Mulu.

F R I . 1 8 . Early breakfast at Johnny's after walk with Wilfred along the Baram shrouded in mists. Wilfred talking all the time. Invited me (but not M[arika]!) to stay any March–May in London. I gave him Ivan Polunin, Ken Scriven and Ramzan Dongola [houseboat owner in Kashmir]. A treat to know him.

S A T . 1 9 . No radio as Miri Control out of order. FEGs [Forest Ecology Group] left early by longboat for Sabang's wedding. We rushed round sorting things out. Sue [Proctor] was ill with undiagnosed fever and so decided not to come. We whizzed down through the rapids with Phil driving, learning the route. Arrived at Sabang's bride's house to find preparations well in hand and 2 Penan boys from Long Seridan with a note from Raban [David Labang] asking me to employ them. We sat and talked and sipped borak until the ceremony began. Sabang and wife both sat on one gong – and were motionless for the next hour. Wife v. pretty in nice orange sarong and pretty shirt. Sabang in smart striped shirt – both barefoot. A succession of old men came and harangued them in Berawan about their future together, responsibilities, etc. They listened, eyes downcast. Uncle Melai came last and went on longest, ending with English version for us and some rather obsequious comments of gratitude to us/me. Then they drank borak – and so did we! Said N[igel], P[hilip], Nicola and I had to slip away as Sue was ill, but didn't escape without 3 more glasses of borak being forced down me by Mrs Usang – blast her. Nice atmosphere, everyone sitting round on floor, sexes segregated. Back horribly drunk – trying to pee over back of boat very difficult at speed – lay for a few minutes in hammock, ate a sandwich and, after P had taken 2 Penan + Sarah home, set off to Deer Cave. Remember nothing of getting there, but found a nice camp set up by Engan at G. of E. end. Some on camp hammocks, some on ground. N and P away under a rock. Colin on the Bertram Shelf, Kate [Clark] in Kate's Hollow, where she got ticks, and Hilary and I on the ground next to Shane. Great view of bats leaving. Counted and took photographs religiously for Gathorne from 6.30 when bats started until 6.55 when they 'streamed' out. Reckoned it took 2–3 seconds for them to pass the gap in picture and they continued for 7 minutes. Then did extraordinary aerial displays. Probably a nervous thing, due to being chased by bat hawks. Spiralled round in rings, higher and higher and faster and faster in v. tight circles up in the sky. Amazing sight, but not a total blackening, as I remember at Niah. After excellent supper – Kate is v. competent – N, P and I went off to explore the siphon where the river runs underground. Saw no big footprints, but spiders and swiftlets (which flew into us) and clambered back all along far side. Heart-stopping in pitch dark. Slept well on ground.

SUN. 20. Bats came back regularly but not in a stream from 6.30 to 7.10 a.m. Not as dramatic as in p.m. but may have been caused by misty morning. Main party set off home, George [Argent] and Ross [Kerby] botanising + Hilary. N, P, Shane and I went off to find Green Cave. First climbed high up to right on a bearing of 60°. Got to high cliff with fine view over G. of E. but could go no further. Backtracked round to the left, past the cave I had found twice before (rope needed) and forged on up past several promising-looking small cave sites. Then up and up towards the white cliff face until suddenly we came over the lip and looked down into a great green hollow. 80 m down steep slope past white tablet with Osmastons, Usang 10/9/77 on it (nice) and into cave proper. A wonderful place, really one of the most attractive places I have ever been. Green, not because of light filtered (as say Os) but because of green ferns and other plants growing all over the inside. Got to extraordinary limestone formations on floor and rocks, like 6′ [1.8 m] fragile flowers which are easy (all too easy) to crush under foot. I went to see if I could reach the back of cave and after 2 turns and about ¾ mile [1.2 km] reached a tall scree slope. V. hard work and frightening alone – some v. big spiders – then fast all the way home.

TUE. 22. Relaxed start in a.m. Had a bathe in the rocky river – good place. Set off 7.30. Reached Camp 2 at 8.10 to find George and Ross preparing to leave. They reckoned the rats moved the tins about from the rubbish tip – not the scientists! John Dransfield was last man there and there were tins everywhere! N having trouble with his leg – pulled muscle and tendon. Aloi also had swollen ankle, so I changed for Luis [Aloi and Luis were Berawan workers], leaving them to come on slowly. Left at 8.45. Overtook George and Ross 9.30 and reached Camp 3 at 10.30 with George. Ross arrive 11.20 and Luis 11.50 to say N and Aloi had turned back to Camp 2. Made tea and makan, read rain gauge – new instructions needed. Moss forest v. different. Wet and steamy, moss hanging on trees – a mysterious place full of medium-sized trees, bamboos, ferns, etc. Hard time starting a fire with damp wood. I set off again at 1 – meaning we had stopped for 2½ hrs – that's how long it took to prepare a meal, after waiting for the others. 3–4 much the hardest leg of the journey. Moss forest getting more so all the time. Lots of steep stretches and rain or wet mist all the time. Began to think of going on up to the top, and had just written a note at Camp 4 to George, having arrived at 3.15, to say 'Gone on to photograph the sunset, if there is one! Back by 6 at latest. If not, better send someone + torch to look for me – I have one – on summit path', when G arrived. Set off again 3.30 with just camera and torch. Crossed helipad and began to climb. Much steeper, harder and further than I expected, but clouds clearing in west and some fine views over the Tutoh. Also glimpses of Api and the white cliffs. Some quite hard stretches, where v. steep and at one point a rather precarious pole ladder, which could be improved. Nice and open on the top when eventually reached, but jolly cold. I emptied and measured the rain gauge, then found I had no pen to write it in book. Will do so tomorrow. Left at 5 while thunder boomed from storms around, and hurried down seeing flashes of sunlight and some fine views. Masses of nepenthes on path. V. cold on return, but good to be in shelter. Hot meal. Full moon and warm sleeping bag.

WED. 23. A little blue bird is flying from perch to perch outside the camp. It has a blue back and head, brown tail and wings, yellow front/orange almost and white spectacles – more like goggles – round its eyes. It behaves like a robin and is very tame. George suggests we may have usurped its normal shelter when it rains, as it is doing now. We watched the dawn from the helipad. Lovely pink clouds and a view of Api, but the sun rises behind Mulu, so no sunrise. One would need to be at the top for that. Luckily we didn't kill ourselves trying to get up there before dawn, as the clouds and mist swept over before the sun was up. Took it easy after breakfast, as I felt fairly weak after yesterday. Then climbed slowly to the top (1½ hrs) photographing the extraordinary quantity and beauty of the nepenthes on the way. The sun was warm on the top (I had overtaken G & R collecting happily) and I slept for ½ hr under the trig point, but the clouds below never cleared and I got no scenic views. When George arrived we followed and cut the trail along the ridge beyond and down some way. Different, impressive country and, although I couldn't see much for the fog, a competent team of 4+ men would, I think, be able to cut along quite quickly down to the real ridge. Some very thick patches of vegetation at first but also open natural paths. Didn't reach the end where Bob

Hoskins, presumably, had cut to. [Nigel later pioneered this route all the way to the Melinau Gorge.] Back down ahead of the others and arrived before the rain began at 2 to eat and rest, reading 'Pursuit of Love' [by Nancy Mitford]. George arrived at 3.15 in pouring rain. No sign of Ross and Herbert. Did the rain gauges at 4 and summit. The atmosphere in a sub-camp can be very pleasant. Tea, rice and some meat, eked out with Provita [synthetic mincemeat], is being cooked over the wood fire by the boys. The smoke curls up through the drying firewood, past the damp clothes spread on top and hanging up to dry, the botanists (or entomologists) sort their day's collection and, if at Camp 4, one huddles in one's sleeping bag for warmth.

THUR. 24. Porridge and jam for breakfast and then high speed off downhill, leaving Camp 4 at 6.30, reaching Camp 1 at 10.20 and, after ½ hour with Kevin [McCormick], chatting and drinking tea, back to BC by 12.25 (5½ hrs). Gratifying surprise and pleasure to see me back and all well. The run down the mountain was stimulating, hard on the feet, and the last stretch back to BC a bit tiring, but not otherwise. Wore plimsolls going up which were excellent, gave no problems, but split and wore out. Boots coming down, probably a better idea, gave me some blisters and bruises, but more protection. Never fell over, although the speed involved a good deal of leaping and occasional trots. Took it easy in p.m. and read Love in a Cold Climate [by Nancy Mitford] in my hammock. Had my blisters treated, a good wash in the river and long peaceful evening not thinking about the work waiting to be done tomorrow.

FRI. 25. 'Very peculiar atypical presentation' (G. Argent). Lots of people returning. George and Ross from Mulu, Harry [Vallack] from Camp 5 and Joan [Cramphorn] from Medalam, where she had been for 2 weeks + 2 men and had had a good time collecting fish – sparse in the Terikan. The Temenggong arrived with the new DO [district officer], Marudi. He seemed a nice man and we had quite a long talk about the exped. He wants to have lists of members coming. Couldn't stay to lunch. Had a meeting for admin people to decide future dates. All dovetailed well and N[igel], P[hilip], S[hane], K[ate] and Nicola all seemed happy with plans. We should have pretty good admin cover for the rest of the year. Wrote a lot of letters and cleared my desk which seems to pile up almost as badly as at home whenever I leave it. In a way it's harder because the heat stultifies initiative and so many things need an effort to get started. Time has a lovely way of passing busily, but that can easily be an illusion if one is not careful.

SAT. 26. Male operator at Miri Control is excellent and takes great trouble for us. Spent most of the rest of the day doing a press release to go with Nigel's report to sponsors and the 1st article for Geographical Magazine. This then had to be watered down – my superlatives turned to cautious 'possibles' – mainly by John Proctor, but good PR to be discussing this with them. Rather strained feelings as Mark and I plan to make a quick dash for Api next week and John regards it as a 'glittering prize' which all should share to bring colour into their lives. The point I'm sticking to is that Mark and I are the fittest at present and so will have a go. Harry, at Camp 5 anyway, will join us. John [Proctor], George A., Mark, etc. all had a go 2 weeks ago from Melinau River crossing but found it too hard. Kevin back and group sat up late talking.

SUN. 27. Picnic for Kate [Clark] (cook), Katie, Nicola, Shane, Joan, Esther [Penan girl from Long Iman], Philip [Leworthy], Harry [Vallack] and me. We took a longboat without any men and I drove with Philip in front. River quite high so no problem. Stopped at lower end of an island where there was a sandy and gravel beach. P and I got a fire going with great difficulty as everything was wet and we had no paper. Used petrol and cooking oil in small doses, but not a good system. Bathed in racing current, blew on fire, ate sandwiches, blew on smoky fire, tried unsuccessfully to catch fish (Joan), blew more on fire, and at last boiled kettle for tea. Got back safely before rain. Before we left Joan had assembled her electric fish gear for the first time and stunned one whopper off the raft, but too much water. Rained hard.

MON. 28. Heavy rain in night and river up to and over banks in a.m. – and still rising. Standing water under jamban, rubbish pit, etc. but under house still dry. I set off early to fetch 2 Penan and Arun from L. Iman in JB. Tutoh also v. high – able to cut behind island with ease. Later Tu Au arrived with sick Bangah in boat who Nicola looked after for a long time – pleurisy? Worked on Geog. Mag. article and accounts during the day. Found reprint of chapter from 'Borneo Jungle' by Eddie Shackleton and read it to Engan and the other men, in their house, after dinner. [Engan was the grandson of Tama Nilong, who climbed Mulu for the first time with Shackleton in 1932.] They remembered and were interested. They also told me that banteng [a species of wild cattle] had been often seen by T. Nilong when he farmed near L. Birar – and I remembered Usang pointing out the spot between there and Camp 5 where he saw 4 in 1957.

TUE. 29. Went in longboat up the M. Paku + John [Proctor] and Tama Weng to visit Camp 1 for 2 days. Shane came too and walked there and back + Engan and Lipan and Kevin's resupply. Sandra and I stayed near the waterfall – all looking ravishing up there today – we collected a begonia, photographed a cauliferous fruit and climbed up to the cave in the cliff. Back down the lovely Paku for lunch seeing gorgeous male paradise flycatcher swooping from tree to tree. Unmistakable long white tail.

SECOND ATTEMPT ON MOUNT API

WED. 30. Mark ready to set off right away, so after a short radio contact with John M[aidment] and Johnny Leong [the Chinese shopkeeper in Marudi from whom we bought most of out supplies] we started loading the longboat. I dropped my parang in – it fell out of its sheath – so Lang lent me his. Nice run up to L. Birar and 2 hrs' walk, some in rain, to Camp 5. Lots of talk about best route to try. Whether to get up to 4,000 ft [1,200 m] easily by going to Pinnacles [a spectacular limestone feature which became the Mulu logo] by prepared route, but then having problems getting up on the ridge across country said to be very hard, like that the last party ran into further south. Or to try a new route I had heard of from the Penan Ta'ee and his brother Abeng up the next ridge up the gorge, which certainly looks easier on the map and seems to run straight up to the summit ridge. Harry had talked to them the day before and they had said they had been up there before and described looking over and down to Cave of Winds and across Melinau, so likely true, but untried route. Ta'ee arrived and said we could do it in 3 or 4 days from Long Taba'un and that there was water up the ridge. Not that that looks like being a problem as it set in to rain early evening and kept on into the night. Long talk with Mark about John Proctor's problems/hang-ups. A pity he feels this way as it's the first sour note on the exped. so far – as we agreed it's really amazing how well everyone gets on considering almost none were chosen by me, but were appointed for scientific ability. Rapid turnover has helped a lot with this. Well there probably won't be time to snatch J's glittering prize from him, but hopes are high for the other two. Perhaps the best thing would be if I were to pull out just before the last assault, but I don't think I'm noble enough to do so without circumstances forcing it.

THUR. 1 DECEMBER. Up at 5.45 and all packed and ready to go by 6.45, with only a cup of tea inside. Due to stop in 2 hrs for makan. Walking up and down over steepish ridges through very attractive alluvial forest. Past Ta'ee's old camp where some were still living and on, through dawn sunlight slanting through the trees, to Long Taba'un, where Ta'ee's wife was living. We cooked rice at base of ridge (9 [a.m.]). Said to be water far up from here. Should always cook rice before leaving and eat cold, but forgot today. Off again at 10.30 and up surprisingly easy long ridge. Kept thinking it was going to turn to limestone but stayed sandstone all the way. 10.30 = 250 m; 12.00 = 500 m; 2.30 = 1,150 m. Camp. Passed lots of signs of pig and wild sago, which had been cut by Abeng almost up to where we camped. This was under a tall cliff, but with more behind. A gully leads up just above the camp. I went some way up and felt it could be climbed but dangerous without a rope. Should take one to the ridge. From highest point I could see part of Mulu rising above us to the SE into the low cloud. Also good view to NE of Benarat. Fine tall trees, one with damar resin on it, growing right at the base of the cliff. Another ridge, higher than our one, lies across a fairly deep valley and that's the way the Penan says we must go. From there he says we can see down to Clearwater River and 'reach the top' although he has not done so and nor has anyone else. So we are a bit worried that he may have just looked round behind the mountain. Still, there is nowhere else to go, so we'll try it in the morning. Mark got a lot of leeches. He and Harry quite tired but I feel full of beans. Nice camp on level ground.

FRI. 2. Porridge for breakfast. Set off at 7.30, down to stream, heading south. Crossed a low ridge, another valley and then climbed up another steep ridge. The ridge ends abruptly at the cliff we saw yesterday and there is no way anyone but a full-scale rock-climbing team could get up it. The cliff goes on as far as can be seen to the south, dropping some 3,000 ft [900 m] into what Mark has named 'Hidden Valley'. This view was our reward. We could see right down to the high cliffs of the gorge, the sump where the river disappears and even, across all that, to the tall rocks by Camp 1. Beyond, Borneo stretched away, steppes of endless forest to the horizon. 9.20. We took photographs and trudged back to our camp. 10.00. There we ate rice and pusu and stripped our packs down to the barest essentials – sleeping bag, 1 dry shirt and sarong, cape or hammock bed, camera equipment, torch, odds and ends, food (basic), water bottle. Also lots of climbing gear. We started the great climb at 11, going up the gully near our camp, which I had investigated the evening before. The first bit I had stopped at was harder than it looked and we needed ropes. Mark went up first, anchoring himself with crabs to various trees on the way, but still dangerous – grade Severe to Hard Severe – because of the lack of protection during the first 30 feet [9 m] or so. Whole climb about 80–90 ft [25–27 m]. Sabang went next with one of the packs and did well, but Harry was painfully slow and so was Sabong. We had all been taught how to tie bowlines round our waists and Mark was holding us at the top. We decided to take Sabang instead of Sabong, as he was the better climber, sent the packs up and then I came last. Shinned up the steepest part without looking down and then nearly died of fright when I stopped at the ½ way ledge and did look down. Had to unrope and send Sabong down from there. Then up the last bit. Never have I been so consistently frightened for so long. However, there we 4 were + packs and it had taken 2 hours and 20 mins to get up so far. Then we started up the gully, still steep, but climbable without a rope. At first through some wild pinnacles and holes, tricky but not difficult. Then steeper and care needed not to get into impossible situations at either edge of the gully. Pushing through undergrowth with bare hands – no thought of snakes, scorpions or centipedes – and getting fairly scratched and pricked in the process. I led for a time, annoying the way the frame of one's knapsack and one's parang or sheath got caught in everything, but a stimulating scramble for all that. Not much view as everything had clouded over and a fine drizzle falling most of the time. One would have been far worse scratched in an equivalent overgrown English wood. Began looking out for somewhere to camp but no flat ground at all until 4 when at 1,550 m we came up against a sheer cliff where the root matting had fallen away, exposing the bare rock. There we found a little shelf where there was just room for our 4 hammock beds and our camp sheet. Pretty wet and cold, but we managed to get a fire lit thanks to some damar gum Harry had with him and a candle. On this we brewed tea in Mark's water bottle and then mixed up some porridge and jam. Sabang used my cape as a hammock and it split in the night. I had promised he could keep it and so must get him another.

SAT. 3. More tepid porridge and off by 7. Cut downhill a bit to the right first then much more steeply up. Constantly looked hopeless, but Sabang was fearless and cut on ahead. We left the camp up and just took climbing gear, the flags and water bottles. Some pretty scary places and sheer drops on all sides. No apparent alternative ever to the route we were taking and that was risky. By 9 we were at 1,650 m on my altimeter and it was very frightening. We seemed to be on a bulge over an overhang and although it was all covered in roots and rotten vegetation, so that there was plenty to hold on to, it often broke off and we only had to slip and fall, or have a whole clump come away with us to, one and all, plummet out of sight. The ground, some 2,000 ft [600 m] below, seemed straight down and indeed we were not sure that in zigzagging up we had not moved across away from the gully to over the sheer cliffs on either side. Not that it would have made much difference once we started slipping. We came to a place where Sabang skirted round over space outside the vegetation – somehow crawling under it seemed safer – and disappeared out of sight. I didn't like the look of it at all and waited for M[ark] and H[arry]. After much talk M followed and climbed on about another 30 ft [9 m] to where Sabang was, but returned to say it was all much the same and much too dangerous – all unprotected and likely to slip off. Reluctantly, but with some relief, as I had begun to count my responsibilities (always a bad sign), we decided to go back down and see if there was another way. No sign any more of our 'gully', although there was a ridge to the south, but that, too, was very steep. Back at camp by 10 and made some tea – now out of sugar. I recce'd a way down to the right further and climbed into a limestone chimney to try and look round the corner. Wasn't sure if it could be done, even lower down. Went back for the others who came to look and agreed no way. So back, broke camp and went down fast. Past a green, broad-headed snake (Wagler's pit viper?) with brown dotted stripes down side just below the camp (1,500 m) but it just watched us and flicked its tongue. Reached the steep section above our camp by about 1 and went down one by one on the rope. I'm quite beginning to enjoy it. The security of the rope means that one can do outrageously dangerous things and somehow not fall, although one certainly would without a rope. Filthy, caked in mud, as we had spent most of last two days on all fours in slush, and covered in cuts and scratches, it was good to have a total wash and scrub in the stream below the camp, then treat wounds and feet and stretch out on our beds. Much talk about whether we could have gone on, but on the whole I am pretty satisfied. We did our best and it's still there to beat. According to H's calculations we were only 300 ft [90 m] from the top.

33   The limestone cliffs of Gunung Api. Some are 1,000 metres high.

SUN. 4. Mark rather depressed and wondering inevitably if we couldn't have made it after all. But it would have been too risky and I have no regrets. Also it's more tactful all round from J[ohn] P[roctor]'s point of view. Perhaps if we'd had, as planned, 2 men and the 2 of us instead of Harry we might have done better, but it was nice for H to be along. Heavy rain in a.m. so sat eating porridge and tea without sugar, as we had run out, until 8 when M[ark], H[arry] and I set off in rain + Ta'ee, leaving the others to follow. We whistled down the ridge – it really is very easy going, through open beech-wood-like mixed dip-terocarp forest. Crossed river at base onto another ridge, down that for a bit, then another ridge and mucky up and down stuff into the gorge. Stopped to look at cave near Ta'ee's old camp – they have now all moved to Long Taba'un. A nice small dry cave 65 m deep × 30 m wide at deepest, narrowing to 15 m at mouth. A perfect place to do a population study and mist netting, etc. of bats, of which there were quite a lot, so we named it Bat Cave. Back at Camp 5 by 11. Ate lots of biscuits and golden syrup and drank tea.

MON. 5. Walked back fast in rain – floating on air, feet going so well and feeling so fit – to Long Birar, where found Spurway and Tama Engan waiting + longboat. Also Mark's canoe, in case we hadn't been able to cross the river. Arrived back to find JB had run a main engine bearing at Long T, probably due to oil blockage, and so out of action, and other problems. Helicopter due next day for lifts to sub-camps. Arranged for Nigel's rubber boat to be taken to Camp 5, as crossing there can be dangerous. Down to just 9 stone [57 kg] on scales! [This was the lightest I had been for more than 20 years.] There had been a fight in the middle of last night between Tama Engan and Tama Weng which John had had to go and sort out. Everyone got drunk and broke into the store. Not pleased, but Engan apparently in control. Much else to do. Store finished.

[I flew home for Christmas.]

WED. 25 JANUARY 1978. Collected first 15 boxes of stores from high commission [in Brunei] and just squeezed them into L/Rover. No room for a mouse, but somehow we also got the three newcomers and their bags on board as well. Sensational driving along beach between K. Belait and border – smooth sand, no rivers visible at all – and monkeys running inland from the water's edge. Fishermen standing like statues, hazy light and endless sound and distance.

THUR. 26. Raced round Miri in a taxi, dropping passports, shopping for rain capes and having hair cut. Met Shane at airport + 15 boxes and sweated to transfer all 30+ baggage + 8 drums of fuel to a big heap next to helipad opposite Borneo Skyways, where we then sat and waited. V. jolly crew and Capt. Rahim who gave Shane his spare uniform during the flight (and made her get into it) and said the RMAF [Royal Malaysian Air Force] were desperate for more jobs!! So good to arrive so quickly and unload, then Capt. R. stayed while heli went back for drums. Then an evening catching up with news. My things had stood up pretty well to absence and S. had taken good care of my bilek. Everyone seemed pleased to see me back.

FRI. 27. Dr Giles [David Giles, a Cornish GP] seems very well settled and is another Jo Anderson-type Mr Fixit. V. useful and reliable. Lots of improvements while I've been away, handrails to raft, new shower and pump designed by Philip [Leworthy] from a lavatory plunger. Got carbide lamp working – a good light but a bit messy and complicated to start and carbide is not nice stuff to handle – it burns if your hands are wet, which of course they usually are.

SAT. 28. Raban [David Labang] is trapping at Medway's old site and we took the longboat up the Melinau Paku to see him. He has caught 3 v. nice fireback pheasants (2 m. and 1 f.) which are in a chicken house behind the men's new house.

SUN. 29. Raban came in the morning with a masked civet in a basket which had been caught in a pheasant snare.

MON. 30. River v. low – island appearing and ideal for swimming. Nigel has fixed a greasy pole – floating log for games while I have been away. Difficult to sit on, let alone stand.

TUE. 31. Ricky, twin of Dicky, Engan's son, was brought in with deep gash in chin which clearly needed stitches. John P. and I cleaned it up, tried pulling it together with suture strips, packed it with powder and covered with plaster. He was v. brave. But typical that that should happen when no doctor or nurse in camp. When he got back in the evening D stitched it up v. expertly while I helped. This time Ricky became hysterical and I didn't really blame him.

WED. 1 FEBRUARY. Double birthday for John P. and Jeremy Holloway. I had brought back v. splendid boots for JP which I had persuaded Berghaus [bootmakers] to give and which he badly needed as he has trouble with his feet. Also crippled at the moment with a septic hole in his shin caused by a kick before climbing Api, but deep bruise became infected on the mountain and forceps could still be inserted an inch or so.

THUR. 2. Before I went away for Christmas I had dropped my good Tinjar parang in the river when getting into a longboat. Yesterday we spent quite a long time diving to look for it as the water, though deep there (12 ft [4 m]), was clear for once. Lots of dead wood and branches to hold on to as I peered around and felt the sandy bottom stirring up some mud, until I met a yellow-and-black-striped snake with a painted face and decided that my ears had had enough and it was time to abandon the search.

FRI. 3. Dr David and I went fishing in p.m. I caught a v. large carp-like fish with my first proper cast at the junction of the M. Paku and the Melinau, where the Melinau was full and muddy and the Melinau Paku clear blue and backed up. Had another bite, which took hook, spinner and all in one gulp, and only caught one other tiddler.

SAT. 4. Nigel, Harry and I went off to try and get through the Green Cave, but in spite of a thrilling day and lots of excitements, failed to reach daylight. However, we did get further than anyone else has and saw amazing stalactites and stalagmites, like Indian phallic, fertility totems at far end.

SUN. 5. Raban has a paradise flycatcher's nest behind the men's jamban, which he is recording. If the eggs hatch it will be the first recorded observation. Gathorne's birds abandoned their nest. I went and photographed the male on the nest, his long white tail drooping down.

FIRST VISIT TO HIDDEN VALLEY

MON. 6. I walked fast ahead to Camp 1, arriving at 10.25 to find only Jeremy [Holloway] there + Joseph [a Berawan]. I watched him sorting a colourful night's collection of moths. The men took nearly an hour to catch me up. They had collected a large amount of white toadstools which I had seen on the way growing on a fallen tree in midstream. These they cooked and we ate. A pleasant bland rubbery taste, but very elastic and chewy and I found I had to spit the chewy bits out, but they swallowed. Walking quite fast up and down steep ridges following the trail blazed by Nigel, I got unaccountably exhausted, thought I was going to have a heart attack and had to lie down. But I recovered by the time we reached his tripod at the river junction. A nice spot with a fine view of the limestone tower which we agreed, as he was the first there, should be named Batu Nigel. The river joining the M. Paku there is the S. Bessalay. We went on another ½ hour to the S. Hutan, another true-left-bank tributary. It seems Lupung knows this area well and gathers sago here. In fact we found marks he said he had made in recent weeks. He said once he walked all the way on to the Melinau Gorge this way, so he should be able to find Hidden Valley for me. We camped at S. Hutan and the men had the sheet up and platform made in no time. A good stream for washing with deep pools. Party now consists of Usang, Tama Engan, Sabang, Lupung and me.

TUE. 7. Set off 7.30 after makan nasi [rice]. Enchanted woods, open and with a 'Mediterranean pinewood' feel to them in the sunshine. Glimpses of the cliffs/steep limestone hills on our left all the time. The night before, when I washed in the S. Hutan, I saw several small crayfish, just like the ones at Lough Bawn [my home in Ireland]. Maybe 3 ins [8 cm] long but I couldn't get anyone to catch them although I said they were a great delicacy. We saw a large snake looped in a bush we had all except Sabang passed under. It had a round head stuck out about a foot and flicked its tongue outwards and downwards as Sabang nervously ducked under. Then he poked it with a long stick and it glided slowly away. Stretched out it was 6–7' [around 2 m] long and quite thick (my wrist) in the middle, greenish-brown mottled. Lupung said v. poisonous. A nice pigs' nest made of green 'lily' leaves with a clear hole about 18" [45 cm] at one end – the whole about 2' [60 cm] high and 4' [120 cm] long. A perky grey squirrel, not a bit afraid of us, chirruped happily past, flicking its tail and doing physical jerks up one tree after another. 10 [a.m.] reached the 3-way junction of the M. Paku, the S. Iman and an unnamed river. A tall batu visible from here almost due north may mark the edge of Hidden Valley. We crossed the M. Paku a short way upstream. The bed is full of huge rocks and it would be hard to cross if much water flowing. Should fix a rope, perhaps. 10.30 saw a large binturong ambling about high in the trees. It had not seen or heard us, in spite of our making quite a lot of noise, and was easy to watch. The men were excited and we all dropped our packs and rushed under it to look. It looked a bit like an anteater or sloth at first, slowly creeping about. But when Usang banged the tree it was on it moved off along horizontal branches, not v. fast and walking like a fox with its tail straight out. About 5 ft [1.5 m] long with a long tail with rings. I could not positively see the tufts on its ears. A pointed face and pricked ears. Berawan name Paseo; Penan, Pasui; Iban, Inturin. We climbed endless ridges, it rained and we sheltered under a big rock overhang, the roof of which was covered in little cone-shaped wasps' nests, like tiny Malay bats upside down. Thinking the rain was going to stay I suggested camping, but they said the wasps would get angry at the smoke and sting us. The rain let up and we crossed some steep gullies working round to the N again. At one point had great view out over the Deer Cave complex to the Tutoh and far beyond. Then started seeing into the Hidden Valley gorge with no sign of a ridge. Either we were much too high or the map was wrong. At last able to turn left and start going down. Now heading straight for high left-hand cliff at gorge's mouth. The ridge began to narrow until there was at least 1,000 ft [300 m] sheer drop (with trees on either side, while the top of the ridge was like a garden path much of the time and often no wider – 6 ft [1.8 m] was common. We reached the sheer wall of limestone and the ridge just stopped dead with no possibility of getting down our side and not much the other. Frustrating, as I could look far down into the valley I wanted to reach below. So we retraced our steps and went down as soon as we could – maybe ¼ mile back. Now getting late, but easy going though steep and we reached the first stream (marked on map) at 4.30. Made camp on a narrow flattish piece. Still no rain at 6. I had a complete and cold bath in the pool. In the afternoon we saw a large black gibbon which came to almost the tree above and looked down at us. Lupung blew a wah-wah noise through a leaf and it came closer, then saw us, took fright and swung off, gathering ½ dozen others up and shouting an agitated version of the morning and evening call: 'Whoop, hup, whup.' Rather stiff and back rubbed raw by pack. Just noticed that this camp is actually at the junction of two streams. I'm tempted to walk round Api, as it's not much further to go back that way.

WED. 8. 7.50. Latish start, but then we had a pretty hard day yesterday. A good camp, no rain and I slept v. well. At first v. hard going along steep side of ridge – sometimes almost sheer. Then, suddenly, at the bottom of a particularly steep slope, the sandstone ended and the limestone began. For a time this made hard going, scrambling over sharp outcrops with holes between. The river running on our left seemed to grow and shrink. I think part is already underground. Then the valley bottom levelled out a bit and the going became easier, walking through open cover made up of low vegetation with only occasional big trees. Some ulu/sago at the mouth of the valley and also several nilong [palms] – limang is Berawan/Penan name. Tall palm trees. They say the Penan have not been here for a very long time and none is collected from here now, but limang is also edible. It seems that when Usang and Tama Engan were with Robb Anderson they followed the ridge down from Mulu. They say they never came down into the valley and nor did he, so it seems that I am the first here. I stopped to measure large rusa [deer] footprints. They were 4′ [1.2 m] wide and 4½′ [1.4 m] long and quite fresh. Usang said that one that size would make almost 3 pikuls of meat (about 4 cwt [200 kg]). He said he killed one that big on the Melinau once. At the junction I found the place where, at this flow, the water disappears. Here is just a nice pool, with a small waterfall feeding in a good flow of water, but only a little trickle goes on out and that soon disappears, too. The water seems to flow back under a big rock, though there is no sign of a cave. The riverbed meanwhile continues through a bed of boulders and clearly taking water in a flood but empty now. Here we made camp. I told them to make a nice one as the speleos will probably live here a while and it's not a bad spot. The riverbed is good for washing and has some open views of the cliffs. The camp itself is a few yards back from the river and a bit overgrown, but it could be opened up quite easily. I left them to make the camp and went off alone across the river to see if I could find a cave. There must be lots here but the going away from the main valley bed is quite difficult and it's going to be a hard job finding them. It's always different being quite alone in the jungle and I enjoyed myself not getting lost and reaching the cliff edge, but not finding a cave there either. Just as I was about to turn back, I saw something out of the corner of my eye and stopped. There, not 20 feet [6 m] from me was a large sambar deer standing perfectly still and looking straight at me. He had big antlers and a shaggy ruff of dark hair around his neck, so that he looked very like a Highland stag, and I could see every detail of the grooves on his horns and his wet, black nose. We both remained motionless for an endless, breathless age and then he tossed his head, as if to say that I was an intruder in his domain, and vanished. When I got back they were still building and so I took yesterday's grubby clothes down to the river to wash them and me. I almost trod on a pretty green snake about 3 feet [1 m] long, which reared up and adopted a threatening pose. I went back to get my camera and took some pics, but it stayed nearby watching me all the time I washed. I was not sure if it was a pit viper. The green turned to yellow underneath and the skin was wrinkled. It was still there when I got back at 5.30 and Tama Engan said he had nearly trodden on it as well. Usang is afraid of snakes. Sabang and I walked through easy jungle due W for 5 mins then joined the stream bed. At first boulders, it soon turned to gravel and was like walking along a rough leafy lane – a refreshing sensation with open views of the cliffs and sun dappling through. All too soon (½ mile from camp max) we reached the final end, a soft muddy area thoroughly rootled by pigs. Beyond was a steep barrier of broken limestone, which looked harder to climb than it actually was. High on the north wall we could see the mouth of a medium-sized cave, but it looks unreachable. Over the top of the rubble hill, about 100 ft [30 m] high, we could see into an apparently lozenge-shaped sinkhole, maybe 300 yards [275 m]

34   Hidden Valley from the air.

across. We skirted the left (S) edge and soon came to the first cave opening. [We found six cave openings, some of which have later been explored extensively by the speleologists and have proved to be the entrances to vast cave systems.] Several times today I was startled by ants rattling inside lianas. One sounded like a rattlesnake. Another like rapid heavy breathing. At one rest stop we heard what sounded like pigeons cooing. Lupung started imitating them and soon an adult pair of white-crested hornbills came very close and perched looking down at us and continuing to coo – almost like a cuckoo.

FRI. 10. Peter Ashton [about to become professor of Forestry at Harvard] full of enthusiasm and talk all day. Very interesting about future of park. Agrees about value of park as a scientific centre with lots of ideas about how to put it across, e.g. many valuable fruit (potentially) trees will grow on otherwise infertile kerangas. But they are pollinated by monkeys which play a necessary part in their survival by eating – and cracking the nuts. Eliminate the monkeys and you lose the trees. Therefore reserves like this are necessary. Interested to read in Everest the Hard Way [an account by the British mountaineer Chris Bonington of his successful ascent of the south-west face of Everest in 1975] that sherpas only get about £1.30 per day as against our men's £2.50.

SUN. 12. An old man called Balan arrived with Lusing's wife and children. Lusing was on the way to visit Nyapun near Camp 1 to ask his permission to bring his own family there to cut sago and hunt. Even between brothers there is the sense of territoriality and the courtesies are observed. Later in the day he returned to say his brother had agreed to their going there.

MON. 13. A whole lot of Penan arrived led by Lusing and his family with Balan and his wife, etc. All on their way to join Nyapun. Very photogenic. I talked about tigers, which they recognised from pics but said hadn't been seen for some time, other animals – and collected names and family links. [Tigers have never been officially recorded in Borneo, but everywhere people said they had existed recently.] The legendary Seng, with nice earplugs, was one of the party.

WED. 15. Raban has been spending 3 days with Nyapun's and Lupung's families. While with them they have shot 3 babi, 1 rusa, 10 monkeys, 1 porcupine. Also cut down 3 wild sago trees. Nyapun has built 3 new large sulaps on stilts 5' [1.5 m] high and using 700 sticks (excluding firewood) as against usual 70 per house (210 for 3). But where a temporary house lasts 2–3 weeks, these ones should last 2–3 months, so not using more timber and anyway general feeling it is not too important. Raban says they never save food, but work very hard when they are hungry.

THUR. 16. Ivan [Polunin] and 6 men set off at 1.30 to take heavy loads of equipment to Camp 5 – plant presses, etc. and stores for 2 weeks. After about one hour with Spurway driving and a Penan in front, they went under an overhanging tree, the current took the bow over to the side and the boat capsized. Ivan jumped onto the tree – the men were worried he would drown, as he had heavy boots on – while the rest dived in and rescued everything except one parang. After some time they were able to restart the motor and return to BC in heavy rain by 3.30. It was bad luck and bad management. It is doubtful if it was altogether Spurway's fault. They looked utterly miserable, soaked and frightened when they got back. All wet barang was deposited on the veranda, which is of course ideal, being made of bamboo.

MON. 20. Went to photograph the Penan moving camp. When we reached Seng and Lusing's camp, we found as expected that they had decided not to do so in view of the rain. Seng is a fine-looking smiling man with big earplugs. He posed with blowpipe and we took family groups. Dr D. [Giles] examined a squalling sick child. V. interesting walking with Raban showing Margaret [Wise] different footprints. We saw mouse deer, big and small (tiny dots), wildcat, rats, mongoose and civet. Afterwards David and I walked fast to Camp 1. Detoured to visit Nyapun in his new camp. 3 new houses on tall stilts and framework of another few ready to go up. Quite a solid permanent village, where he says he will stay for at least 3–4 months. This seems to be a new departure for him and may be connected with plans to settle. He told me how it was a good base for hunting, collecting sago, etc. We sat up in Nyapun's house and he pressed us to eat and drink. The children were all over me, thrust forward by their mothers and very friendly. A magical experience always to be with this family who are so very pure and nice. I find myself overcome by a series of conflicting emotions when with them – happiness, peace, understanding, pity, sadness, inadequacy, etc. – if only there were some way of really helping them, but I know that the chances of anything succeeding are small, yet something must be done. The numbers now there and those coming in are incompatible with the park. Yet without the park there would be nowhere else for them to go. A catch-22 situation. [Today I know that the answer is for the Penan's land to be recognised as their own, protected by law and safe from logging. This is a better solution than creating more national parks, but it was not seen as even a remote possibility 40 years ago. Now it is.] Home to find Raban, diving in the river, had found my parang, which I had dropped off the raft at the end of Nov. 2½ months ago. A bit pitted but good to have back. Phil had polished it. Amazingly, heard part of 'Savages' on Radio Brunei and it sounded like me talking when the anthro spoke. [*Savages* is a play by Christopher Hampton that deals with the systematic slaughter of Brazilian Indians. It premiered at the Royal Court Theatre in 1973, and was partly based on interviews with John Hemming and me.]

WED. 22. In the morning Lang came back with a cock fireback pheasant and a tiger bittern caught in traps. Raban weighed, ringed and later released them. Margaret having a good time looking for and finding

35   Life at Base Camp with scientists in
from sub-camps for the weekend.

footprints of both the small-clawed and smooth-coated otters. There
is also an almost never recorded hairy-nosed otter, but that would be
a real coup. [Seen for first time, after being thought extinct in Borneo
for 100 years, in a camera trap in 2010.]

FRI. 24. Hair-raising story of returning party who had set off in one
of the rubber inflatables and got stuck between fallen trees. Capsized
and boat swamped. Margaret swept away on the current, but rescued.
Almost all barang saved except two parangs. [Lucas] Chin and two
professional tree climbers [brought in by Paul Chai to collect plants
from the canopy] observed after the drama perched in a tree over the
river watching it all with cool detachment. I posted 4 rules on notice-
board. 1. Barang must be tied down, preferably under a camp sheet.
(This not so much to avoid losing it as so that people don't spend time
trying to rescue it when they could be holding the boat.) 2. Don't wear
boots, wear plimsolls or bare feet (danger of drowning). 3. Two boats
should never be closer than 100 yards [90 m] from each other. 4. If
you capsize, hold on to the boat.

Sat. 25. One of heaviest nights' rain yet with river rising 3½ m in the night. Usang and I had to get up and bail and rescue the longboats. Water level with the banks at dawn. Jamban and rubbish pit flooded, but holding out and no smell.

Sun. 26. Sue feeding her leeches and we all dutifully stuck them on our arms and legs. If they were tiger leeches we hopped about to begin with from the pain. John and I are the only 3 tiger-leech men. As they dropped off we all bled, looking as though the camp had been bombed. We weighed them before and after.

Nyapun arrived in a state because his son Tinaw was very ill – probably chickenpox – but too weak to walk in to BC. Also, the baby girl had cut off a toe with a parang and Lusing had a bad splinter in his foot. Dr David [Giles] gallantly and uncomplainingly set off to spend the night in Nyapun's camp with Jacob as interpreter.

Mon. 27. A message came in from David saying Tinaw might have smallpox and should be medevacked out. I radioed Miri (DMO [district medical officer]) and then checked with the control tower and amazingly the flying-doctor helicopter arrived within 1 hour at 1.30. [It flew on to Camp 1 to pick up the patient and take him to Miri. David Giles walked back.] David had had a great night in Nyapun's temporary camp around the sick boy. He was lavishly entertained by Nyapun, who gave him lots of different sorts of sago, which he didn't like, babi, etc., but he got little sleep with the sick boy and crowding and Nyapun himself in pain from a bad back and a stitch in his side. Interesting speculation on implications of it really being smallpox.

Tue. 28. Fascinating dialogue on radio between David [Giles] and Dr Mosca Reuben in Miri. At first Dr R. said he thought it an infected eczema, but when Dr D. described the speed with which the infection had developed he agreed that it could be smallpox. This was astounding news, delivered over an open radio. They discussed the unmentionable disease quite freely for all Baram ears to hear. The last case in Sarawak was in 1968, but the last in Indonesian Borneo was in 1972 and so isolated pockets very probably still may exist. [We had all been told that it did not occur in Borneo any more and so we had let our vaccines expire. It was not, in fact, officially declared eliminated for another two years, when the World Health Organization (WHO) put out this announcement on 8 May 1980:

> Having considered the development and results of the global pro-gram on smallpox eradication initiated by WHO in 1958 and intensified since 1967 [...] declares solemnly that the world and its peoples have won freedom from smallpox, which was a most dev-astating disease sweeping in epidemic form through many countries since earliest time, leaving death, blindness and disfigurement in its wake and which only a decade ago was rampant in Africa, Asia and South America.

If Tinaw really had had smallpox, it would have caused a world sen-sation and we were in a state for few days wondering how we could get ourselves revaccinated, but the excitement fizzled out when it was established just to be a severe case of chickenpox. I should also empha-sise that we took scrupulous precautions to make sure that all members of the expedition had health checks before joining us. I was assured by our doctors that none of the outbreaks of disease which occurred while we were there was as a result of contact with us.]

Margaret saw two otters on the Melinau on the way back from Clearwater Cave. The giant tree behind Base Camp was cut down by Usang with only six well placed cuts. It fell exactly right along the path. It measured seven 'spans' (arms outstretched), enough to make a good big longboat. [I recorded the whole process, which was done impressively using only rule of thumb and adzes, assisted by the chainsaw.]

Nice stick insects and moths were collected from its canopy. Also a pretty black and white snake, a squirrel and a little green frog.

36 Usang, the Berawan who built Base
Camp, making us a new longboat.

WED. 1 MARCH. There is a ½ grown tame female rusa being kept
as a pet at L. Terawan and also a flat-headed cat. Both are healthy.
Wrinkled hornbills seen from the batu and a Malayan fruit-eating bat
brought in from mist net.

THUR. 2. Flat-headed cat brought back to BC. A good-looking cat
with a brown neck and shoulders and an angry savage face. We put its
small cage in the bath under the house, tipped up so that it had water
and with a sack round it. We put a chick in the cage, which pecked
about unconcerned for a time before, just as it was climbing out, being
seized and eaten with loud crunching. In the cave behind the lab, we
saw several bats and lots of traces of civets, wildcats, rats, pig, etc. We
also saw the biggest spider I have yet met. By climbing on Margaret's
shoulders I was able to reach a ledge near it and I caught it in a net.
Then had to scramble down via Bis [S. C. Bisserot, a photographer]. We
brought back the spider and a huge cricket, which Bis photographed.
Then the spider, which had a large egg sac clutched in her forearms and

which we named Ruby after her eyes, escaped from the plastic tub in the night and was later seen near the water tanks by Dr D. Sandflies bad, but Uschi [our Swiss cook] a v.g. cook, which is good for morale. Nyapun staying in the annex with his family. I bought two bark loin-cloths from him ([M$]5 each), a selabit and some damar, which we burned for light and smell this evening.

SAT. 4. Built a cage outside for the cat where Bis could film it in natural surroundings. Pressure on me not to give it to RMAF, but I was able to explain my reasons for doing so. [These, I think, were that the RMAF were vital to our whole expedition, and extremely helpful. While we may not have approved of them wanting to keep captive a very rare cat, letting them have it was a bit like giving it to a zoo and would earn us lots of Brownie points with them. Frankly, when we desperately needed a helicopter we were ready to sell our souls!] Today we anaesthetised the flat-headed cat in its cage by putting a pad of ether in and enclosing all in a plastic bag. It fought to the last and took a long time to go. Was then measured all over before being put back in a new cage where it was a bit groggy for a couple of days.

MON. 6. In the night (11.30) Nyapun came to tell me they had caught a civet in a snare and put a basket over it. We went in flip-flops and the fire ants were very painful. It, too, was very savage, but we got the snare off its leg and put it in the cat's old cage without trouble. Later we anaesthetised it too – a much better patient, who just dropped – and measured it. Huge balls and scent glands. Both it (Malay civet) and the flat-headed cat are males. Civet striking and healthy with vivid markings, graded black spots all over its body and white rings around its neck and tail. While anaesthetised, David [Macdonald] put a blue collar with transmitter on the civet. Then in the evening we let it go and worried throughout the night that it had died, got caught up or got the collar off as the signal seemed to be remaining static. While all this was going on, the cat had to go back into its little cage ready for the heli flight tomorrow, where it sat with a sour expression and growled at everyone who passed.

Also a green pit viper which Bis handled confidently and I took pics of before taking it across to the helipad, as it seemed a bad idea to let it loose under the longhouse. When I tipped it out of the clear plastic box it was in it hurried up the nearest tree, which happened to be a stump only 3 feet [1 m] high. At the top was a fern into which it draped itself trying with some success to become invisible. The only trouble was that it had picked a spot exactly at hand height on the path along the river's edge, so I warned everyone. When I went back in the evening, it was still there.

During the day the speleos went to explore Deer Cave and came back ecstatic and firm in their opinion that it is the biggest river-passage cave in the world.

WED. 8. Splendid views of the Deer and Green caves from the RMAF helicopter with charming Capt. Affendi; then dropping a drum of fuel at Camp 5. Spectacular sinkholes and big caves high on Api. Even with my earphones on I could hear the speleos baying like a pack of hounds behind the open door and window at all the wonders they were seeing. Striking Neuschwanstein views of towering white cliffs, rainbows, storm clouds and distant da Vinci views of the lowlands with limestone hills rising out above the forest, with far hazy vistas.

David [Macdonald] and Margaret tracking their civet with the radio signal and pleased to see it was moving. The culmination came at 8.30 p.m. when it seemed to approach the longhouse and at last they actually saw it in the torchlight among the bananas by the riverbank. 10 p.m. and we have all just seen it with its collar strolling unconcernedly across the front of the longhouse towards the men's house – amazing – looking twice as large in the wild. [Over the next months, it kept to a fairly regular schedule, so that we could impress visitors by saying at 10 p.m., 'Let's turn on the outside light and see if there is anything out there' – and sure enough there it would be, ambling past.]

THUR. 9. At 4.30 p.m. I decided it was time to set off for the Deer Cave, where I planned to spend a couple of nights underground with the speleos. Everyone should walk alone in the rainforest in the evening or early morning, if only a short way and not far from camp. One's awareness is sharpened and stimulated, and everything is more thrilling. The sounds of the jungle seem louder and more immediate and one notices much more. I heard bats leaving the main entrance of the Deer Cave long before I got there, but couldn't see them. The slightly nervous anticipation of knowing I would be going through it on my own added spice. With only a small torch it seemed even bigger but quite friendly and to my surprise I was not at all frightened, although I picked up a good many earwigs on my high route. The speleo camp was welcoming and I found Dave [Brook] and Ben [Lyon] there full of enthusiasm and really excited for normally phlegmatic characters. Ben: 'Anyone who wanders about on the surface of the limestone is wasting their time. The whole story and history of it is in the caves.'

They told me that the Garden of Eden was once all filled with sediment, which had since been washed out. They had found trees at high levels in the caves parallel to Deer Cave, which they had been investigating and surveying. Ben: 'Anyone who says they've had trouble catching bats just hasn't looked.' But this was after they had just climbed up to a high cave never before disturbed by man, as it involved some quite severe climbing, and this may have been significant. They had found a new cave which they thought might lead to the waterfall on the Melinau Paku, but had been stopped by a long snake on a ledge, which appeared to live on bats. So they named it Snake Cave.

FRI. 10. A very long day, although they are not early risers. First we went to Snake Cave. Caught some small blind catfish in the stream and some troglodyte insects. Then, after a winding passage, reached the snake which, after some discussion, I caught quite easily with two nooses made of pink string. We put it in one of my green Robert Lawrie boot bags and, leaving the others, Mike [Farnworth], Andy

[Eavis] and I hurried back to the camp, had a quick makan and set off again for Green Cave.

Reached there by midday, found my torch left behind from last time and quickly made our way by carbide light to the far end. After we had caught some blind white crabs, we needed rope to go on, me using a figure of eight for the first time and finding it quite easy except for having to trust the rope completely and lean back against it into space. We went on down and along and down again exploring different chambers and getting deeper and deeper with some quite difficult drops. Cut the rope three times and left it fixed. Very patient and efficient with the ingénue. At the bottom we seemed to be getting into nothing but sump holes and returned to the first rope. Halfway down a big dark hole seemed to open on one side. I scrambled up to

37   Andy Eavis in Green Cave on a later expedition.

look and peered over into another huge cavern, while the other two disappeared again into the bowels for another look. I came down to a watercourse, now feeling very confident alone and sat at the top occasionally seeing a flicker of light below and waited for them to come up. Wrote notes. Sound of water splashing, trickling, rushing exaggerated and always somewhere. I expect big waterfalls but often there is only a little trickle, or drips, although today in two places heavy showers had to be crossed, soaking one completely. Huge spaces above, large caverns ending in little passages. An almost intestinal feeling. Drain plugs getting smaller and smaller, down and down, ending in a sump with a corkscrewing effect. Every now and then we felt a little breeze, which encouraged us to believe there was an opening ahead, but often it was only caused by water falling.

Carbide lamps excellent. No trouble when one understands them. They cast huge shadows. Not frightening in such big caves, but always a sense of danger – the darkness, steepness and the unknown. The threat of spiders and snakes all adds to the spice. Time always passes v. quickly underground (as under water). I feel we could go on indefinitely. It's nice we don't have to be home for tea. 4.30 p.m. already.

Sense of direction goes easily without a compass. At the end of last series we were heading back south towards the entrance – but much lower down and underneath. Sitting at the top of the rope alone, carbide flame small and v. dim as saving it. Smoking a cheroot and waiting. The rope starts moving, goes tight. It's belayed back onto a second rock. Now a flicker of light and it starts thrashing about, slapping the cliff as Mike climbs up.

'Whew! Ridiculous situation. I slid down a steep little hole into a sump. Had to pull myself out by the old system of looping the rope and putting my foot in it. Phew!'

I can't quite imagine what he was doing but it all sounds very dangerous.

We go on to investigate 'my' big cavern. Looks good, but we pass an even larger snake than this a.m. on the way and lose our dignity. I must have stepped over it on the way to the watercourse. Over a ridge and down the last rope, then along a short way and stopped by a huge wall, maybe 65 ft [20 m] high, of rubble. Sheer or overhanging and no way up. Sheer white limestone on either side. Like a plug, only there looks to be a way over the top. No way to go but back and time to go home. We take a fork to avoid the snake, but it had the same idea and is ahead of us. We wait while it stops and looks round in the exit hole. About 7 ft [2 m] long. Two big long-legged centipedes are on the other wall and I don't like the look of them. At last the snake slides down a steep smooth slope, it seems able to grip – and off across the main floor. Thought it was going to stop and make friends with our white rope as it crossed it, but continued on. We flog on fast, leaving ropes behind, and, through driving rain, get back to camp at 7.30. Welcome rice and curry, a wash and a warm sleeping bag. Pretty tired but a great day. Rather wet in night and spray blown in.

Sun. 12. Bis handles the cave snake well and we can all feel how it seems able to cling to a smooth wall. Last night Margaret caught a white moonrat. [Moonrats are related to hedgehogs and give off a strong smell of ammonia. We quite often saw them in moonlight when following paths by night.] We photographed it with its fangs wide open and released it with a radio collar. Sat still after release. Not so with 6 ft [1.8 m] monitor lizard, caught in a fish trap out of the water. After being released on the beach with lots ready to photograph, it ran off very fast through the netting and into the water.

TAKING CAVERS INTO HIDDEN VALLEY FOR THE FIRST TIME, THE FIRST CIRCUIT OF API ANTICLOCKWISE AND MY SOLO ATTEMPT TO REACH THE SUMMIT

Tue. 14. Two days' walking into Hidden Valley. Took Lusing, who knew a short cut which made the Berawans nervous, but on the way suddenly, just as we reached a small stream, we saw little Anyi and her sister Taree catching prawns in a pool. I was surprised, as I thought they were miles away. It made the Berawans look a bit foolish. Soon after we reached Nyapun's camp where there were four large sulaps on quite high stilts and a lot of Penan. Had a good wash in a very nice pool, poised on top of a steep waterfall down to the main river, but a bit dark and overhung by trees for a long-term camp.

WED. 15. Lupung kept wanting to camp and saying 'Joo, joo' (jau = far) but unfortunately for him I knew exactly how far it was! I found a good new route and reached Hidden Valley camp at 3.30. Washed, bathed in the sump pool, deep and cool with no danger of being sucked down and no sign of my friend the pit viper, but I cut my chest diving across. About 4.30 I climbed to look for the Wind Cave; 20 mins climb and a v. small opening and fresh breeze. The speleos pleased by winding passage made by water, which we followed until a deep hole which Andy got across while Dave [Brook] and I waited. A promising cave from the mouth of which we could see a likely one opposite. Back in camp I decided to stay another day as everyone was tired. Lupung could scout a way towards Camp 5 and I could see more of Hidden Valley. I kept telling Andy and Dave how privileged they were to see Penan in their natural state: Nyapun's family and children all living in sulaps; Lupung padding off barefoot to hunt with blowpipe and poison darts, returning by firelight, just one man and his cawat, calmly taking the dart from the barrel and putting it away.

THUR. 16. Had a long argument with Lupung this morning, which really goes to the heart of the Penan problem. I am sending him off to find a path to the NW ridge. He has not brought any meat (there wasn't time, he says) and now he says he must have some or go home – and I need him. He won't/can't eat our tinned meat or the Berawans', partly because he doesn't like it – and it is pretty horrible – and partly because the stylised picture of a pig on the pork tins looks like a dog to him. I say OK he can shoot a babi. No babi here, he says. OK, well just this once a deer, as the Penan are allowed to. He tried last night, he says, and failed. No chance now, by day. He says 'Why not a monkey?' I say not allowed inside the park. He says 'But I have been killing monkeys here for 40 years. You/they can't stop me now.' He knows nothing of the law. So he goes off saying he will kill a monkey if he can and I have to say no you mustn't. Impasse.

[I hated having to lay down the law to Lupung like that, but at that time I felt it was what I had to do since our brief in writing a Management Plan was to design a sustainable system and I could not see beyond the fact that more and more nomadic Penan were coming into the park as their land outside was logged. Working with them to ensure sustainable hunting, while campaigning for their land rights to be recognised, was what I should have been doing. All over the world we are at last beginning to realise that parks created by evicting their indigenous inhabitants are not the best solution. Tribal people are the best conservationists and only by working with them and using their deep knowledge of their environment will we really save each whole ecosystem in the long run.]

We cut across direct to the overhang opposite and S of the camp. Went up a steep scree above rubble at the base; an open area of low plants, flowers and rocks, almost like a meadow. Should be interesting botanically. Also superb views. Then we edged down the cliff face easterly and came to a cave mouth with a dry pig-rootled area outside. Many tracks in almost dusty earth. Went in. At first it looked unlikely and we had to crawl under a low overhang. The cave mouth had collapsed and the bed was full of rubble. Then Andy got through and shouted excitedly, his voice echoing. Dave and I followed, walking bent double and crawling. A very big chamber smelling of guano and with the roof out of sight. Easy walking on level earth until the drop off. Then another crawl and another big chamber, filled again but with an 'Inca road' along the side. [In some places, flat ledges looked man-made and we called them 'Inca roads'.] A long time exploring this and finally, after 3 hours, returned as rope was needed to go any further. Great excitement, as this is the biggest cave they have found so far and not much smaller than Green Cave, but very filled.

38 Sarawak Chamber, the largest known
cave chamber in the world by area.

[Years later, after Sarawak Chamber had been discovered, it was realised that this was the original passage that formed the chamber. To date, there is no way through the blockage, but at some time in the future cavers may well dig a route through and make a much easier way of getting into Hidden Valley.]

Back to camp, nice under their big camp sheet, for some makan. Then I took them down to the end of the valley, further than I remembered. We saw four maroon leaf monkeys and heard more leaping and chattering at us. Also had a good sighting of a rusa. We scrambled over the end wall and through the first doline (sinkhole) before getting into the second doline, but it was very full of vegetation and hard to see where it went. Then back in pouring rain to the cave at the end of the valley which, as I thought, doesn't seem to go anywhere. Back to find the others all arrived at the camp and a jolly speleo atmosphere.

FRI. 17. Dep. 7.45 up path cut yesterday by Lupung. Staying close to cliff and climbing steeply from the outset. Great caution past a wasps' nest. Ate nice fruit with peachy taste but floury texture which dried up my mouth. Pink inside outer shell. Called 'buah liang'. There is water at the top camp, or near. Then it seemed to take forever and we didn't reach Camp 5, v. tired, until 2.30. A good place to be.

SAT. 18. About 12 maroon leaf monkeys came down through the trees at the upstream end of camp, just beyond the overhang, presumably on their way to drink. They stopped and looked at us, sitting close together and peering down as we stood or sat still. A little chattering but no alarms or crashes and after about 5 minutes they swung easily off. Lupung, who had pointed them out, said there are lots here, there and there (pointing at 3 compass points – not on Api). When trees are in fruit, lots come; when not in fruit they go farther away.

8.20 depart with 3 men. Reached Pinnacles on my own at 11, alt. 3,600' [1,100 m]. Would have liked to go on, but had to wait for the men to catch up until 12.20. Lupung tired and upset by limestone and saying he didn't think he would go on any further. When I arrived at the Pinnacles camp I heard a rustling round the corner. I thought it was rats but when I came round I saw it was a v. big maroon leaf monkey rummaging about. He looked very surprised and raced off trailing his long red tail. Chattered nearby for a bit and then I saw a troop on the way up. Now after a good start everything seems to have gone wrong and the outlook is pretty bleak. It is always hard to imagine when the sun is shining, the rocks are hot and clothes are drying, what it's like when it rains. We got the camp sheet up. Plenty of room, even on the rather awkward 2-tier site, and it was almost too hot under it on the exposed mountain. I chose a rock basin for the fire so that the earth around the campsite should not be burned. Then the clouds rolled in, after we had eaten, and with wind and heavy rain it was hard to stay dry.

SUN. 19. Start from Pinnacles camp. Lupung quite useless, complaining and probably frightened, so I said he could go back. Had to take his selabit to share out the load between the 3 of us. Now Sabang painfully slow and moaning. Herbert [today the headman of Long Terawan] OK but something wrong when I, who am no climber, have to keep waiting for them. Now doing so at Ridge camp at 4,000′ [1,200 m]. After good views and several photographs, mist seems to have rolled in for keeps. No need for rope yet, only one spot where we handed up the rucksack but no problem to climb. Waited until 10.30 then went back to see what the matter was. Sabang sitting at bottom of steep bit refusing to come up. I threw down the rope, pulled up Sabang's barang and told him not to be silly. He climbed up and I carried his pack up to Ridge camp again. As a result of this we didn't get off again until just before 11; kept waiting for Sabang to help him over the difficult bits – ridiculous me doing this for Sabang – I thought it all very easy – and even so we reached Little Api camp at 11.35. Alt. 4,400′ [1,340 m]. Sunny and misty and no water so let's pray for rain. Pandanus [prickly palms] not as bad as expected. Gloves nice but not essential. Some thought of going on, but boys v. tired and so better be sensible. Herbert says he is too frightened to go to the top again. 12.15. Doesn't look like rain so decided to go back to Ridge camp and fetch some water. H & S both much too tired, so it has to be me. No problem going down with empty rucksack in 20 mins. Coming up with 2 gallon [9 l] jerrycans rather harder but only took 30 mins, although pretty whacked by the end. Back at 1.05 (50 mins up and down). Nice sunny open camp on ridge below rocky summit of Little Api. Just seen two rhinoceros hornbills fly high over Little Api from west to east. Not cutting close over the ridge but easily 5,500′ [1,680 m]. The mist keeps swirling up round Api all day but the sun is v. hot and burning on top. Incredible sunset out over Miri and Brunei. Little regular flecks of cloud far below above the forest catching the last sunlight and going pink and silver while we are in cloud and mist. A shaft of orange light catching the cliffs of Benarat through the Melinau Gorge and lighting up a cave I have not seen before. We sat on a rock next to the camp sheet, watched the mists swirl below us and listened to the evening noises. The river, 4,000′ [1,200 m] straight down (or else it may be a waterfall further upstream) sounds like machinery or traffic. How one would resent it if it really was, and yet it is indistinguishable. The far hum of the evening insects also comes up indistinctly. Up here there are few cicadas, a chirping tree frog or two, the sudden flutter of wings of a bird surprised to find us here, and always the mist moving about revealing tortured Arthur Rackham trees below. At last, just when I had got comfortably settled on the ground in my sleeping bag, the much-needed rain begins. May mean a wet night, but we won't die of thirst. Millions of flying ants look as though reading (Anna Karenina) and writing are out for now. Pretty stiff night lying over a hump but no rain after all and so a thirsty day ahead.

MON. 20. 7 a.m. dep. Little Api Camp 4,300′ [1,300 m]. 8 a.m. summit of Little Api 4,700′ [1,400 m]. False summit on the way, right after the camp, the rest an even ridge – if such can be said of pinnacle country. Herbert refused to go any further and said, rightly as it turned out, that there was no suitable place for a camp ahead and he would set up water traps at the summit of Little Api. Sabang being as slow as ever. 9.10 I reached the summit of Api with no problems on my own. At no point was I frightened, as I had expected to be, and I was a couple of times yesterday, and at no time did I do anything dangerous or feel the need of a rope. Alt. at top 5,020′ [1,530 m] by this clearly wrong altimeter. Nice clear summit with only some sweet papers which I cleared up, and a stick cut like a cross. I went on a bit, but it becomes quite dangerous. Took a lot of pics. Not happy about the ridge and summit far ahead (as far as this top from Pinnacles camp) which looks higher. Mulu had cloud on top but rest clear around at first, then mist rolled up and obscured the ridge ahead. I wonder if they saw it. 9.40 set off back. 11.25 reached Little Api camp, last of tea and nuts. 1.10 arr. Pinnacles camp. Monkeys had unpacked the bag I left here.

TUE. 21. Pretty stiff and tired after yesterday – possibly my swansong as a Mulu exploit. [It wasn't!] I have really seen and done as much in the park as anyone and will be more useful doing other things. Had a marvellous bathe at Camp 5. The pool there at low water really is the best swimming in the park, though the so called sandflies do bother some.

WED. 22. Nyapun arrived with a note from the doc saying that Ben [Lyon] was quite ill and very weak with dengue fever in Hidden Valley and could we try and get a heli to lift him out. Meanwhile they were trying to cut a helipad and could hear us on the radio, but clearly we couldn't hear them. He had got here in one day, arriving at 7.30, which was pretty good going. He deserves the Mulu Medal 1st Class. We radioed Kuching RMAF HQ, as the heli had left, and asked if we could have one Alouette back tomorrow to try and get Ben out. To my surprise they said yes without argument and understood the problems (e.g. why not flying doctor, as no need for hospital). We then radioed Mulu I in Hidden Valley and spoke to Andy [Eavis], who could again hear us clearly, but we could get little more than 'Roger' due to heavy static. Then there is the problem of getting a chainsaw in to them so they can clear a helipad and this is now all crated up and ready to drop. But, as Usang pointed out, there is no one there 'pandai' [adept] with a chainsaw, so we ought to drop him in, too, but can't do so without a helipad. Catch-22 again.

THUR. 23. RMAF new Alouette arrived unexpectedly early at about 10.45 and were ready to go straight on and try. They had a winch and Nigel had spent the morning packing up the chainsaw in a tripack [our strong waterproof containers], painting it yellow, etc. The crew of 3 were all necessary so only I went with them, expecting to be winched down (and Ben and doc out). There was low cloud (2,000' [600 m]) and we couldn't get over the ridge so I said no good let's go back. The pilot – a mad, smiling Chinese, but brilliant – suggested trying the other way, over the pitted bit of Api. I was sure it wouldn't be on, but he went and we found a narrow winding valley of dolines with cloud at the tops – like a tunnel – which we zoomed down. Had v.g. view into a big sinkhole. Made it into Hidden Valley, also cloudy like a tube, and saw that they had made a tiny helipad, with 5 parangs in 48 hours. Turning round in the valley was quite tricky and losing altitude involved three circuits. Then a slow and agonising creep into the little hole they had made with no more than 6′ [1.8 m] on either end of the blades/props. Quite brilliant and I never thought we would make it. Pilot laughing all the way. I jumped out and Ben and the doctor were loaded on and off they went again. The speleos and their 4 men (Nagan, Sawing, Timo and Lupung) were shattered, with heavily blistered hands from all the paranging. They had done an amazing job, including cutting down three really big trees – the biggest they said they had ever heard of being cut down with parangs. We set to work with the chainsaw and cut several more down before, much to my relief, the crew came back and fetched me – having been to Miri to refuel. Andy wanted to be lifted out as well, but they wouldn't take him. I took his camera and some pics of the dolines. Ben started improving at once, the pilots came over for a drink – a very different and top-notch bunch, we thought – but so young! They left and I wrote another thank you note to A/C Welch [Air Commodore Sam Welch].

TUE. 28. Long talk about Penan with Raban [David Labang]. He has been talking with a lot of people in government about it and is either very naive or very brave. He tells people how much better things were for them under British rule; how the DO [district officer] used to come up to Kuala Melinau and trade with them and how badly off and forgotten they were after independence. They are, apparently, very happy with the help they have had from the RGS. Not much bothered about education, but interested in doctors and settling. I summarise their needs as follows:

Doctor/clinic – also help with birth control.
Agricultural advice – sago planting, pig breeding, fish farming, etc.
Employment – also help with crafts and marketing
Housing in family units to create villages
Work as forest guards to pay for food

Education – Penan school only
Teaching them what they need to learn
A few selected for higher education

WED. 29. Sue [Proctor], having been dosed by the doctor, produced a worm 7 ins [18 cm] long, fat white and curled up in a bottle of formalin. Katie had a smaller one. Most people here a long time probably have them. Proposal made to have a 'worm of the week' award. Nyapun and his family were present when the worm was being admired in its bottle and Raban had to explain to them that they should look and see if they had them, too. I'm worried about Nyapun. He looks tired and the doc thinks he may have TB. Should go to Marudi for an X-ray. He and all his children around. Elder wife sat on veranda and virtually completed and designed the back of a selabit during the afternoon. They have also made about a dozen of the ones with figures of men on them.

THUR. 30. Anyi came to sit on my lap and all the rest of Nyapun's family under the age of 7 climbed on too, so that I was swamped. They are very devoted and loving and follow me around.

THUR. 4 MAY. Philip Chapman spent the night alone in Deer Cave and returned in am, just as a search party was setting out.

FRI. 5. [David] Wells and [Sandra] Hails bird-netting, bringing in chirruping bags and taking out and measuring exquisite little king-fishers and so on.

SAT. 6. Happy speleos returning from about 14 miles [23 km] into Clearwater Cave, where they had walked all night trying to find their way back to their camp.

SUN. 7. My 42nd birthday. [Some weeks before this, on one of my trips to Miri, I had been given an adorable beige puppy, about eight weeks old. On arriving back at Base Camp with him, the then doctor, I forget which, pronounced grumpily that she was a health hazard and would just contribute to our problems. I called her Hazard, Haz for short, and everyone soon fell in love with her. But for some days she had been ill, listless and not eating her food.] Haz was looking poor today and could barely walk. She couldn't make it up the steps of the longhouse without help. John Ogle, the doctor, examined her but came to no conclusion. She just seemed bloated and lethargic, and she hadn't eaten for three days. Worried about her lack of liquid intake, I gave her some glucose by tube, but it did no good and in the afternoon she died, giving just one spasm. Margaret and I took her up the batu and we dug a grave for her near the path. Dr John came and did a post mortem beside the grave and found she was full of fluid. It seems she had a perforated gut and he found a small hole in it, which could have been made by a worm. Very sad.

39 Haz, my puppy; so named because our
doctor said she was a 'health hazard'.

MON. 8. Great excitement today when the civet came round too soon after its anaesthetic and escaped. It ran down to the raft with Margaret in hot pursuit. She nearly got it but then it dived into the river and swam off with Margaret wailing 'It will die if it gets wet!' – meaning after the anaesthetic. I jumped into a longboat and paddled after it, heading it off from the far bank. Luckily Laing, the Kayan boy, dived in from outside the men's house and caught it by the tail so that between us we got it in a sack and safely back home, where it was dried.

TUE. 9. It seems that I am viewed with great suspicion in Kuching because of my previous writings. Lucas Chin, curator of the Sarawak Museum, is especially afraid of what I may say about the Penan.

WED. 10. Cavers return with lots of stories. Andy had lowered himself 800 feet [240 m] into the big sinkhole on Api and abseiled far down into the depths. A flying snake had flown past him while he was in mid-air a long way down. They are all pretty pleased with the way things are going.

FRI. 12. Stopped to watch Raban ringing the birds he had caught (a bulbul and a flycatcher) at his camp, where he had mist nets and traplines. I set off to fish alone at 6.10 with the spinning rod. Cast about 30 times at the mouth of the Melinau Paku, where the water was mixing, and caught a nice 2 lb [900 g] barb on the last cast.

SAT. 13. Marvellous warm safe tropical feeling going slowly by boat up the dark overhanging river by moonlight and a bit of torch. Mist rising from the water, the night noises and our shouts echoing back, seemingly imitated by the hoots of crickets and frogs. Phil Chapman had been catching bats at the mouth of Deer Cave and had seen our hornbills.

SUN. 14. Late at night. All but admin were in bed when we heard a row from the chicken house. We investigated and found a large pit viper (actually identified by [Bong Heang] Kiew next a.m. as a racer – a rat snake – colubrid – back-fanged – only quite poisonous). It was brown-and-beige-dappled. Sandy [Evans], Phil [Chapman], Kevin [McCormick] and I caught it with a loop of cord on a stick (I am getting quite good at doing this!) and put it in a canvas bag. Sandy bravely held it by its tail. It was left in a box outside my bilek all night.

MON. 15. Clearwater is a fine underground stream and can be walked for a mile or so along ledges. A boat could be used if carried in and the whole cave is 15 miles [24 km] so far. A very fine world-class passage!

TUE. 30. Went through the draft Management Plan with Robb Anderson. He is a nice man under his gruff exterior and it was very generous of him to make me feel that I was actually contributing to it.

Went up the batu to watch the sunset. A clear evening, the river low after no rain for several days and the sun illuminating the canopy and the limestone jumble beyond. Looking through Phil's powerful binoculars brought everything close and I was able to watch the activity in the canopy below. Three species of hornbill, especially the very noisy pair of rhinoceros ones, arguing over a great distance, maybe 1 or 2 miles, about which tree they were going to roost in. Just like a cross old couple. Kept changing trees until they finally got together. I spotted a long-tailed macaque in a tree near the camp and I'm sure as I watched it through the glasses it became aware of being watched and leaped down to join the others below. Very good, mostly low-flying, flocks of bats. And a charming pair of bat hawks, which I thought landed above my head, but they certainly circled close calling loudly like squeaking rubber. Decided to sleep up there.

WED. 31. Slept well on batu. No need for sleeping bag – I just lay down on the ground. No trouble from mosquitoes, etc. as others have complained of. Fantastic dawn, with mists swirling and changing below for ¾ hour before the sun came up behind Api – actually between Api and Mulu. No wildlife, but an experience all members should have, as it is quite different from sleeping at a sub-camp, or even under a normal camp sheet.

SUN. 4 JUNE. Cocktail party on the batu with a punch using up the BBC's remaining drink and watching the sunset. [A film crew from the BBC, led by the great Barry Paine, had spent six weeks with us.] Bats, which were better than ever, coming out in long lines which corkscrewed and twisted through the air, smaller clusters, which hurried off in a close group, and big sweeps like a bird's wing rushing past overhead. As each bigger batch emerged from behind the Deer Cave complex we all clapped – reminiscent of Eton on 4th of June when we used to cheer the fireworks and count 1, 2, 3, 4. [Strange that it was 4 June!] Barry made a nice speech of thanks and about the honour and responsibility he had to 5 million viewers to interpret such beauty. I made a short speech in reply saying how nice and trouble free their visit had been. [The film, which was excellent, apart from the ghastly title, *Mysteries of the Green Mountain*, has been shown many times on television since.]

TUE. 6. At about 9 p.m. I went along to give Sue a letter and then looked into the room next door, where Ralph [Brown] and Paul [Chai] were sleeping. As I went in there was a crash in the passage, but I couldn't see anything. I talked for a bit and then set off back along the gallery. A big mattress was drying upright and it had fallen across the passage with a big tear in it. I felt along the top rail to see if there was a nail there and touched what felt like snake, but thought no more of it and found no nail. So I lifted the mattress up and there saw a very big snake coiled around the top bar. I called the others and we shone torches at it which seemed to make it wish to approach, as it slithered towards us across the mattress. Sue said she thought it looked poisonous by the things on the top of its head, so I shooed it away. I thought we should catch it, but got little support for the idea. It began to climb towards the roof, which didn't seem such a good plan if poisonous and so I suggested I shoot it, which was approved with acclaim especially, I suspect, as it was headed for the rafters directly above the other 4's rooms, and Katie's bed. So I got David's gun and the only 4 cartridges I have (his, too, I think) and shot cleanly through it about 1 foot [30 cm] behind the head. The body writhed across the handrail and dropped to the ground leaving a fair bit of blood. But where was the head? Not attached... Ralph said he thought he saw it blasted off into space and so I stepped forward onto the mattress (in bare feet) and avoided stepping on it by about 6 inches [15 cm]. Couldn't find Mark's identification book, so put both bits in a Manor plastic bag and cleaned the gun.

WED. 14. Eddie [Lord Shackleton, son of the great Antarctic explorer, patron of our expedition and the first man to climb Mount Mulu, in 1932, as part of Tom Harrisson's Oxford expedition] flew in an RMAF helicopter to visit us. We used it to take him up to Camp 5 and, from there, to the kerangas plot where John Proctor was working. [This was probably the most significant work of the whole expedition and the key to our understanding of how a rainforest works. *Kerangas*, which means 'land which cannot grow rice', is extremely poor in nutrients but very rich in diversity.] The kerangas has a quite distinctive appearance, being a vista of a mass of mostly small, straight, thin trees. A very tranquil glade-like place. In each plot there are 35 litter traps and the collection of leaves and other detritus falling into them is a most important study. They are emptied every two weeks and are producing interesting results. We saw several of the dangerous Anacardiaceae trees oozing black sap, of which John Dransfield tells the dreadful story of the lecturer in tropical botany who rubbed some into his arm as an experiment and is now totally paralysed. The sap is very toxic and should be avoided like the plague. Foresters are frightened of it – it can act like itching powder if poles for beds are made of it. And it is quite common. Saw a dear little saprophyte – a tiny plant with no leaves, which grows like a small toadstool as a parasite on fungus. And an exquisite purple and blue toadstool – and the wax horn of a wasps' nest. Also a stinkhorn puffball covered in jelly and called locally 'mata babi' which means 'pig's eyes'. Eddie had to be helped across the river back to Camp 5. He is slowish but very game and interested. He had brought a bottle of whisky, which we shared with the men.

THUR. 15. Eddie and I walked back to L. Birar, which took 3½ hours and he went well. It gave us a chance to talk about Survival/Australian matters [Eddie was vice chairman of Rio Tinto, whom Survival were criticising for mining uranium on aboriginal land without their permission, and he was very angry with me!] and about Nigel's future at the RGS, etc. [That evening a party had been arranged for him at Long Terawan, when five of the six survivors of his 1932 expedition had gathered to meet him again. But the jetboat let us down for once and we never made it. He flew out next morning.]

SUN. 18. Interviewed Tim Whitmore which was very interesting because he had a lot to say about the ill-feeling which is being generated in Sarawak. He says it is because of the way the expedition has grown far beyond what was originally planned. They are so touchy and sensitive and almost seem to want everything to be a failure and certainly to see us all fall flat on our faces. He has lots of ideas about how to troubleshoot and he will have much to say at the next RGS committee meeting in July.

TUE. 20. [Beginning of a three-day trip cutting a new path up a ridge to the Mulu summit with Nyapun and three other Penan: Nor, Musa and Sabin. It was extremely hard work, but took us through some fascinating terrain, as well as giving me a chance to travel alone again with just Penan companions.] Off at 8 with quite a heavy pack. I sent Nyapun ahead to kill a pig/babi with his blowpipe. On the way to Philip [Leworthy]'s ridge camp we saw a dozen Hose's monkeys, 4 giant squirrels (they looked like binturong but greyer with striped tails). Also a couple of maroon leaf monkeys, which called above me near S. Hutan. We heard and saw lots of gibbons at S. Iman. The Penan were getting tired and so we camped early in a nice cool place.

[That night I wrote the following by candlelight.]

NYAPUN. Oh my friend Nyapun! What will happen to you after I have gone? True friendship is a rare enough thing between people with the same background. For those of different cultures, with only limited language in common and a totally separate view of the world, it is something strange and wonderful, something brought about in spite of, rather than, as is usual with friendships, because of shared interests and outlooks. The love and trust I believe to exist between Nyapun and me is something not to be explained away in normal terms. There is certainly nothing profane about it. There are no undertones of the emotional and physical attraction sometimes felt between perfectly 'normal' people of the same sex. It is not based on any great experience we have shared together, a danger overcome through mutual confidence or a trauma endured through mutual support. It just exists. Our lives are not closely linked at Base Camp, although I see much more of his family than any other. We have travelled together on several occasions, but we do not, I think, either of us, regard these journeys as anything epic or extraordinary. We just like and trust each other more, I think, than is usual even in the unusual circumstances of such a large group of often impressionable Europeans living in close intimacy with such sincere and amiable people as the Berawans and the Penan both are in their very different ways. It is of course immodest of me to think that my departure represents a threat to Nyapun's future. He may do very well without our special relationship, but there is much I would like to do for him and his family which circumstances make difficult, if they do not totally prevent. To do anything permanent, such as opening a modest bank account for him or paying for one or more of his children to go to school (and there is a long tradition of this), is impractical, dangerous politically and probably not what he needs. Maybe the best I can do is to resolve this time to remember, to try and keep in touch, to send things – and to return one day.

WED. 21. Early start – 7 a.m. – after getting up at 5.30. 3 hours easy going up the ridge. A lot of gibbons about. At 1,500 m began to get into difficult tangled moss forest. Lots of pretty red rhododendrons and nepenthes began to appear. Hard cutting and scrambling. At 1,550 [m] at 11 a.m. an excellent view across to Camp 4. Helipad clearly visible, but summit of Mulu in cloud. Good view out over Deer Cave complex, Tutoh and plains to Lambir hills. Batu Pajang, steep hill over Camp 1, Batu Payau, Penan name for hill over Deer Cave. Rivers in order from here: S. Paku, S. Iman, S. Hutan, S. Bessalay (bessalay = landslide in Penan). Batu Labang Tapun (tiger) is the name of hill cliff at mouth of Deer Cave right round to little one already so named.

Stayed in really difficult but just possible montane scrubby forest along ridge and going up and down little summits. In the dips Leptospermum; on the tops rhododendron and shrubs. Some bits awful but there was always an animal track along the ridge and sometimes, gloriously and suddenly, it would be very easy for a while. I went first, cutting with my Gurkha knife, which is excellent in such crowded conditions but was, I feel, really made for killing people. Then Nyapun, toiling loyally as always, and widening the track. Then the boys, chattering away. Musa is an interesting character. He speaks quite a lot of English, though he denies going to school for any length of time. In 1974 he went to Kuching and saw gibbons in the museum there.

Reached the last but one knoll before the two very steep ones below the summit at 2.15. Everyone pretty exhausted and no water all day. Altitude still only 1,650 m, but we have covered a lot of ground and I've decided to stop. We are clearly not going to reach Camp 4 tonight, a heavy mist has come down which will make deciding where to leave the ridge difficult and we want to be ready to catch any rain there may be or it will be a thirsty night. It's pretty here and the views, when not foggy, are charming. Quite cut and tired. We made a small camp on the path. The wind blew stronger than I have ever known it and nearly took the camp sheet away. Very cold in the night. Never found water, but it rained later anyway.

THUR. 22. My poor old sleeping bag isn't what it was. Had some Nestum [a cereal milk drink] and hot milk which helped aching bones and off by 7.30. The ridge just went on and on over more and more little peaks. The altimeter crept up to 2,000 m mark but still ground fell away steeply on our right and no good trying to cut across. Camp 4 helipad now very clearly visible and later the roof of Camp 4. Splendid views every now and then. This must be the best route in the park for views. Luckily an animal trail – civet? – follows the crest of the ridge and makes life a lot easier. Often it is open and easy walking but sometimes there are tunnels under roots and usually there is cutting and pushing through the undergrowth. A couple of times there were steep places which might have bothered Sabang, but my Penan never faltered. I cut just about the whole way, only catching the top of a finger once, but getting very scratched and some blisters.

By 2 p.m. we had reached 2,000 m by Nigel's altimeter. Here the ridge at last seemed to end in a good open place under big trees with a mass of tangled small bamboo ahead. Now was the time to cut off and try to reach the main ridge and path down. No point in going on in same direction anyway as no more ridge. So I started cutting. Now it was really hard going – soul-destroying tangled undergrowth when you think you will never get anywhere and were a fool to start. But I kept on a bearing of 210° which seemed from the map to be where following the contour at 6,500 ft [1,990 m] would go to intercept. We skirted the top of several landslides (bessalay), crossed two stream valleys – one of which had water – and kept climbing all the time. Then at 3 p.m. and 2,050 m we struck the path. I did not think it would be so soon. Saw Croxalls [John and Barbara] soon after and hurried down to Camp 4.

FRI. 23. Icy-cold night with rain passing through the camp sheet outside Camp 4, where I slept, to soak my sleeping bag and things. Hot milk and Nestum again and off at 7 leaving two Penan behind to cut the trail back to the ridge and follow next day, 2 to follow me down while I trotted ahead without barang or even parang. Camp 3 by 8, Camp 2 by 9, Camp 1 by 9.30. Stopped for ½ hour with Kevin [McCormick] and Rosie [Sadler, who married Philip Leworthy] and reached BC at 11.15. So 4½ hrs in all or 3½ hrs travelling. Fairly knackered but an enjoyable trot with only a couple of blisters. Found an empty and relaxed BC.

SAT. 24. One of best parties ever at L. Terawan. Started with tea and cocktail-party atmosphere in main room. Much easy sitting around and talking and bustle behind the scenes. Then a snack of rice in banana leaves and a good peanut sauce like saté, followed by a huge and quite delicious feast of mainly tame pig. Really excellent food. Then after a while the singing to people began and we all had at least 3 glasses of borak, but not too much, and after that no need to drink more borak and plenty of beer. Najat dancing by everyone – all quite painless – followed much later by rock music, to which everyone freaked out until dawn. Not much recollection of the night but was up most of it, I think. About 5 of us did see it right through. I remember dancing a lot and getting a big blister on my toe again – teaching Agnes [a Berawan], Betty, etc. how to rock and roll – long talks with people – Imelda [a Berawan] and Jane [Marshall]. Sandy [Evans] given new name, Pada-ulay, youngest brother of Senan (John Proctor), Oyau Abeng (me), Tebengang (Nigel), etc. Then I made a speech in English, followed by JP in Berawan. Exact anniversary of my first time in L. Terawan on way upriver to build BC. [It was at this party that I was presented with what I was told was their most treasured possession as thanks for all we had done for them over the past year. It was a superb ancient *parang* in a wooden sheath with a handle carved in the shape of a hornbill. I was told that the blade, which was, and still is, razor sharp, had taken 100 heads. I have since presented it, together with all the other artefacts collected on my travels, to Eton's Natural History Museum, where it may be seen in a glass case.]

40 The Berawan *parang*, which had taken 100 heads.
Now in the Eton College Natural History Museum.

SUN. 25. Rather naughtily slipped away at about 6 with Fred [Wanless], Paul [Chai], Jane [Marshall] and Nathan [Sammy] and sped home in the jetboat. Incredible feeling flying through the thick dawn mist on the river, with dazzling views of Mulu and Api rising above. Feeling pretty ghastly, but Nulacin had prevented the worst and I was not sick, for once! However, I was good for nothing for the rest of that day and not much cop the next, so perhaps although one suffers less by taking the magic pills, it also prolongs the agony.

MON. 26. Found about 30 huge cockroaches in my boxes and clothes and put down mothballs. Also met a 7 inch [18 cm] centipede which I chopped in half with my parang. Both ends went on wriggling and fighting until they were pushed down between the floorboards.

MON. 3 JULY. [I flew in an RMAF helicopter from Miri to Mulu.] Collected 3 more drums of fuel from the airport. Picked up 4 scientists and 3 Berawan from Base Camp for Camp 5 and had a recce of Benarat after dropping them. Then flew straight to Bario, seeing Long Seridan and Long Patik on the way. Dramatic Shangri-La arrival over a high ridge to see down into the shining valley where wet padi fields glint in the sun. Landed and a friendly reception from the Kelabits while we shopped for rice and artefacts and the MAS 'plane came in and left. I decided to walk to the salty spring with Affendi, the co-pilot, Malcolm [Coe] and three police Field Force. It was said to be one hour, but we took two with stops. I walked fast ahead. Very different swampy stunted forest with lovely rhododendrons – white and red – nepenthes, birds and a completely different vegetation and general feel to things. A good path on white sand, elevated above ditches running with tea-coloured water with lots of wet places, so that I was hard put to it to keep my feet dry in silly suede shoes, but there had been no time to change at Base Camp. Passed a swing bridge and longhouse before the spring, which was unattractive, being a concrete tank and corrugated hut, but interesting. There are eight half oil drums in which the salty water is boiled until only the salt is left. Said to be a better one – hot? – where the resulting salt is white – about five hours' walk further on. Had excellent army compo makan cooked in minutes by the men on solid fuel – rice and curried chicken flavoured with bunga kantan – like a lotus, a big water lily, pink and white and bulbous – all eaten with the hands. Solid fuel a good idea and only costs 10p for a packet of 10 here. Walked back fast and reached airfield in 1½ hrs. Then walked a long way along a road to the pengulu's house on a hill. David Labang's cousin, a nice sensible youngish man who was pleased to see us all. Quite cool in the evening. Showered and given mattresses.

Saw a smallish brown bittern flying over the padi. Longhouses here built like fortresses – often on a square. Everything here has an Alpine atmosphere. The individual houses are solid, often two-storey and chalet-like. It is cold at night and there is something solid and secure about the people – reliable.

Tue. 4. Took off about 9.30. A memorable flight skimming very low through the gap over the ridge out of the valley. Then over very wild country, some limestone at first, then jungle for a long way – impenetrable hilly country. Then up above 6,000 ft [1,800 m] with only the top of Mulu appearing through the cotton wool. A glimpse of L. Seridan and a sight of a great many big landslides in the Mulu foothills. Just able to get down to Base Camp, where I was dropped off.

THUR. 6. Nigel never fails to amaze me with his constant good humour and hard work. He is still very much the rock upon which the expedition is founded – and he has no apparent jealousy, which is refreshing.

My own personal most lasting memory of life at Base Camp will be the walk I took most nights down to the steps above the river at about midnight. The sound of frogs and crickets is much louder there and it's much lighter than one realises inside the longhouse – on moonlit nights light enough to read. Looking back I can see the sleeping longhouse, with the trees towering above it and behind. An oil lamp burns in the kitchen to light the way to the jamban and there is another in Nigel's bilek where he is always working until the small hours. The most remarkable thing about him is that he can be so good-tempered with so little sleep.

41 Base Camp from the air. Note the floating raised walkway and landing raft to cope with floods.

These have been my happiest and most contented moments on the expedition. The constant minor worries and problems of the day seem very insignificant under the vast dark sky in the middle of so much night activity. There is also a deep sense of achievement in standing back and looking at all we have built up here and knowing that some 30 people are sleeping safely there.

FRI. 7. Boat from L. Iman with Tauee and his son – about 8 y.o. – who had been bitten on the toe by an 18′ [5.5 m] black snake, described as being as thick as a big toe. The foot was very swollen and they had tied on a tourniquet above the ankle. I gave him 1 Piriton and 1 Veganin, laid him out on the bench by the clinic bilek with his leg hanging down. Took his temperature and pulse every 15 mins – fairly steady and just above normal. They had covered the bite with powdered 78 gramophone record – a well-known local cure which, when removed later, seemed to have burned off all the skin around – although snakebite itself can have the same effect. Later Rosie [Sadler] and John Masterton [a vet from Jamaica] came back and took over. Main danger is shock and renal failure.

SAT. 8. Made a board from the lid of a stores box and a handle for waterskiing. Stood up on the board easily and made several passes of the longhouse but failed to turn round. Board of very rough planks with nails sticking out. Sped down to below rapid 7 and drove back in minutes. A very thrilling boat [belonging to Ralph Brown, who later left the RGS more than £1 million in his will to support future expeditions]. Slide show in evening with homemade projector Phil [Leworthy] had made up out of a biscuit tin, a bulb and an old camera lens. Really quite good. Heavy rain over commentary by Nigel.

SUN. 9. It is still – and always will be – sheer magic when a group of Penan arrives at BC. Father first, whose name I know by now, and who greets me with a smile. Three small children next with packs on, then the mother, bent under hers and not looking up, and lastly the eldest son carrying a blowpipe, selabit and spare quivers and walking proudly at the back. Barefoot all with sarongs and shorts or loincloths and no shirts.

The tropical lethargies get one increasingly often as time goes on. I still feel as well as ever in my life here, but some days it is impossible to generate energy and the temptation is to sleep all the time. I feel guilty when there are scientists in camp who have only a few weeks here and are trying to fill every minute, but one shouldn't really fight it too hard. Fred [Wanless] today commented that when I got back from Bario I was 'chirpy as a cricket' for a couple of days, but it was noticeable that I wasn't any more.

MON. 10. Almost alone in BC. Katie playing somewhere – a background childish chatter. It was good idea to bring a child along. The cats making a sudden miaow or a quick race and tumble along the veranda. Always something happening in the men's house – wood being chopped, dogs scrapping, cocks crowing. And behind it all always, but noticed less as time goes on, the birds and frogs and crickets and insects of the forest.

WED. 12. [Lord (John) Hunt, the then president of the RGS and leader of the successful first Everest ascent, and his wife Joy arrived by helicopter. They had brought out with them from England the 300 gilded medallions we had had made by Spink, the coin and medal specialists, to reward all who took part in the expedition. This was the first time an RGS expedition had presented medals to their team since David Livingstone's day.] Sam Welch [Air Commodore], wearing a six-shooter on his hip and in battle fatigues, and two other smartly turned out RMAF officers arrived with the Hunts. Hunts very gentle and pleased to have arrived. Sam kept calling John Hunt 'Your Lordship' and was delighted with his medallion [he was probably the first person to receive one].

FRI. 14. John and Joy Hunt climbed both Batus Pajang but he had a bad fall on the way down, cut himself and lost his gold Rolex. Rosie and I set off from the Paku bridge and walked through dark luminous forest quite fast – monkeys and argus pheasants calling and a very loud underground cricket – to Camp 1. We brought whisky for John H., which was very welcome. I slept on the floor next to him.

SUN. 16. Deer Cave picnic. Tony Lamb [a visiting botanist] found an Arachnis lowii orchid, one of the most interesting orchids ever found because of its size and an amazing scented yellow flowers and unscented red flowers hanging down up to 10 feet [3 m] on the inflorescence.

I had a long session helping Alan [Lloyd-Smith] remove a tooth from a very brave and pretty lady, wife of a man from a logging camp (Nam Hua). It was rotten and kept crumbling and v. painful. I had to hold her head blindfolded, comfort her and hold her hands very tight. A nice evening sitting next to Nyapun on the veranda with Anyi on my lap and all the rest of the family round, playing Penan musical instruments.

WED. 19. All the Penan turned up to see Mark off. I was near to tears. Very much the end of an era and the best of the scientific bunch leaving after a year.

FIRST CLOCKWISE CIRCUIT OF API

[WED. 19. CONT.] Nyapun and I set off upriver [the others had gone ahead], but when we reached the Melinau crossing we found it flooding down and much too deep to ford. I tried and was soon up to my waist. Nyapun started building a tiny sulap for us, which he finished in about an hour and he got a good fire going. We then had a simply delicious supper. Tender mouse deer, which N had gone and shot with his blowpipe. This and the rice were cooked inside bamboos which, after pouring out the meaty juice from one, were then split open revealing the tightly packed steaming contents. Also ready was boiling water in a third bamboo, for coffee. As a side dish he had tasty strips of smoked babi, which is always good, but one does need a toothpick badly afterwards. I lay and read and dozed while he set off to try for another mouse deer, armed only with a parang.

THUR. 20. Woke every hour or so through the night – but in utter heaven being self-sufficient with Nyapun. Went and had a look at the river before midnight, but still up and so slept on and off until 4 when I went out and had another look and found it right down in the still faint moonlight. Woke Nyapun, sleeping on the ground beside me, and we easily waded across, holding on to the rope. Walking on in the dark was pleasant and exhilarating. A big fright at one point when a large unidentified flying object (it looked about 2 feet [60 cm] body with a one foot [30 cm] tail, beige and furry) jumped across from one tree to another in front of me. Tony Lamb, later, after much thought, said it was probably a civet. Reached Camp 5 at 6.15 just as everyone

42   Ta'ee, Edmund, me, John and Joy Hunt, Nyapun and Sabang on the first clockwise circuit of Gunung Api. Taken by Tony Lamb.

was waking up. Splendid porridge breakfast. Party of eight, consisting of two Hunts, Tony Lamb, Edmund [a Berawan], Sabang, Nyapun, Ta'ee and me, set off at 8 and made fairly good progress up the gorge and the two ridges to Mark's and my camp, which we reached just as it started to rain at 2 p.m.

Had a happy and relaxed afternoon eating, talking and lying in our hammocks. All went at Tony's call to watch a fine view of Benarat from behind the camp. [This was the cover picture of my subsequent book, *Mulu: The Rain Forest* (1980).]

FRI. 21. Straight across the two valleys and up to the 3,000′ [900 m] ridge where the sky was blue, the sun out and the views sublime, which was excellent for the Hunts. Took group photograph. Carried on down the steep hill – lots of loose stones and John H.'s foot swollen and painful – but easier than I remembered from going up the other way before. Tony being very interesting about flowers, fruit and birds. Reached Camp 6 at 11.50. Bathed in the pool (the Hunts in privacy in the deep one), washed some clothes and spread them to dry in the dappled sun, discussed going on to Philip [Leworthy]'s camp and decided to eat and stay. Able to relax and read for a bit – and also to treat wounds. A lot of leeches on the way down. Walked with Joy and Tony to the end of Hidden Valley.

SAT. 22. [...] Rather tired out the Hunts, who felt that four hours without a break or drink was too much. But we reached the Hutan and crossed the Paku to find Limin, Lusing's comely wife, making sago in the most decorative way imaginable on the river's edge. A pool of squeezed water, leaves spread on top for stamping sago through, brass bowl for scooping water over – and Limin looking as pretty as a picture.

Spent a pleasant time drinking tea at Seng's settlement and talking to him. Then trudged non-stop back to Base Camp talking quite a lot. Both JH's foot and Joy's shoulder giving quite a lot of pain. Brave work to get back by 5.

43 Limin, Lusing's wife, making sago.

44 John Hunt's hand being examined by our nurse, Rosie Sadler.

[John Hunt later wrote in the foreword to *Mulu: The Rain Forest*:

I have prided myself on being a competent navigator in thick weather and being reasonably fast and footsure on a mountain; I was clumsy and sluggish in the forest, disorientated, humbled by the speed and easy economy of movement, the intuitive sense of direction displayed by the forest-dwelling Penans and the Berawan people, by the skill of Robin himself and those who had adjusted to the conditions during more than twelve months' experience. I felt oppressed and exhausted by the sheer difficulties of travel beneath the dense, dark canopy, in humid heat and torrential rain, without a vista to lift my spirits. Yet at the end of a four-day journey across those rugged mountains Robin, who had escorted us, seemed to be as spruce and fresh as before we had started out.]

TUE. 25. A dear little slow loris (Nycticebus coucang) was collected from a logging camp and brought back to Base Camp.

SAT. 29. Big party followed by the prize-giving, which went like a bomb but took a long time. Some 54 people got medallions, handed out by John Hemming with a few words from me and a glass of borak from Nigel. Then a slide show entirely of people and faces, which was quite literally a howling success.

MON. 31. As I was coming back from my daily 6 a.m. bathe and wash, I heard Wilma [Lloyd-Smith] crying and chirping and running up and down the balcony from her room. I knew at once what had happened. A giant centipede we had been trying to catch for a couple of days and which lived between bilek 6 and the kitchen, had bitten her on the finger when she went to dry her hands on the towel. She was already in great pain, shooting right up her arm and with a bloody finger she kept shaking about. Embarrassed and sorry but clearly the most painful thing imaginable. It had hung on for a bit before dropping off and racing away. [Alan, her husband, and also a doctor, gave her an injection to knock her out and she slept all day!]

WED. 2 AUGUST. Walked to Green Cave with John Hemming. Saw the outline of Abe Lincoln in the Deer Cave for first time on way back.

45   Vast silhouette of Abe Lincoln. First spotted by John Hemming and me, this is now a main tourist attraction.

FRI. 4. Wilma's centipede was caught at last (or one like it) in Rosie's bilek. Phil pinned it down with his parang and Raban picked it up with two sets of tweezers. I rushed about and held the plastic box. A very frightening angry creature which charged around its prison at high speed and had horrible big jaws which would clearly cause a lot of damage even if they weren't highly poisonous. But clean and magnificent in its own way.

SAT. 5. In the afternoon Engan caught a delightful turtle about 9″ [23 cm] long off the raft. It had webbed feet with little claws at the end, a quite soft shell and a long neck which could reach its own length to the surface so that it could breathe through the inch-long trunk at the end of its face. I called it Jumbo as it was straight Disney, but it proved to have a very hard bite, though only hard plates, no teeth. We made a nice sandy bottom to one of the aquarium tanks, where it tried to paddle itself underground to hide. By raising the water level we were able to find out just how far it could stretch its neck up to breathe above the surface. Almost 10″ [25 cm] before it had to leave the sand and swim up a bit. Unkind, but interesting – and then we released it back into the river. Later, one very old Penan lady, Jawé Lewee, Nyapun's mother, and Lupung's wife Tina Ukau arrived with amoebic dysentery. Jawé was very weak and took a long time to reach the Penan house, having to stop and rest several times on the way. Alan put her on a drip, collected stool samples when she had to go off with diarrhoea and diagnosed amoebic dysentery. Meanwhile, I spoke to DMO [district medical officer] at 5.45 just before radio went off and started ball for flying doctor rolling.

SUN. 6. Carried Jawé across to helipad wrapped in a blanket and the flying doctor heli duly arrived. Tina Ukau didn't want to go at the last moment, but was bundled in as well as Ukau, who was going to look after her. All Penan gathered to say goodbye to her, as a good chance they won't see her again.

MON. 7. Climbed Batu Pajang slowly, collecting with Clive [Jermy]. Interesting watching him at work. Very capable and hard-working, fit and energetic and fearless of heights (apparently!). He found a lot of ferns and was very pleased. Also collected several millipedes and snails. We talked a lot about the future. I found some of the climb quite frightening going up – not technically difficult, but a long way down. Incredible views of Api and, on the other side, across to Usun

Apau and Dulit. Danny and I went to look for John Hunt's Rolex watch and FOUND IT! Almost halfway down the ridge and so didn't have to climb the 2nd batu. Reached Camp 1 at 4.45 and set off alone to walk back to BC. Thrilling walking and running fast alone in the dusk, so that I saw a lot of wildlife. About 6 silver leaf monkeys, a 3 ft [90 cm] monitor lizard surprised in one of the riverbeds. Several small squirrels in the trees and once, after Deer Cave, a black low animal loping along the path in front. Could have been a sun bear. During the day, Raban, swimming off the raft, came back with a 5″ [13 cm] scorpion from under the driftwood in the river; then went in again and caught a very dangerous 5′ [150 cm] krait with a red tail and red head (Bungarus flaviceps), an elapid. Raban (David Labang), when questioned or alert, puts his head on one side to listen, like a bird waiting for a worm.

TUE. 22. Chris Saunders, a veterinary student collecting blood samples from people and animals, saw a 4 ft [120 cm] long snake suspended in the narrow doorway as he was using the jamban, cutting off his escape and apparently ready to strike. He identified it as the dangerous common or Malayan krait (Bungarus candidus), reputedly even more poisonous than the notorious banded krait (Bungarus fasciatus) [made famous by Sir Arthur Conan Doyle in his Sherlock Holmes story 'The Adventure of the Speckled Band']. As he backed away into the farthest corner of the small square hut, the snake lost its balance and fell out through the door. Shane is back having walked from Kuala Tabuan, perhaps the longest walk anyone has done in a day. Raban back from Long Birar camp. Rather monstrous reports of deputy chief minister and party killing 2 mouse deer, one pig, a porcupine and catching lots of fish. All inside the national park. Should be mentioned without comment in a report.

WED. 23. In the evening we had a big party for the Penan. Very tranquil and relaxed; about 70 of them, mainly children, sitting round the veranda and being waited on by all of us. Just simple rice dishes, orange juice, barley sugar and cigarettes. Only Penan music and candlelight early, by which everyone danced in a gentle way. Such a relief not having to drink. Kayan did two long mime dances, the second one as funny and professionally timed as Marcel Marceau, which had us all rolling on the floor. Much talk later with the men about garu [incense wood], of which they say they have 44 katis [a Malay measure equivalent to 605 g] and which they want to take to Marudi and so avoid being ripped off by Usang!

THUR. 24. Long meeting with Penan and Raban talking about their future. Talk with Dr Alec Anderson who has very good and strong views on the Penan, which he is not afraid to express and which we must try and get him to write up for us, even though his nutritional info may not be released by the Sarawak govt.

SUN. 27. So this is my last evening and although it has been a great and memorable year I leave with no regrets, except for Nyapun, to whom I may not be able to say goodbye.

*

He did come to say goodbye and his whole family came with him. As the last helicopter landed across the river from Base Camp to take the last of us out, I saw them standing clustered close together in the shade at the edge of the clearing. With great dignity, each in turn came to me and hugged me, forcing woven bracelets over my hands as we cried unashamedly. Little Anyi, laughing and weeping at the same time, flung herself into my arms. Nyapun and I just held each other for a long time, until a shout from the helicopter crew made me break away. We took off and our Berawan friends, who had helped us load our final baggage, crouched under the wind of the rotor blades. They were staying behind to clear up the charred remains of our Base Camp longhouse which, as agreed with the Temenggong, we had burned to the ground, so as to leave as little trace as possible of our having been there. As we rose into the air, I could see a row of slight figures carrying baskets and blowpipes as they trooped in single file out of the sunlight and back into the cool shade of their forest home.

46   Nyapun and his family waving goodbye
at the end of the expedition.

PART III

TODAY

The government says that it is bringing us progress and development. But the only development that we see is dusty logging roads and relocation camps.

Anderson Mutang Urud of the Kelabit people of Sarawak, address to the UN General Assembly, 10 December 1992

I have been back to Mulu several times since 1998, when I was first able to return. Most recently, I went for a few days in November 2015, as I had heard that Nyapun was not well, that he was asking for me and might not have long to live. I brought him some good large photographs of him and his people taken when we first met and told him that I was writing a book about him. I told him that his name was already known all over the world to people who cared about Borneo, its rainforest and its people, especially the Penan. I didn't tell him that I had recently been on a BBC radio programme called *The Museum of Curiosity*, in which guests from all walks of life donate fascinating exhibits to a vast imaginary museum. I had chosen to donate him, so that he would live forever. Another guest on the same show, Ronni Ancona, donated Humphry Davy, the Cornish inventor of the miners' lamp. I found Nyapun frail and almost deaf and blind, but with the same sweet smile and evident affection as we hugged. Surrounded by his family in his little house on stilts by the Melinau River, in the Penan village of Batu Bungan, we looked at the photographs together and he was able to identify several of the people in them, including himself, looking strong and handsome, which made everyone laugh excitedly. To my great surprise, one of his grandsons, Kalang Noh, spoke excellent English, which he had learned at the village school, and he started translating as we spoke, so that we were able to communicate easily.

I told him some of the stories about him which I was putting in my book. How we had first met and how he had taken me to meet his family. He remembered it all clearly and said that he had waited a long time before stepping out of the shadows, as he had been very frightened, not knowing what sort of reception he would receive. 'But then,' he said, 'we met...' and I knew just what he meant. He remembered that I gave him an orange which he later shared with his family, giving each a segment. He told me they had never seen an orange before. Then he launched into a long dialogue about those times. 'Before you arrived,

I was always the one who had to provide for my family. After you came, it all changed. I remember how we travelled together and how I never needed anything. We always went faster than the others, like the Labang brothers, who came along behind. We were very strong then... When I was ill, you took me to Marudi in the jetboat and made me better. When Noh [Kalang's father] was ill you arranged a helicopter for him. I tried to find as many of my people in the forest, who were still nomadic, and to persuade them to come and work for a good white man.'

Ouch! Was I really responsible for so many uncontacted people coming in from the cold? Lots of Penan did come and work for our expedition and they earned good wages, but it gave me a pang of guilt to hear it put that way by Nyapun. I had many conversations in those days with Nyapun and other Penan about the pros and cons of settling and I always tried to give balanced advice, while warning them that if they did decide under pressure to settle it would not be easy. I asked him if he missed nomadic life.

'Yes!' he said, emphatically. 'They were happy times and I was young, but it was hard, as we were constantly on the move looking for food. Now I have a house and there is always food. We can still hunt and, now that the logging has stopped here, game is still fairly plentiful.' I was surprised to hear him saying this, as I had expected him to be more nostalgic about the past, but he is a realist and, although consistently one of the leading fighters against logging and other imposed change, such as missionary activity and being made to move into a longhouse, he had come to believe that it was inevitable. I asked him what he thought of the national park. Was it a good or a bad thing? 'Good,' he replied. 'It has created 400 jobs where there were none before and we can still use the land for hunting.'

It was sad to hear the resignation in his voice while we discussed this. The Penan in the Mulu area have had their land taken from them without any compensation and, as far as I know, there has been no movement to have any of it given back. But in other parts of Sarawak there are Penan campaigning to have relatively undisturbed territory, over which they have traditionally hunted and gathered, restored to them, and this would be an even better conservation solution than more national parks. Elsewhere in the world vast areas of land have been demarcated for tribal people, who now protect and manage it far better than those without their intimate and deep-rooted understanding of it ever could. At last the unassailable truth – that the best way to stop deforestation is to give back their land rights to indigenous people – is being recognised internationally. As I was writing this in July 2016, I read the following report from the news agency Reuters:

> Indigenous people are better than governments at preventing forests from being cut and should be seen as a solution, not a barrier to protecting them, the UN Special Rapporteur on the Rights of Indigenous People said [...]
>
> Indigenous peoples and communities have claims to two thirds of the world's land but are legally recognised as holding only 10 percent [...]
>
> Without title deeds, indigenous communities may find their land is taken over for major development projects such as palm oil plantations and logging.
>
> 'Society thinks that indigenous peoples are claiming land that they shouldn't be having because it should be used for expanded food production,' UN Special Rapporteur Victoria Tauli-Corpuz [said].
>
> But giving indigenous peoples rights to land was a guarantee that forests, which store carbon and contribute to food security would continue to exist.

Sadly this thinking is only now beginning to gain a glimmer of understanding again in Sarawak, although the Brookes practised it effectively for more than 100 years, even though it is politically incorrect to say so!

I asked if he had met Bruno Manser and Nyapun said he had. 'Was that when you were arrested for blockading a logging road?' I asked.

'No,' he replied. 'Bruno was not there then, but he sent us a message of support from Limbang. One hundred and five of us from Long Iman and Batu Bungan were sent to prison, all men and boys. No women.'

We talked of the *pantuns* he sang to me just before we left in

1978; how in the first one he had recalled all the good times we had had together and what fun it had been. As I looked into his rheumy eyes, I could see that he was remembering those days with delight and he squeezed my hand, which he held all the time we talked. Then I reminded him of the stories about his life, which he told me in the second one. I asked about the time of the Japanese. Although he had claimed in that *pantun* that he had taken their heads, he now denied it, but he looked embarrassed as he did so and I didn't press him. Maybe it is wise of him not to admit to having been a headhunter for a while.

'We were warned by the Berawan that the Japanese were on the way and Temenggong Mayang advised us to run away to Bario. I never killed any Japanese. I took care of my family. I met Tuan Sandy then and took him to see some waterfalls. I met Tuan Tom far up the Melinau and he asked me where I was from and he told me to go back and collect my family and take them to Bario. He said it would take 200 days, but we did it in 100. There were about 30 people in our group and the headman was Seng.' [Seng was still the headman of the Mulu Penan in 1977.]

I asked him about our Base Camp being called Long Pala ('the place of the heads') because so many Japanese heads were taken there, and he said:

47   Seng, the Penan headman.

'No, that was the name long before, because it was an ancient headhunting trail of the Iban and Kenyah people.'

When I taxed him on Rodney Needham he couldn't remember anything – he was getting tired – but he recalled well the meeting with the British Army during Confrontation and how his cousin Sugun had said that they were good people.

I visited him each day for three days while I was in Mulu. Sometimes we talked and someone interpreted. Sometimes we just sat in companionable silence, as we had done in the past. He gave me a small piece of gum wrapped in newspaper; he said it was a very powerful sacred charm which had belonged to his great grandfather and that it would protect me from storm and lightning, wherever I was.

I slipped him £100 in Malay ringgits 'in case of emergencies' and I gave him my book of photographs 'to remember me'. Only one of his two wives, Itang, the old and wrinkly one, who always looks rather grumpy but who clung lovingly to me, was there. Awing, the younger, was away in Limbang, but I had a momentary double take when I thought I saw her, devastatingly lovely and holding a young baby,

48   Two old men in 2015.

sitting near us. I quickly realised that it couldn't be Awing and asked who it was. Sure enough, it was Aren, Nyapun's youngest child, whom I had last seen as a baby. She was the spitting image of her mother and I told her so, to much delight and laughter.

When Nyapun grew tired, King, his eldest son and now head boatman at the park, took me by longboat a short way up the Melinau River to visit Anyi, the sweetest of Nyapun's daughters, who had been my rather bossy little protector during the expedition. The river was high and brown with flood water. Speeding over the surface, I was transported back to the days when we were exploring it for the first time. Now there were boats for hire to tourists moored along the bank and we passed other craft with rows of people in orange life jackets. But I was with a Penan and above such petty regulations, so that it was like old times as we passed the still beguiling and unspoiled landscape on the protected bank which was within the park. The next day I returned with just one guide, Veno, the park's head ranger, to the Garden of Eden, which I had first entered and named so many years before. I made it through Deer Cave, beyond the walkways and then up to the mouth of Green Cave without too much effort, but the slopes have grown steeper over the years and I thought it wiser not to try any more cave exploration that day, being in my eightieth year. I felt a deep peace being back among the sights and sounds of Mulu, and especially in a part where absolutely nothing had changed. During the day I was able to hear the distant whoop, whoop cry of gibbons, still there, deep inside the park. In the morning the first sound was often the familiar song of the babbler we called the Beethoven bird because it sings, over and over, the first four notes of his Fifth Symphony: da-da-da-dum, with the last note always slightly off-key. In the evening the reliable six o'clock cicada broadcast its deafening, chainsaw-like message that night was about to fall. And in the darkness there was always a cacophony of frogs, especially one which sounded just like a very loud and determined person shouting 'WHAT?' as I walked past, making me start. Others answered, equally urgently, from all around and I was tempted to yell back at them.

I stayed in one of the excellent bungalows at the park headquarters. The changes to Mulu since we were there in the 1970s have been monumental. Most of the forest around has been clear-felled and several of the little limestone hills (*batus*), including the one we used to climb behind our Base Camp, have been bulldozed to allow bigger planes to land at the now quite large airport. There is a bridge across the Melinau right by where our Base Camp was, and a luxury modern hotel, recently acquired by the Marriott group, has been built on the opposite bank, just on the edge of the park. The headquarters is a model of its kind, with a good cafe/restaurant as well as the bungalows. There is also a very well-designed interpretation centre and I had a nostalgic time wandering through and quietly congratulating myself on what we had helped to bring about. One of the most recent contributions we were able to make was to have Mulu, the largest national park in Sarawak, designated a World Heritage Site. This was largely due to the efforts of Ian Swingland, who had been the herpetologist on our expedition and who went on to found the Durrell Institute of Conservation and Ecology (DICE). Most of our continuing relationship with the park has been through our cavers who, under the leadership of Andy Eavis, have been back year after year to confirm Mulu as arguably the greatest caving site in the world. It is full of superlatives: Sarawak Chamber is the biggest cave chamber in the world; Deer Cave is the largest cave passage; the Clearwater Cave System may contain the largest volume of cave anywhere. The caves teem with life. At the top of the food chain are the snakes, cave racers 2.5 metres long, which feed on the cave swiftlets, the largest colony in the world, and the 3 million bats of 28 species which fly in and out each day. Deer Cave alone has 12 species of bat, the highest number of species occupying a single cave ever recorded. Bats are vitally important as pollinators in the rainforest, where they comprise half the mammal species to be found there, globally. Among the more than 500 species of plant that rely partly or often wholly on bats to pollinate their flowers or disperse their seeds are kapok, eucalyptus, durian, mango, clove, banana, guava, avocado, breadfruit, ebony, mahogany and cashew. Bats range in size from the largest, with a 1.5-metre wingspan, to one of the contenders to be the smallest mammal in the world, which is the size of a bumblebee. The guano produced by all the bats and birds using the caves produces vibrant life down below, too, from blind white fish and crabs in the underground streams to the myriad insects and beetles, spiders, cockroaches, centipedes, moths and earwigs.

Outside the caves is tropical rainforest supporting some of the greatest diversity of living organisms on earth. Half of all life on the planet is to be found in rainforests, which only cover 2 per cent of the earth's surface, and much of it is in Mulu. There are more than 80 species of mammal, including tarsiers, which haven't changed for 45 million years, the longest record of any primate. There are 17 vegetation zones, from the towering dipterocarp forests on the lower land to the soggy moss forests high on Mount Mulu itself. Only coastal mangroves are not represented there. Mulu is one of the richest sites in the world for palms, with approximately 111 species and 20 genera recorded. To date more than 4,000 species of fungi have been recorded and 1,500 flowering plants. Of the 81 mammals recorded, several are endemic to Mulu, and the other contender for the title of smallest mammal in the world, the Savi's pygmy shrew, *Suncus etruscus*, which weighs only 2 grams, is also found. In addition, there are 270 birds, 20,000 invertebrates, 55 reptiles, 76 amphibians and 48 species of fish, as well as 80 per cent of Borneo's Lepidoptera and an infinite number of smaller plants and creatures yet to be discovered.

One evening, I was invited by the park director to give an illustrated talk at the airport, that being the largest venue. Several hundred people turned up: familiar Berawan faces, many now working for the park or the hotel and some recalling the time they worked for me; lots of Penan from Batu Bungan, including rows and rows of very well-behaved schoolchildren from both communities; and some tourists from many nations. I was introduced flatteringly as 'the founder of Mulu', and at first in my rusty Malay, then through an interpreter, I told them how there had been nothing there when we arrived in 1977, except for a simple forest hut marking the Forestry Department's commitment to research the newly created national park; how more than 100 top scientists from all over the world had studied everything and how we had all grown to love Mulu. I showed them the BBC film we had made 38 years before, *Mysteries of the Green Mountain*, and presented to the park the large portfolio of photographs from those days. Everyone crowded round to help identify the people in the pictures. Shyly, a wrinkled old lady pointed at one of a group of pretty girls by the river and said: 'That was me!' A young man pointed to a baby and declared: 'That was my father!' It made us all realise just how long ago it had been, but everyone was eventually named and the pictures now grace the walls of the park headquarters, with captions below.

Next day I toured the primary school in Batu Bungan, a modern building with many classrooms, each of which I visited, and I had fun getting those whose parents or grandparents had been part of our expedition to put their hands up. There was a good atmosphere and, apparently, no discrimination against the Penan children, who made up about half the pupils. It was not always so. On my first return visit in 1998 I had found the school just starting, but with no provision for the special needs of the Penan, who had no funds for uniforms, books and so on, and so they were not going there. We started a Penan Fund after I lectured about Mulu at the RGS and we were able to send some £10,000 to help the children of the then only recently settled Penan get a fair start in life. Now the headmaster, a Kelabit from Long Seridan, said all were treated equally and he found the Penan children just as bright and ready to learn as the rest, if not more so.

On my last night in Mulu, I lay awake thinking about all that had happened since I had lived there for 15 months. I rehearsed the dreadful story of our heavenly *batu* behind Base Camp: all the times we watched the sunset from there, how we sometimes slept there, and how much of our research was done right there, next to Base Camp and actually just outside the park; and then how, to expand the potential for large aircraft to land, it and two others nearby were bulldozed down, leaving a horrid scar which has not healed. This was just happening when I returned in 1998 and it was a terrible sight, which made me very angry. In spite of international protests and proof of a rare, if not unique, orchid being found there, it all went ahead. As ever in Sarawak/Malaysia, commercial potential (often not fulfilled) trumped scientific and environmental sense, let alone the preservation of beauty. One of the Berawan I spoke to about it this time said he never understood why the airfield had to go where it is today. We and they had always understood that it would be on the large area of flat and pretty useless land down towards Kuala Melinau on the true left bank – the same side of the river as the park and so no need for a bridge and all the development that went with that. But then again, after such a wonderful, loving visit, I couldn't help feeling a warm glow that we had played our part in saving at least a small piece of Eden in a huge, now ravaged, country.

If all human endeavour is dictated by the pursuit of happiness, then how does Sarawak stack up? On the one hand, there has been massive environmental destruction, on a scale we could never have imagined in our worst nightmares when we first came to Mulu. If wildlife and vegetation can feel happiness, then those running the country for the last 40 years have done a very bad job. From being perhaps the richest place in the world in biological terms, much of it has been transformed into a desert, where the best trees have been ripped out over vast tracts of country, leaving behind logging roads, erosion and much less diversity. This has also caused the rivers, once so rich in fish and other aquatic life, to become brown and often virtually sterile, the effluent staining the sea far out from the coast. Elsewhere, swathes of landscape have been converted to palm-oil plantations, a virtually sterile crop which, once our global passion for its products (detergent, soap, lipstick, ice cream, margarine, pizza dough, and so on) ends, as it certainly will one day, the land will never recover, because it is a terminal crop. Biodiesel and other biofuels will before long go the way of petrochemicals and gas, to be replaced by clean, renewable energy as electric cars become the norm. The lifestyle of the people has also been changed beyond recognition. Where once they lived lives which have been described in glowing terms by anthropologists and travellers as among the richest, most stable and – yes – happiest of any on earth, now the remaining game in the forest, fish in the rivers and soil along the eroding banks are not enough to support an increasingly demanding existence in the twenty-first century. As a result, rural areas are being depopulated and, as in so many places around the world, we see a massive migration to cities and a different way of life.

It didn't have to be like this. The huge wealth of the country could have been exploited sustainably and in a manner that benefitted all in the long run, and not just filled a few obscenely fat Swiss bank accounts. Of course, a large part of the problem was caused by Britain's postwar urge to divest itself of all colonial responsibilities as quickly as possible. Many people believe that Sarawak should never have been made to join the Federation of Malaya, and that the Brooke family should never have been treated so cavalierly. If it were to join, it should at least have been allowed to keep a fair share of the oil, if not all of it. Then it could have become one of the richest and best-preserved states in the world, both environmentally and culturally. Look at little Brunei, the fifth-wealthiest country on the planet and with nearly all its forest still intact. The obsession with 'development' has caused much more damage to the country, at the same time wrecking the rainforest. Sarawak's existing dams can already provide more power than the state needs, but plans have been made to build one on the Baram, which would flood 388 km² of forest and drive 20,000 people from their homes. Following years of protest by tribal people, not least the Penan, and supported by Survival International, this dam has been shelved for the time being. But despite having no market for the electricity they will produce, the government still want to build this one and many more, which will have a devastating effect on the remaining lowland forests as well as their traditional inhabitants.

It didn't have to be like this. Over the years leading scientists and thinkers, statesmen and politicians, as well as campaigners, have raised their voices to protest at what was going on. In 1990, when the destruction of Borneo's rainforests was at its height, Prince Charles made a major speech at Kew Gardens pleading for the world to take notice of what was happening. In it he drew attention to tribal people, and especially the Penan:

> It seems to me important that any discussion about the tropical forests should start by looking at the people who depend directly on them for their livelihood. This includes both indigenous people and relatively recent settlers, but the main focus of concern must be

on the remaining tribal people for whom the tropical forest has been their home for many generations. Their story has been told many times, and it is one of which we must all be profoundly ashamed. Ever since the first explorers from Spain and Portugal set foot in South America, and the British visited the Caribbean, the people of the so-called 'developed world' have always treated people as total savages, be it to enslave them, subdue, 'civilise' them, or convert them to our way of religious thinking. The latter activity seems to be remarkably widespread and can cause unimaginable confusion and suffering. Even now, as the Penan in Sarawak are harassed and even imprisoned for defending their own tribal lands, and the Yanomami in Brazil are driven into extinction by measles, venereal disease or mercury poisoning following the illegal invasion of their lands by gold prospectors – even now, that dreadful pattern of collective genocide continues. It is not just those who depend directly on the tropical forests who suffer from deforestation, but the entire population of tropical forest countries.

Sylvia Earle is one of the world's great oceanographers. She has been a heroine of mine ever since I had the delight of hosting and interviewing her before a large South Bank audience during the 2010 London Literature Festival. At the end there was a question about the recent oil spill in the Gulf of Mexico, which was the main horror news item at that time, with pictures of oily birds and ruined fishing communities. It was her main research area and so she was probably the top expert on it. She replied that it had not been bad enough. There was an appalled gasp and absolute silence in the hall. She let it ride for a bit and then explained forcefully that in a few years it would all be forgotten and drilling would continue as before. We needed a major man-made catastrophe to shake us out of our complacency. How right she was! She went on to write, later:

> Fifty years ago, we could not see limits to what we could put into the ocean, or what we could take out. Fifty years into the future, it will be too late to do what is possible right now. We are in a 'sweet

spot' in time when the decisions we make in the next ten years will determine the direction of the next 10,000.

Compare this to rainforest destruction. We may not be in a 'sweet spot', as with the oceans, but there is a similarity. Although not as obviously, in that there is no equivalent of our dependence on the oceans for fish, we do depend on rainforests in many ways – from charcoal to climate – and we are beginning to feel the pinch. Stopping commercial fishing would pretty well solve the marine crisis, although the pollution and plastic issues would still be severe for several hundred years, even if all pollution stopped now. Ending deforestation wouldn't solve the problems it has caused for a long time either, as so much damage has been done, although if it could only happen with the informed consent of the traditional landowners, there would be a lot less of it! Neither is going to happen immediately, of course, but it is interesting to speculate, and to hope that sense will prevail.

We came to Mulu at the end of a golden age. We were so lucky to be there just then. There were worries about how the logging industry was beginning to accelerate, but no one imagined how bad it was about to be. It was only 15 years after independence and everyone, from the chief minister to the local civil servants, the RMAF and especially the local Dayak people, was supportive of what we were doing and sterling in their help. After we left, having produced perhaps the most definitive Management Plan ever of a national park, one which demonstrated scientifically and unequivocally the dangers of uncontrolled deforest-ation, things began to go downhill. At the same time as our research and publications were sparking the global movement to protect rain-forests everywhere, in Sarawak the granting of logging licences and the rate of destruction accelerated exponentially. Meanwhile, almost immediately after we had left, having deposited our last samples at the Sarawak Museum and handed out medals to all who had helped us, we heard that we were being accused of 'neocolonial exploitation'. Totally unjustified stories circulated that we had stolen plant specimens and sent them home, without leaving a first example at the museum. We were told, after a time, that we were not welcome, and it was many years before we were able to return. The devastation of Sarawak's forests had begun and no one was going to stop it. Over the next 20 years and thereafter, according to *The Economist*, Sarawak has lost more than 90 per cent of its lowland primary forests to logging and has had the fastest rate of deforestation in Asia. This has been accompanied by abuses against indigenous groups, including harassment and illegal evictions, while allegations of corruption and abuse of public office have dogged successive chief ministers, who have retained firm control over the granting of logging licences.

In November 2015, the twenty-first Conference of the Parties (COP) took place in Paris. We now have the best chance of saving the planet from the damage we are doing to it. More than 190 countries agreed in Paris to keep global temperature rise this century well below 2 degrees Celsius and to drive efforts to limit the temperature increase even further to 1.5 degrees Celsius above pre-industrial levels. And the role of rainforests is not only being highlighted once again, but their significance is being quantified. Because at last the scientific community is beginning to accept and put up-to-date figures on what our Mulu scientists were saying 40 years ago. Not chopping forests down is the best way of controlling levels of carbon dioxide in the atmosphere and limiting the impact of climate change. Trees capture carbon more efficiently than any man-made technology. It is pretty obvious really, when you think about it for a moment, but it has taken until now for the scientific community to wake up to this fact. What we are all trying to do now, rather desperately and at the last moment – to recycle and reduce carbon dioxide – has been done throughout the ages and is being done today by the world's plants and trees. They pump out 120 billion tonnes of carbon every year. (Man-made emissions account for about 10 billion tonnes.) But even better, they then breathe it all in again plus another 1.6 billion tonnes. In other words, they scrub global carbon-dioxide emissions more effectively than any man-made procedure can. And yet every year we cut down, clear or burn 32 million acres of forest, an area about the size of the whole of Sarawak.

This releases huge amounts of carbon dioxide into the atmosphere, about the same amount as all the cars, boats and planes in the world. Worse, it weakens the planet's natural ability to cure the problem. In Paris this ridiculous state of affairs has at last been addressed seriously, but, as ever, short-term politics and greed are likely to get in the way.

It is self-evident that when practising hunting and gathering the Penan do live in harmony with nature. The very idea of doing this has become a cliché in modern times and yet, without having to emulate their lives, which Western people would find impossible, we live in an era when it is once again possible to do so. The Penan move through the forest harvesting the sago and wild boar in a cycle which, provided the forest remains intact, is eminently sustainable. Their energy requirement is minimal: just some damar gum, gathered from a dipterocarp tree to light their *sulaps* at night and perhaps some torch batteries acquired by trade. Twenty-first century society demands a lot of energy for almost everything we do and this has been a major contributor to the environmental destruction the world has experienced. Coal and oil have fuelled global warming, while biofuel production from palm oil in South East Asia and soya beans in Brazil has contributed to the removal of rainforests. The replacement of fossil fuels with renewable energy, a substitution which is happening faster than most of us can still barely comprehend, means that we can continue to enjoy modernity – everything from travel to iPhones to heating and air-conditioning – without ruining our environment in the process. What is more, if we could just stop fighting each other for long enough, we could design a world where there would be ample food for all, and that is the only way to start reducing our population. Because the only effective birth control is prosperity, whether for a self-sufficient nomad with no need to produce excess children, or for an affluent Scandinavian.

The demographic density of a society like the Penan living well off a rich habitat can be greater than the same land will produce when cleared. We established a nomadic Penan population of almost 500 in and around Mulu when it still had an extensive buffer zone. Although they were largely invisible, they were just as numerous as the various Berawan, Kenyah and Kayan people living away from the rivers. Research in the Amazon basin is increasingly revealing just how large the Indian population was before the conquistadores brought the European diseases which wiped most of them out. Today the substitution of the forest Indians with a handful of cattle ranchers when the rainforest is cleared and replaced with poor grazing on barren laterite can be compared with the supplanting of not just the Penan but also the self-sufficient longhouse communities on the rivers with indentured labourers toiling in the palm-oil plantations.

The Penan have been aware of the surrounding societies for thousands of years and have evolved their own extraordinarily highly developed cosmos both of beliefs and of knowledgeable relationships with all life. Is anything more important than this? All we, as human beings, can really do is to attempt to understand our environment and then manage it in the most appropriate way. This is what makes us different from animals: consciousness.

Nyapun, when I met him, epitomised this. He was the most compleat man I have ever known. He understood and managed everything about him: his family, his daily life. He was acutely aware of each plant, animal and insect. He was intensely at home in his world. Beyond that, he had a spiritual aura about him, the sort of subtle radiation described in much religious art – in Christianity as a halo. In group photographs he glows – look at him in the background of image no. 49.

He was also very mindful of the changes looming on his horizon. That was why he regarded the arrival of our expedition in general and me, as his special friend, in particular with such intense interest and affection.

In a way, my special feelings for Nyapun have informed my general desire, through Survival, to try to endorse the right of all tribal people to be recognised as at least as advanced as any of the myriad human societies that have evolved over time. The comparisons in terms of quality of life with our own Western materialism are ones we should all consider with due humility.

Of course, there have been many places where efficient agriculture has replaced forest clearance, although usually without the consent of any tribal people living there, and not all deforestation results in

49 Nyapun surrounded by his family and
a friend soon after we first met.

desertification. However, today most of the richer lowland has been
taken over by modern agriculture, for better or worse, and only the
more inaccessible and higher land is left and still clothed with rich and
diverse vegetation. This should not just be preserved for conservation
reasons. It should be recognised as belonging to the people who have
always lived there to cherish and manage, which they will do far better
than any modern scientists or development engineers ever could.

When we lived in Mulu in 1977–8, Sarawak was still a Garden of Eden,
occupied for millennia by man but largely undisturbed by him. Borneo
was the richest, greenest island in the world. In 1959, in an article titled
'An inward journey' for the *Sarawak Gazette*, Tom Harrisson described
the view from 3,000 metres:

> not a trace of human life anywhere below, just endless [...] jungle,
> mountain, and torrent, ineffably dark green [...] For thirty or forty
> miles, run range after range after range of sandstone ridges, cut with
> waterways, aged and feeling infinitely ancient. This way, quite lost in

the air-world, one realises the tremendous scale of Borneo's interior
and the almost insignificant effect man has had upon it.

This was how it still looked to us 20 years later. Alas! No more. Today,
flying over the country is a depressing business. Large swathes are covered in the regular patchwork quilts of palm-oil plantations and most
of the remaining forested areas have ominous red scars winding through
them, as the loggers prepare to invade the last and most inaccessible
regions. There are still pristine places to be found, like the remoter
highlands and Mulu, although few are privileged, as I was in 2014, to
travel through the rarely visited interior of the park. An impression
of what most of Borneo used to look like can be gained from the
raised walkways and the well-marked paths, and the 'Interpretation
Centre' is a model of its kind; but the immense lungs of the country
are gone, most of the rivers no longer run clear and blue, and far too
much of the diversity upon which all life, not least man, depends
is no more.

The reasons I have written this book are to record what life was like
at that time in a still-pristine rainforest in Borneo, with people who were
still leading their traditional lives; a time when the scientific research
we were doing was changing the way rainforests were viewed; when
Survival International was young and still seeking its role in defending
the rights of tribal people, so that my time spent among some of the
last truly nomadic people in the world, who were also highly articulate
and aware of their problems, was intensely rewarding and stimulating.
That environment and those people have changed so rapidly since I was
there that a glimpse into that past, partly seen through the eyes of my
dear old friend, Nyapun, who showed me so much, may be of interest.
It is never too late to begin to put things right. Nature is wonderfully
resilient, and so are the people of the forest. Even today, when everything looks so bleak, the forests that are left would expand if they were
allowed to do so, and those who have lived there for millennia would
cherish and manage them better than we ever could, if they were put
in charge. That is all we ask.

The River

by Robin Hanbury-Tenison

There is a river of the clearest blue
Which runs from deep inside a limestone mountain.
Its water, filtered by the ground-down shells
And skeletons of untold millions of once molluscs,
Has no sediment or particles to cloud its purity.
Fish swim in full view, even in the deepest pools,
And when it rushes over shallows no froth forms.
The banks are wide and low, giving views
Of high white cliffs on either side.
Broad reaches dapple slow and islands form,
Where giant trees grow, free to spread
Unhindered by the usual forest crowd.
Some came to fish or hunt for pig;
And later others came with nets and boxes to collect
The rich and varied fauna and the wealth
Of plants and ferns, mosses and flowers
Nurtured by river, rain and heat.
Centuries have come and gone and seen no change;
The river free from settlement, guarded by rocks
And rapids, made the trees safe from the axe,
The land from fire and spade.
Now they have found it and the world is hungry.
The river's days are numbered as a paradise;
For Eden is but produce in the eyes of greedy men.

(written on the Medalam in Mulu, October 1977)

50   Anyi.

Members of the Sarawak Government and Royal Geographical Society Mulu (Sarawak) Expedition, 1977–8

The Mulu (Sarawak) Expedition 1977–8 was an international field-research programme organised by the RGS, London, and sponsored and supported by the Sarawak government. The team, led by Robin Hanbury-Tenison, adopted a multidisciplinary approach, enabling scientists from many universities and institutes to contribute to a geographical survey of the Gunung Mulu National Park, to assist its future management and long-term conservation.

For 15 months scientists and volunteer field assistants from 11 nations operated from a temporary purpose-built 'longhouse' at the edge of the park. More than 100 field scientists surveyed the soils, rivers, caves, plants and animals of this 52,864-hectare park, on foot and by longboat. This research was co-ordinated by the tropical botanist Clive Jermy from the British Museum (Natural History), forest botanist Paul Chai from the Forestry Department, Kuching, and zoologist Lord Medway (now Earl of Cranbrook). Research projects varied in duration from a few weeks to 15 months.

The results of the survey were published in the *Sarawak Museum Journal* (vol. xxx, no. 51, part 1 (1982) and part 2 (1984)) and in many peer-reviewed journals. Original copies of these are held by the RGS together with the Management and Development Plan (edited by Clive Jermy and Lord Medway) presented to the Sarawak government in 1979 and the book of the project, *Mulu: The Rain Forest*, written by the leader, Robin Hanbury-Tenison.

The model of field scientists, young and old, from different nations and many disciplines working together closely in the field, with the common goal of a detailed geographical study of the whole Mulu landscape, was scientifically productive and cost-effective. Much of the success was due to the support and hard work given by the local Berawan and Penan communities, who joined as guides, rangers, boat drivers, interpreters, field assistants and logistic-support personnel. The scientific results, biodiversity inventory and mapping of the unique Mulu caves and pinnacles led to the park being designated a UNESCO World Heritage Site in 2000. This successful format was developed by the RGS for subsequent research programmes in many parts of the world from 1978 onwards, under the overall supervision of Dr John Hemming, the director and secretary.

Nigel Winser, deputy field director

ABBREVIATIONS

ADK	Department of Agriculture, Kuching
BM(NH)	British Museum (Natural History), London
DID	Department of Irrigation and Drainage, Kuching
FDK	Forestry Department, Kuching
NPWO	National Parks and Wildlife Office, Kuching, Miri
RBGE	Royal Botanic Gardens, Edinburgh
RBGK	Royal Botanic Gardens, London (Kew)
RGS	Royal Geographical Society, London
SMK	Sarawak Museum, Kuching
SMS	Sarawak Medical Services, Kuching, Miri, Marudi
UM	University of Malaya, Kuala Lumpur

NAME	PROGRAMME/ ROLE	UNIVERSITY/ AFFILIATION/PLACE OF RESIDENCE
Alec Anderson	*Human Ecology Survey*	SMS, Kuching
Jo Anderson	*Forest Ecology (litter fauna)*	University of Exeter
Robb Anderson	*Forest Survey (director)*	University of Edinburgh and Singapore
George Argent	*Forest Survey (flowering plants and mosses)*	RBGE
Peter Ashton	*Forest Survey (flowering plants)*	University of Aberdeen
Gary Bagong	*Soil Survey (assistant)*	FDK
Ian Baillie	*Soil Survey (co-director)*	North London Polytechnic
Henry Barlow	*Faunistic Survey (moths and butterflies)*	Malaysian Nature Society, Kuala Lumpur
Colin Bertram	*RGS Expeditions Committee (chairman)*	RGS
Junaidi Bolhassan	*Human Ecology Survey*	SMK
Barry Bolton	*Faunistic Survey (invertebrates/ants)*	BM(NH)
Dave Brook	*Speleological Survey*	University of Leeds
Ralph Brown	*Field Support (jetboat team)*	Hamilton Jet Boats, New Zealand

NAME	PROGRAMME/ ROLE	UNIVERSITY/ AFFILIATION/PLACE OF RESIDENCE
Jameson Buaw	*Human Ecology Survey*	SMK
Paul Chai	*Sarawak scientific liaison officer (trees and flowering plants)*	FDK
Phil Chapman	*Speleological Survey (cave biology)*	University of Bristol
Kate Clark	*Field Support (catering)*	RGS
Algy Cluff	*RGS Mulu Sub-Committee*	RGS
Malcolm Coe	*RGS Mulu Sub-Committee*	University of Oxford
Mark Collins	*Forest Ecology (termites)*	Centre for Overseas Pest Research, London
Brian Coppins	*Forest Survey (lichens and fungi)*	RBGE
Joan Cramphorn	*Faunistic Survey (fish)*	Field Studies Council, Shrewsbury
Barbara Croxall	*Forest Survey (ferns)*	University of Cambridge
John Croxall	*Botanical and Faunistic Surveys (birds)*	British Antarctic Survey, Cambridge
Geoffrey Davison	*Faunistic Survey*	UM (pheasants)
Mick Day	*Landform and Hydrology Survey (geomorphology)*	University of Wisconsin

NAME	PROGRAMME/ ROLE	UNIVERSITY/ AFFILIATION/PLACE OF RESIDENCE
Rebecca Day	*Landform and Hydrology Survey*	Wisconsin
Constance Dennehy	*Field Support (medical doctor)*	London
John Dransfield	*Forest Survey (palms)*	RBGK
Julian Dring	*Faunistic Survey (amphibians and reptiles)*	BM(NH)
David Dunkerley	*Landform and Hydrology Survey (geomorphology)*	Monash University
Victor Eastop	*Faunistic Survey (insects)*	BM(NH)
Andy Eavis	*Speleological Survey*	Yorkshire
Sandy Evans	*Secretariat and Field Support*	RGS
Tserng Goong Farn	*Soil Survey*	DID
Mike Farnworth	*Speleological Survey*	Ribchester, Lancashire
Chin Fook	*Forest Survey (pathologist and fungi)*	FDK
Hans Friederich	*Landform and Hydrology Survey (water chemistry)*	University of Bristol
Hilary Fry	*Faunistic Survey (birds)*	University of Aberdeen
Rosemary Fullerton-Smith	*Field Support (catering)*	RGS

249

NAME	PROGRAMME/ ROLE	UNIVERSITY/ AFFILIATION/PLACE OF RESIDENCE
Naen German	*Human Ecology Survey*	SMK
David Giles	*Field Support (medical doctor)*	Bude, Cornwall
Chris Hails	*Faunistic Survey (birds)*	UM
Sandra Hails	*Faunistic Survey (birds)*	UM
Abang Abdul Hamid	*Forest Ecology (entomologist)*	FDK
Jon Hamilton	*Field Support (jetboat team)*	Hamilton Jet Boats, New Zealand
Michael Hamilton	*Field Support (jetboat team)*	Hamilton Jet Boats, New Zealand
Marika Hanbury-Tenison	*Field Support (catering)*	RGS
Robin Hanbury-Tenison	*Leader and field director*	RGS
Carlo Hansen	*Forest Survey (flowering plants)*	Botanical Museum, Copenhagen
Ilkka Hanski	*Faunistic Survey (beetle ecology)*	University of Oxford
John Hemming	*Director and secretary of RGS*	RGS
Amy Herbert	*Field Support*	
Dave Hollis	*Faunistic Survey (insects)*	BM(NH)

NAME	PROGRAMME/ ROLE	UNIVERSITY/ AFFILIATION/PLACE OF RESIDENCE
Jeremy Holloway	*Faunistic Survey (moths and butterflies)*	Commonwealth Institute of Entomology, London
Lord Hunt (John)	*President of RGS*	RGS
David Iboh	*Human Ecology Survey*	SMS, Marudi
Nicola (Hokey) Ingram	*Field Support (nurse)*	RGS
Hamdan Abang Jawi	*Field Support*	NPWO, Miri
Clive Jermy	*Scientific programme co-ordinator*	BM(NH)
Walter Jülich	*Forest Survey (fungi)*	Rijksherbarium, Leiden
Tuton Kaboy	*Human Ecology Survey*	SMK
Abang Haji Kassam	*National parks and wildlife officer*	NPWO, Kuching
Peter Kedit	*Human Ecological Survey (director)*	SMK
Ross Kerby	*Forest Survey (flowering plants)*	RBGE
Then Thiat Khiong	*Soil Survey*	DID, Kuching
Bong Heang Kiew	*Faunistic Survey (amphibians, fish, reptiles)*	UM
Ruth Kiew	*Forest Survey (flowering plants)*	Universiti Pertanian Malaysia, Kuala Lumpur

NAME	PROGRAMME/ ROLE	UNIVERSITY/ AFFILIATION/PLACE OF RESIDENCE
Ben King	*Faunistic Survey (birds)*	American Museum of Natural History, New York
Mumin Kundi	*Human Ecology Survey*	SMK
Joseph Yong Kim Kwee	*Director of forests, Kuching*	FDK
David Labang	*Faunistic Survey (birds and mammals)*	NPWO, Kuching
Lian Labang	*Human Ecology Survey (assistant)*	SMK
Wan Laeng	*Soil Survey (soils)*	ADK
Martin Laverty	*Landform and Hydrology Survey (water chemistry)*	University of Oxford
Sandra Leche	*Forest Survey (flowering plants)*	RBGK
Bernard Lee	*Forest Survey*	FDK
Gwilym Lewis	*Forest Survey (flowering plants)*	RBGK
John Lewis	*Forest Ecology (invertebrate fauna)*	Dover College
Philip Leworthy	*Field Support (transport and workshop)*	RGS
Roger Ley	*Landform and Hydrology Survey (geomorphology)*	University of Oxford

NAME	PROGRAMME/ ROLE	UNIVERSITY/ AFFILIATION/PLACE OF RESIDENCE
K. S. Liew	*Faunistic Survey (amphibians, fish, reptiles)*	UM
Tie Yiu Liong	*Soil Survey*	DID, Kuching
Lim Eng Hua	*Soil Survey*	DID, Kuching
Lim Chin Pang	*Soil Survey (co-director)*	ADK
R. P. Lim	*Faunistic Survey (freshwater fauna)*	UM
Alan Lloyd-Smith	*Field Support (medical doctor)*	Uckfield, Sussex
Wilma Lloyd-Smith	*Field Support (catering)*	Uckfield, Sussex
Ben Lyon	*Speleological Survey*	National Scout Caving Centre (Whernside Manor, Yorkshire)
Kevin McCormick	*Faunistic Survey (bird community analysis)*	University of Aberdeen
David Macdonald	*Faunistic Survey (mammals)*	University of Oxford
Roy McDonald	*Landform and Hydrology Survey (geomorphology)*	University of Oxford
Jane Marshall	*Faunistic Survey (beetle larvae)*	BM(NH)
Margriet Maurenbrecher	*Field Support*	
Lord Medway (Gathorne), now Earl of Cranbrook	*Faunistic Survey (director)*	RGS

NAME	PROGRAMME/ ROLE	UNIVERSITY/ AFFILIATION/PLACE OF RESIDENCE
Keluni Mejeni	*Soil Survey*	ADK
Andrew Mitchell	*Faunistic Survey (primates)*	University of Bristol
Geraldine Mitton	*Field Support (medical doctor)*	Cape Town, South Africa
Abang Haji bin Morshidi	*National parks and wildlife officer*	NPWO, Kuching
Ricky Nelson	*Field Support*	NPWO, Miri
Ivan Nielsen	*Forest Survey (flowering plants)*	Aarhus University, Denmark
John Ogle	*Field Support (medical doctor)*	Brighton, Sussex
S. T. Ooi	*Landform and Hydrology Survey (geology)*	UM
Henry Osmaston	*Landform and Hydrology Survey (geomorphology)*	University of Bristol
Nigel Osmaston	*Landform and Hydrology Survey (assistant)*	University of Bristol
John Owens	*Landform and Hydrology Survey (assistant)*	Keele University
Alec Panchen	*Faunistic Survey (butterflies)*	Newcastle University
Richard Padan	*Soil Survey*	ADK
W. Peters	*Faunistic Survey*	

NAME	PROGRAMME/ ROLE	UNIVERSITY/ AFFILIATION/PLACE OF RESIDENCE
Cajetan Phang	*Landform and Hydrology Survey (pedologist)*	FDK
Ivan Polunin	*Field Support (medical)*	Singapore
John Proctor	*Forest Ecology (director)*	University of Stirling
Sue Proctor + Katy (3)	*Faunistic Survey (litter survey and bats)*	University of Stirling
Mohd Suleiman bin Razali	*Human Ecology Survey*	SMS, Kuching
John Richardson	*Field Support (medical)*	
Rosie Sadler	*Field Support (catering and nurse)*	New Zealand
Bryan Sage	*Faunistic Survey (montane birds)*	Potters Bar, Hertfordshire
Abdul Manaf Sairi	*Advisor and Field Support*	NPWO, Kuching
Nathan Sammy	*Forest Survey (lichens)*	Dampier, Western Australia
Chris Saunders	*Faunistic Survey (vertebrate blood parasites)*	Liverpool
Lee Hua Seng	*Forest Ecology (silviculture)*	FDK
Paul Sepping	*Field Support (medical doctor)*	London

NAME	PROGRAMME/ROLE	UNIVERSITY/AFFILIATION/PLACE OF RESIDENCE
Lord Shackleton (Edward)	*Patron of the expedition*	RGS
Michael Pengiran Sia	*Field Support*	
Patrick Sibat	*Soil Survey*	ADK
Peter Sie	*Forest Survey*	FDK
Mike Singer	*Forest Ecology (insect herbivores)*	University of Texas
David Stoddart	*Chairman of the RGS Mulu Sub-Committee*	University of Cambridge
Ben Stone	*Forest Survey*	UM
Marjorie Sweeting	*Landform and Hydrology Survey (director)*	University of Oxford
Ian Swingland	*Faunistic Survey (reptiles)*	University of Oxford
Yeo Eng Teck	*Forest Survey*	FDK
Yiu Liong Tie	*Landform and Hydrology Survey*	Kuching
Dries Touw	*Forest Survey (mosses)*	Rijksherbarium, Leiden
Ursula Trosch	*Field Support (catering)*	Bottighofen, Switzerland
Harry Vallack	*Forest Survey (litter survey)*	University of Stirling
Yau Kwok Wai	*Field Support*	
Trevor Walker	*Forest Survey (ferns)*	Newcastle University

NAME	PROGRAMME/ ROLE	UNIVERSITY/ AFFILIATION/PLACE OF RESIDENCE
Rory Walsh	*Landform and Hydrology Survey*	Swansea University
Tony Waltham	*Speleological Survey (director)*	Trent Polytechnic
Anyi Wan	*Human Ecology Survey*	SMK
Fred Wanless	*Faunistic Survey (spiders)*	BM(NH)
Peter Wedlake	*Field Support*	Chippenham, Wiltshire
David Wells	*Faunistic Survey (birds)*	UM
Shane Wesley-Smith	*Secretariat and Field Support*	RGS
Tim Whitmore	*Forest Survey (trees)*	Commonwealth Forestry Institute, Oxford
Nigel Winser	*Deputy field director*	RGS
Margaret Wise	*Faunistic Survey (mammals)*	Exeter
Colin Woodroffe	*Landform and Hydrology Survey (peat swamps)*	University of Sheffield
Yap Kok Thye	*Landform and Hydrology Survey (geology)*	UM
Robert Jamal Yapik	*Field Support*	
Azahari bin Zainuddin	*Forest Survey*	FDK

APPENDIX 3
Survival International

Survival International has been campaigning for many years for the Malaysian government to recognise the Penan's rights to their land, and to halt all logging, palm-oil plantations, dam construction and other development on their land without their consent.

We are Survival, the global movement for tribal peoples' rights. We're the only organisation that champions tribal peoples around the world. We help them defend their lives, protect their lands and determine their own futures.

Tribal peoples have developed ways of life that are largely self-sufficient and extraordinarily diverse. Many of the world's staple crops and drugs used in Western medicine originate with them, and have saved millions of lives. Even so, tribal peoples are portrayed as backward and primitive simply because their communal ways are different. Industrialised societies subject them to genocidal violence, slavery and racism so they can steal their lands, resources and labour in the name of 'progress' and 'civilisation'.

Our work is preventing the annihilation of tribal peoples. We work in partnership with them. We give them a platform to speak to the world. We investigate atrocities and present evidence to the United Nations and other international forums. We support legal representation. We fund medical and self-help projects. We educate, research, campaign, lobby and protest. We won't give up until we all have a world where tribal peoples are respected as contemporary societies and their human rights protected.

We depend on you. We need your money, energy and enthusiasm to help us fight one of the most urgent and horrific humanitarian crises of our time.

Survival International, 6 Charterhouse Buildings, London, EC1M 7ET, United Kingdom | +44 (0)20 7687 8700

PO Box 26345, San Francisco, CA 94126, United States | +1 510-858-3950 www.survivalinternational.org

INDEX